Personalized & Database Printing

David Broudy

Frank Romano

GAMA
Micro Publishing Press

Personalized & Database Printing

David Broudy
Frank Romano

Published by GAMA

Bookstore distribution by
Micro Publishing Press
A division of Cygnus Publishing
2340 Plaza Del Amo, Suite 100
Torrance, CA 90501
(310) 212-5802
www.micropubnews.com

Also distributed by
Digital Printing Council/PIA

GAMA
P.O. Box 170
Salem, NH 03079
(603) 898-2822
Fax (603) 898-3393

First Edition: April, 1999
Printed in the United States of America by Malloy Lithographing

ISBN: 0-941845-24-9

Sponsored by **NEX**PRESS ⦂

Acknowledgements

I wish to thank the following people for their valuable assistance with this book. The relative lack of literature on this subject required many hours of interviews and meetings with those who have helped to create this technology and without their time and assistance it would not have been possible: Robert Barclay, Jac Bloomberg, David deBronkart, Peg and Bruce Ganger, Forrest Gauthier, Jeff Gebhart, Rab Govil, Tim Graves, Cheryl Kahanec, Brett Knobloch, John Kriho, Jane Mueller, Marc Orchant, Michael Riordan, Julie Roberts, Peter Takacs, and of course my partner Frank Romano.

—David Broudy, April, 1999, Rochester, NY.

And let's not forget Richard Romano who copy edited our work, Robert Romano and Kristin Murphy who designed the cover and processed the illustrations, and the folks at NexPress Solutions LLC who sponsored it. And especially, Mary Garnett and Joanne Vinyard at the Digital Printing Council/PIA who were its earliest supporters.

—Frank Romano, April, 1999, Rochester, NY

Intellectual Property

There are many product and company names used throughout this book.

To try to list all of them, or to put the trademark symbol in the text, would be an overwhelming task.

Therefore, all proper names, almost always spelled with a capital letter, are someone's intellectual property.

Please respect the rights of the owners of such trademarks.

Foreword

Successful communication is easier said than done. Why is that the case? Perhaps because good communication requires that a clear message be transmitted, and that the message be accepted and understood by the receiver. But in today's world—in part because of improved technology—we have information overload. As a result, it becomes increasingly critical to tailor the message in such a way to get the attention of the receiver and to convey the information accurately and succinctly. Digital printing technology enables communicators to customize their messages, increasing the timeliness and therefore the accuracy of information.

NexPress Solutions LLC, a joint venture of Eastman Kodak Company and Heidelberger Druckmaschinen AG of Germany, is proud to sponsor "Personalized and Database Printing." We desire to be agents of change in the fundamental acceptance of personalized and customized digital printing. We are creating the next generation of non-impact, digital color printing solutions.

Authors David Broudy and Frank Romano, the renowned source authority on digital printing at the Rochester Institute of Technology, spent months interviewing and researching digital printing technology experts. In this book, they have captured both the nuts and bolts of customized printing as well as provided a view for how personalized printing will change business practices around the world through one-to-one marketing. Readers will gain valuable insight into how to successfully embrace the new technologies and to improve the overall effectiveness of their communication.

Venkat Purushotham, President, *NexPress Solutions LLC*

Authors

David Broudy is a Masters of Science candidate at the Rochester Institute of Technology. He received his Bachelor of Arts degree from the University of California, Irvine. He has ten years of prior experience in the graphic arts industry as a designer and production consultant in Southern California prior to beginning his advanced degree studies in Rochester. He has also written several textbooks for graphic arts software applications.

Frank Romano is a professor at the Rochester Institute of Technology. He is the author of almost 30 books on digital printing and publishing technology. He is the founder of a number of magazines and user groups.

Introduction

Personalized, customized, or variable data printing offers a new value-added proposition that has been proven to improve response rates, provide improved customer service, decrease overall costs, reduce time to market, and enhance productivity. Personalization—and color—can yield significant improvements in direct marketing promotional programs. The percent of improvement by using personalized printing combined with color, on the average, has been:

Response rate	34%
Average order size/value of order	25%
Repeat orders/retention	48%
Overall revenue/profit	32%
Response time	35%

On-demand print technology and variable data applications will propel the industry to about $35 billion in revenues by the year 2001, according to a number of predictions. We have already seen 24% growth in black and white impression volume and color on-demand printing is beginning to meet expectations. The U.S. print market, including commercial and in-plant printers, is $100 billion. The overall printing market will increase to $135 billion in the year 2001. Digital printing will surge from $10.5 billion in 1997 to $35 billion in 2001. That's five times the annual growth rate of conventional print.

Color on-demand printing grew from $4 billion to $7 billion from 1996 to 1997. Color now makes up 63% of the on demand market and the retail value of color-on-demand printing is predicted to increase at a compound annual growth rate of 35% through 2001. The total U.S. market for print on-demand equipment, supplies and service was $4 billion in 1997. Digital technology is penetrating every aspect of our lives, with 55 million computers in the U.S. workplace; 15 million networks in operation; e-mail messages exchanged by 30 million people every day; and Internet users in the U.S. at more than 35 million. With the growth of e-commerce, personalized and on-demand printing will grow as well.

In this digital era, companies have more information about their customers, their operations and their distribution than ever before. Some companies are creating database-driven promotions, automated production, distribution and customer service systems. The goal is to reach an individual customer with a personalized message that results in an order for a customized product or service that is manufactured just-in-time, delivered overnight, paid in advance, and leads to repeat orders. This is the ultimate concept of one-to-one marketing. One of the most valuable assets many companies have is the vast amount of information they have about their customers. The key is to apply this information as an integral part of marketing and customer service programs. Personalized print-on-demand is an essential capability in maximizing the return on your information assets.

By focusing on specific industries and niche markets, the printing industry can better provide solutions to the critical applications that drive emerging business models. Applications range from all forms of promotions to direct marketing to on-demand publications and data-driven publishing, including forms, coupons, catalogs, invitations, notices, dealer-specific literature, explanation of benefits, directories, financial statements, and other transactional documents, and others. Each of these applications has a variety of requirements that determine which printing technologies are applicable for personalized printing services.

Factors include print quality, color, capability, total units printed, production schedule, cost-per-unit of printing, available databases, file formats, other printing and production systems in place, such as offset printing with selective inserting or ink jet printing, and many other issues specific to the industry and application—plus the value of the final product in the marketing equation. Over the next decade the amount of personalized printing will grow.

David Broudy
Frank Romano

Table of Contents

4 Tips for Dynamic Printing 149

5 Applying Dynamic Printing 155

6 Variable Data Printing Programs 171

1

Direct Marketing and Dynamic Printing

Eighty percent of everything that printers print is because someone wants to sell something to someone else. We are, in fact, bombarded by advertising messages. In one day we see or hear the following number of ad messages from these media:

TV	112
Radio	21
Newspaper	63
Periodical	82
Posters	31
Internet	17
Mail	12
Other	45

The object of direct marketing is to get messages to defined audiences in a manner that invites attention and engenders actions—that ultimately lead to buying a product or service.

Personalized and database printing is an enabling technology. It is the step in the process called "one-to-one marketing" that generates the paper-based communication that actually goes to a customer or potential customer. Traditional printing is static in that every piece reproduced is the same. Variable-data, or dynamic, printing varies the text, data or images on each piece in response to information in databases. The result is database-driven customized or personalized printing used in direct marketing programs.

The market of one

Despite the fact that customization and personalization are often used interchangeably, they are distinct and separate entities. We define customization as a printed unit targeted to a particular group of people and only your name and address vary. Personalization means that it is targeted to you and other information varies. Here are some examples:

- When you receive a document that says "Congratulations on your new house, isn't it time you thought about insurance" it was customized to a small group of new home buyers, you included.
- When your mail says "You are now 50 and time to join AARP," you received a document that was customized to people in your age group (old).
- When you receive a flyer with your local real estate or life insurance agent's picture on it, that is a customized piece sent to a small group of people based on location.
- When professors at universities prepare coursepacks, they assemble specific book chapters, magazine articles, and notes by the professor; these are customized for that class.
- When Prudential creates an insurance or portfolio report to prospective clients containing 90% boilerplate pages and 10% specific information, it is a version customized to your group. Since other people may be in the same situation it is not a unique document.
- When you receive a catalog with photos of products based on previous purchases with your name on every page, this is now a personalized promotion mailing.

Sometimes the customized content is personally relevant and then the document is both personalized and customized. Take any of the examples above and add personal information such as the recipient's name, street address, or a specific picture and you have created a document that is both customized (going to a small group) and personalized (information relevant only to the recipient).

At other times only one criterion is met, resulting in a document that is personalized, but not really customized. When you see your name printed inside one of your subscription magazines or when you receive one of those documents that say "Congratulations Josephine Blow, you have just won a million dollars" you have received a personalized marketing document (it has your name) and may be customized (the content is changed based on some factor).

There are three distinct types of variable information:
- text
- data
- image

Take an auto promotion. The personal information could be your name and the customized text could be your car model (Ford Taurus). The customized text could also be a description about the latest model of that car (*the 2000 model . . .*). Customized images could include a picture of the latest model car, but become more personalized if you include the car in the same color or with the same extras (tail fins) that you may have selected. Based on data from direct response experts the addition of any one of these items will increase chances of a sale. Adding more will increase the chances even more.

For the service provider the process adds greater complexity to the database as well as the manufacturing time. Creating a database with the customer name, customized text of the car, and image of that car will take longer then a personalized piece with only the customer name. But, the more personalized and customized the piece, the greater the sales potential. The obvious question is how great is the increase in sales?

According to direct response advocates, personalization may increase sales from 1% to 30%. Keep in mind that these direct response campaigns also limit the size or the number of outgoing pieces, which can also decrease costs and increase efficiencies. For example, a 1,000,000 unit "shotgun" mailing may be reduced to a 10,000 "stochastic" campaign. Stochastic means *to aim well* in Greek.

When considering the addition of variable content it is important to recognize the technology challenges and potential complexities for finishing. On one end of the spectrum are the easy applications, such as short runs with very simple demographic versioning; for example, one version for men, and another for women. An additional level of complexity would be the addition of peoples' names, therefore creating personalized product. This requires a database of names and some sort of "mail merging" capability. In this case instead of saying "Congratulations, you just won a million dollars" it would say "Congratulations, Joe Blow, you just won a million dollars."

As direct response advocates know, seeing your name in print is a seductive and potent selling tool. This becomes very obvious the first time you see the your name inkjet printed on the inside pages of the national magazine mailed to your home. Another level of complexity is the finishing considerations. Names could be added with or without labels. If labels are used then a third level of complexity is added, which is affixing the printed labels to the printed pieces.

Moving up the line of complexity we have the multiple versions using customized or personalized pictures. In this case we could have different text and different pictures selling different products based on some demographic profile. For example, six categories could be 17–25-year old single male, 26–45-year old year married male, 46-year old or over divorced male, 17–25-year old female, 26–45-year old married female, 46 year old or over divorced female. For greater personalization the unit could also have each person's name.

The market called "you"
The ultimate demographic customization and personalization would be for each person to receive a separate piece based either on demographics or purchase information. Everyone would get their own unique piece. The ultimate example of "one to one" marketing would be a picture of you wearing or using the potential product. Imagine a day when personal digital photographs find their way into databases along with other information about each of us.

This demonstrates the underlying motivation for using variable information for customized and personalized printing. It is a direct response tool for distribution in retail markets. The market estimates are quite impressive. Direct market applications represent a $460 billion dollar market which includes catalogs, TV shopping channels, and other direct-marketing alternatives.

But that is not the whole story. The $460 billion market is only a small percentage (2.8%) of the $2.1-trillion-a-year retail marketplace, which includes supermarkets, mall outlets, car dealerships, department stores, warehouse clubs, boutiques, mail order houses, and more, and the direct response portion of it is growing. According to *Fortune*, merchants predict that conventional retailing will remain steady or contract slightly, while *high technology* marketing such as interactive home shopping channels and personalized direct marketing could achieve 15 percent of total sales. This would result in revenues of $300 billion and create one of the largest businesses in the world.

Direct marketing

For the first time in U.S. business history, the size and scope of direct marketing in America—direct mail and catalogs, telephone marketing, and direct response print, broadcast, and other media—has been measured as a result of an econometric study undertaken by the Direct Marketing Association.

According to the research, conducted by an econometric forecasting consulting firm in 1995, direct marketing generated an estimated $594.4 billion in consumer sales, and $498.1 billion in business-to-business sales. In employment, more than 19.1 million U.S. jobs are related to direct marketing activity—nearly 10.8 million in consumer direct marketing and nearly 8.3 million in business-to-business direct marketing. By 2000, all of these measurements would increase by 20 percent, it is predicted.

A media-based definition of direct marketing is:

> *Any direct communication to a consumer or business recipient that is intended to generate a response in the form of an order (direct order), a request for further information (lead generation), and/or a visit to a store or other place of business for purchase of a specific product(s) or service(s)(traffic generation).*

Direct Order refers to all direct-response advertising communications—through any medium—that are specifically designed and produced to solicit and close a sale. All of the information necessary for the prospective buyer to make a decision to purchase and complete the transaction is conveniently provided in the advertisement.

Lead Generation refers to all direct-response advertising communications—through any medium—that are designed to generate interest in a product or a service, and provide the prospective buyer with a means to request and receive additional information about the product or service.

Traffic Generation includes all direct response advertising communications conducted—through any medium—that are designed to motivate the prospective buyer to visit a store, restaurant, or other business establishment to buy an advertised product or service.

The focus of this book is on the use of print-based products used specifically for direct marketing, or used to support direct marketing. The print-based technology is that of static and dynamic printing.

Static Printing is any ink, toner or inkjet image on paper or other substrate that is the same for each sheet reproduced through a digital printer or traditional ink-on-paper printing press.

Dynamic Printing is any ink, toner or inkjet image on paper or other substrate that is different for each sheet reproduced through a digital printer or digital press.

Direct mail
Marketing through direct mail is a big business. Because of the one-to-one nature of direct mail, you can target specific individuals or businesses who have a need for your product or service—increasing the likelihood of making a sale. You can also build lasting customer relationships that result in repeat business.

Direct mail is a form of direct marketing. It is marketing that seeks an immediate response. Direct mail is the perfect way to reach selected audiences, from an audience of one to an audience of millions. It is also called *direct response*. You can use this immediate response to measure the success of your campaign.

Direct mail is a complement to your overall marketing mix.

Direct mail is accountable—it is advertising you can justify and track.

Direct mail is adaptable to fit almost any budget.

A direct mail package can be designed to make an instant sale, open a dialogue between the potential buyer and seller, or simply inform the potential buyer about certain products or services.

The list is the key to direct mail. It allows you to select your audience and information about that audience. It lets you target a message to that audience. The list comes from a database; hence, *database marketing*.

Whatever the desired outcome of a direct mail effort—direct mail is a proven, cost-efficient way to reach customers.

- Direct mail is targeted, focused, aimed, stochastic (stochastic: from the Greek "to aim well.") Mass media is a shotgun approach to a galaxy of potential customers. Direct mail can be pinpointed to a single individual at a single address.
- Direct mail is testable, predictable. With testing and tracking on a small scale, you can effectively predict the results from a large-scale campaign.
- Direct mail is, well, direct. It allows you to take your product or service right to the customer. Direct mail can make it easier for a customer to make a purchase in a number of ways. For example, you can alert potential customers to new products or sale items before they come into the store or meet your sales person. You can also include an order form, or web address, or complete the entire transaction through the mail.
- Direct mail is based on databases, data, information. The more data you have the more direct marketing you can do. More data also means better direct marketing.
- Direct mail is economical. Depending on the magnitude and complexity of a given campaign, direct mail can be a cost-effective vehicle to reach a sizable audience of potential customers on an individual basis. Or it can reach one person.
- Direct mail puts you in control. You control the medium and the message.
- Direct mail is personal and friendly.

Direct mail is junk mail. The only junk mail is the mail you throw out without reading. Think of the mail you actually read or save or do something about. The majority of direct mail is at least opened and looked at.

Direct mail is an expensive way to advertise. When performed properly, direct mail is one of the most cost effective ways to get your message to an audience. You only pay to reach the audience that you feel will most likely buy your product or service. If you do it right, there is no waste. All other forms of media have a waste factor based on some percentage of the audience that is not a prospect for your product or service. Magazines call this "waste circulation."

Nobody wants more mail. A survey showed that over 75% of the survey participants preferred direct mail as an advertising medium. It does not interrupt your favorite TV or radio show or hinder your reading of a news article like one of those telemarketing calls. It is read at your leisure. Nobody want more mail that doesn't matter to them.

Direct mail is only for mass marketers. Direct mail is democratic. It is for big and small businesses. It works—if you do it right. Most attempts are half-hearted and not thought out. Direct mail works in small mailings as well as in large mailings.

Direct mail does not work. Direct mail is the fastest growing advertising medium. This growth rate is a testament to its effectiveness. Direct mail advertising offers you unique benefits that other kinds of promotions do not. You can tailor a mailing precisely to your audience. You can make your mailing piece as modest as a postcard announcing a sale, or as elaborate as a letter accompanied by a full-color brochure. You can enclose coupons or gifts or other items to get someone's attention. Look in your mailbox. There is a reason you get so much mail. It works.

What can you do with direct mail?
You can announce sales events, offer discounts, invite consultations, or even supply a sample. Depending on the nature of your business, you may even be able to complete a sale by using mail alone. The recipient gets a sample, tries it, likes it, phones in, emails in, or completes an order form and mails it in.

You can also "target" who receives your mailing, approaching only those people who live in a particular area, or work in a particular industry, or use a related product, or have a job that needs your product or service, or others who most likely to have interest in what your company has to offer.

As more and more small businesses discover the capabilities of mail—and the results they get—direct mail is beginning to take its rightful place as an outstanding way to generate profits.

The first thing on your list is your list
There are two levels of direct marketing:
- front end
- back end

Front end marketing aims for an initial response, a first order. This initial response is sometimes called *prospecting* or *lead generation*—the identification of potential customers. Back-end marketing is essentially repeat business—it is also relationship marketing. Front-end marketing gets them; back-end marketing keeps them.

When you plan to do a front end marketing mailing, the primary decision is to whom you mail. If your mailing is an offer to your present customers, you can simply take the names and addresses out of your files. (If you don't already have such a list, you can build one by taking the names from the computer, or even recording the information from sales slips.) House lists are important since existing customer can be continuing customers.

Attract new customers. Try trading names and addresses with related businesses in your area. If you sell furniture, for example, you might trade customer names with a carpet showroom. Or use the services of a "list broker," a professional whose job is to supply mailing lists of prospects. A list broker can enable you to mail only to people who live in a specific geographic region—perhaps the entire community in which you do business, or to certain Zip codes. With a list broker, you can acquire lists that let you target an audience by factors such as past purchasing patterns.

You might also ask a list broker or mailing house about economical "shared" mailings with other establishments. For instance, if you're offering a discount, it can be included in a collection of money-saving coupons sent to certain business customers or local households.

Mailing lists are rented, usually for one-time use. They are protected with decoy names—these are actual people and businesses with a slight twist in their name who will receive the mailing and report if the mailer had permission. In some cases, you can merge/purge lists. For instance, you can run the list against your customer base to remove existing customers. You usually cannot put the rented list into a new database.

You can, however, use the responding information in any way you want. So you could make a great offer just to get a list of respondents, plus some additional data. These names become your own database for use to your heart's content. Then you can rent your list to others—with decoy names, of course. The nature of the list and the nature of the offer combine to produce the response rate. This is traditionally said to be 1%. However, some organizations do very well with rates well below 1% because they are mass marketers, and other organizations are seeing 10% to over 20% because they are niche or specialty marketers. Back-end marketing response rates are normally higher than front-end marketing response rates due to increased knowledge of the customer.

There are cases where one mailing serves both front-end and back-end purposes—catalog marketing. However, catalog marketers have discovered that personalized messages, or inserts, or covers help to make the existing customer (who previously ordered) feel special.

Lists become databases
Lists may be developed by:
- geography
- demographics
- psychographics
- job functions
- purchasing patterns

Geography refers to where the audience lives or works; *demographics* refers to socioeconomic characteristics (age, gender, occupation, income level, marital status, etc.); *psychographics* refers to lifestyle characteristics (interests, activities, attitudes evidenced by what clubs people belong to, political parties they vote for, or sports they participate in). *Job functions* identifies people who buy or use certain products or services based on what they do for a living. *Purchasing patterns* predicts a sale based on previous sales, like promoting new mufflers to owners of older automobiles, or looking for relationships between any of the four other areas.

It may be that market research will reveal that all three of these criteria can be matched by the area in which people live. The U.S. Bureau of the Census publishes demographic profiles by Zip code. These can be matched against any list that also has Zip codes. Data is matched from different lists and then stored in a database.

Lists are developed in a variety of ways. Most often they are acquired from list brokers, or traded, or licensed from other organizations. In addition you can develop names from:

- advertising in newspapers or magazines
- visitors to your Web site
- calls to an 800 number from the point of purchase, or billboards, or other promotions
- respondents to other direct marketing efforts

When does a list become a database? When it has more information than a mailing list. That information would include what other products and services were acquired from your company over what period of time, combined with other data such as what related products or services the person has acquired, related lifestyle data, and perhaps credit rating or other economic data.

You could use one personalized direct mail program to get the data for another direct mail program. A large automobile maker has a database of users who have leased their vehicles. They use this database to mail a personalized questionnaire with a free offer, like a free service visit, if the questionnaire is completed. The returned information is input and creates a new database that reveals more about the possible decision the user will make when their lease is up. The next direct mailing uses text and images that are specific to the user's needs and desires.

Here is another example of how database marketing works:

1. A Japanese motorcycle maker was about to introduce a new model. Their target audience were people who already owned motorcycles: over one million names.
2. To narrow the list they selected only those people within a reasonable distance of a dealer. This is called a *geographic overlay*, and is usually based on Zip code. This cut the list to about three quarters of a million names.
3. They then applied a profile based on their own research

that compared certain demographic data. This cut another 100,000 names.

4. Then they narrowed the list to those who had bought a motorcycle over three years ago and had not traded it in. This brought the list down to half a million names.

5. Then they accounted for brand loyalty and excluded users of certain models. With a last check of credit worthiness, the final list was about a quarter of a million.

The result: 6% of the recipients took the offer for a test drive. The company did not reveal the sales results.

The data to accomplish the above lives in many different databases. There are compiled lists of virtually every home owner or apartment dweller. Major purchases are usually covered by mortgages or loans, and motor vehicles are listed in public records, and therefore public data is available, which list compilers computerize.

The art of art and copy

To many people, one of the most daunting aspects of advertising is the issue of what to say and how to say it. You want to write compelling copy that sells and put it into an effective layout. Small business people prefer to work with direct mail professionals. But nobody knows your product or service as well as you. And if you have a way with words, or a flair for design, you may want to have a go at it yourself. The best approach may be a collaboration between you and someone who—excuse us—knows what they are doing.

Whether you're putting on your own creative hat or judging the work of others, consider the golden rule of communication that tries to persuade: everything you say, and everything you show, should be guided by the self-interest of the prospect. Think of the people who will be reading your direct mail piece. Show them how well you understand their needs, and exactly what your product or service will do to make their lives better. Avoid overblown "hype" and superlatives that no one will believe.

You must overcome the immediate reaction that the offer is too good to be true. Pay particular attention to the copy that appears on the envelope, cover, or outer wrapper. That's what gets a person to open it and start reading it.

And remember—the best offer written in the best way is meaningless if the recipient has no need for the product or service. Selling car insurance to someone who does not own a car is one example. Offering a lawn tractor to someone who lives in an apartment is another. This is where the database comes in. The copy and its presentation are tied to the target audience.

Many years ago a big computer maker (when computers were big) identified seven potential users in the city of Chicago. One day a messenger arrived at the desk of the secretary of the chairman of each company. The box had holes and there was clearly an animal within. The note said:

> Dear Mr. Chairman: Big Computer Maker has a system that will cut your costs and increase your bottom line. If you are interested, please release the enclosed messenger pigeon at the nearest window.

All seven returned.

How to make an offer they can't refuse

Every piece of direct mail advertising must possess something very important—"the offer." It is the essence of what is being offered for sale. You have heard the old ad line "Always ask for the order." Well, direct mail is no different. What is the offer? What can they order?

Check the offers in the mailings that other companies send you. It'll give you an idea of the variety of approaches out there. Are they clear? Did you understand what they were trying to sell? Or did you have to wade through levels of copy before you finally figure out what they wanted to sell you?

The offer should include at least these items:
- What is the product or service?
- What are the advantages or benefits?
- What is the price?
- How do you order it?
- What are the details?

What is the product or service? This sounds awfully academic. But you yourself have received direct marketing materials and you have not been able to figure out what they are trying to sell. There are gobs of copy and loads of illustration, but somewhere in that mess there is a product or service struggling to get out.

What are the advantages or benefits? All advertising and promotion comes down to three things:
- *features:* aspects of the product or service that describe it to me
- *advantages:* aspects of the product or service that offer me some advantage
- *benefits:* aspects of the product or service that directly benefit *me*

The last two are the most important. Why should I buy this product or service from you now? It could be one of the following:
- a low rate
- a low rate for a limited time
- a combination of items or services that represent a bargain package
- a discount off a normally higher price
- a soft offer—delayed billing, installments, or trial period
- a hard offer—up-front payment based on free gift, special pricing, or other discounts
- a step-up offer—more years on a subscription, a "prestige" level of membership, more product at one time

What is the price? Okay, you have my attention. I am interested in the product or service. Now, how much? This is where the offer comes in. You are going to tell me the price and also tell me why I should buy at this price. Here are some reasons:
- you are a new customer
- you are a member of an affinity group (teachers or auto mechanics, etc.)
- you are a previous customer
- you live in a certain area

How do you order it?
- 800 number
- local phone number
- e-mail address
- secure Web site
- mail-in form with check or credit card information

- drop by a business location
- bounce back (a pre-addressed, postage-free order form in the package with the recently ordered item)

What are the details? You have me. I'm yours. Now, put some icing on the cake:

- free trial
- delayed billing
- additional discount if prepaid
- order now for a free gift
- free alteration, installation, accessories, etc.

Make sure that you provide a mechanism for more information. In some cases, the product or service cannot be ordered directly. There may be more information (perhaps a medical exam or credit check) required. So you make the request for more information the next step in the process.

Engender action

Have you ever peeled a label and pasted it on a sheet? Or licked a stamp and placed it in a box? Or checked boxes? Or torn or cut or de-perfed a coupon? Or inserted a form in an envelope? Or folded and taped or stapled a card? Or mailed anything back to anyone in response to a mailing? They are all actions. Once someone takes the first action, they usually go on to the final action—ordering the product or service. Sometimes the action is merely tearing the reply card at a perforation and mailing it. Your name and address are already printed. There is a business reply mail indicia. The key word is: *easy*. Make it easy. Direct marketing is interactive marketing.

The hook

The offer ties in with another direct mail device called "the hook." This is the enticement that accompanies the offer. It is a reason to act now or to act at all. Reasons to act now all come down to one thing: a time limit. This is usually in the form of:

- a deadline date
- a time period
- limited time sale
- end of model year
- inventory closeout
- price increase coming

A traditional example: if prospects respond by a certain date, you'll allow them a discount on your product or service. Or, if they drop by your establishment, you'll have a modest gift waiting for them. Many offers consist of a promise to send more detailed information. That is not enough of a hook. Perhaps you have an interesting catalog to provide. That is an advertising hook. Or you could offer a free phone consultation. In some cases, you might even consider a free trial of your product or service. That is one of the best hooks. Hooks are inducements. They offer something for nothing.

Of course, the kind of offer you make depends on the nature of your business, the type of prospect you're talking to, and the purpose of your mailing. But there's nothing like a good offer—especially one with a good hook—to induce action on the part of the prospect.

You then have two things:
- offer
- hook

The offer is what you want the potential buyer to buy. It is the deal, the program, the product, the service, or any combination of them. The hook may have a "gimmick." This is something that will get the recipient's attention, like:
- a key
- a sample plastic card
- an imprinted date book
- an ID tag
- a sample
- a coin
- a dollar bill

A gimmick is something that makes the recipient feel that they are getting something for nothing. It may be a "keeper"—something that they will keep and perhaps use. More often, it is something they toss into a drawer and to remain there for ages, eventually dug up by archaeologists who try to figure out what it was.

Be careful with gimmicks. They are expensive and their drawing power fades fast. How often have you received a questionnaire with a dollar bill as a sort of bribe—and then kept the buck and chucked the form. There is a difference between a gimmick and a premium. A premium is an incentive. It is the extra added value that induces you to take an action. And there is also a difference between a gimmick, a premium, and a free sample. These often come down to a *free* offer. You must be careful to explain that "free" refers to a premium of some kind and not, perhaps, to the entire offer.

Contests

You may be a winner. Well, most of us are not. There are stringent rules for the use of sweepstakes and contests:

- Full disclosure: tell the recipient the odds, what it takes to enter and how the selection is made.
- Award all prizes: you really should give away everything you promise.
- Randomness: the selection of winners should not be influenced in any manner.
- Eligibility: Even those who say "no" to the offer should be eligible to win.

Watch those asterisks. Too often there are so many disclosure, rules and other explanations that your copy looks like a legal brief.

Layout for direct response

There are seven main elements of direct response design:

- main headline
- subheads
- dominant illustration or photo
- secondary illustration or photo
- text
- company name and logo
- reply mechanism or coupon

You can arrange them as you wish but the reader's eye should flow from point to point in some logical way. More on layout later.

Measuring results

Measuring a mailing's success often requires only the most basic accounting procedures. It's called counting. Did you earn back more than the outlay for the direct mail? Answering this question is straightforward—such as when you're making the entire sale by mail. You can easily count the responses. If people are redeeming discount coupons, it's also easy to tell how many purchases are related to your mailing. Many mailings are coded in such a way that they can track the list, the mailing date, and other attributes of the mailing.

If the purpose of your mailing is to build store traffic, you should be able to detect an increase in sales shortly after the mailing goes out. Don't be disappointed if a lot of people don't answer your mailing. If you get a 2 percent response you are considered a pro. But sometimes a success rate as low as 1 percent can translate into significant profits. And mailings can have success rates as high as 10 percent or 15 percent. Personalized mailings have been in the 15 percent to 20+ percent range. A lot depends on the list or database, the level of personalization, and the link between them and the offer/hook.

When you gauge the effectiveness of a mailing, try to consider it long term. Check to see if you're getting one time customers or clients, or steady ones. When you have a winner of a program, consider expanding on it. Modify the offer.

A goldmine of data
The people who respond to your mailings can be particularly valuable to you in many ways. Whether they're brand new customers or established customers returning for more, you know one very important thing about them: they respond to mail advertising. You can start to build your own database of direct mail *responders*. Now, what products or services might you offer them?

Wait a little while, and contact them again. You might make them another offer, or perhaps inform them of a sale. Or, from time to time, you can just send out a friendly reminder that you're always ready to be of service. A big city service sent postcards every Monday so they would be delivered in the middle of the week when mail was light. The cards always said the same thing: if you need our service, here we are. It was amazing how many customers they got—most of whom had received the mailing many times, but just one time found a need for the service. One of the keys to direct mail success is consistency.

The more you learn about your prospects, the more effectively you can target their needs in future efforts. Unlike other advertising media, you can use the mail to develop a personal, ongoing—and even lifetime—relationship with customers. The Web is great for collecting or even e-commerce, but mail keeps the customer a customer.

Mail is a trusted medium

Despite competing media, electronic mail and changing perceptions about what arrives in the mailbox, the nation's use of the mails remains healthy. That's the overall impression from a nine-year market research study of mail sent to and received by U.S. households.

People still want hard copy evidence in their hands, particularly when it involves business transactions. People still want paper. We think they want both the mental and the physical experience. As we all know, most of the first class-mail we receive is bills, 2.6 pieces per household a week in 1987 to 2.9 pieces in 1995 to a projected 3.1 pieces in 2001. Banks were the largest users (5.87 percent), followed by credit card companies (5.7 percent), and insurance companies (4.43 percent). Even with ATMs and electronic banking, hard copy continues to grow.

Doomsayers have been predicting the demise of mail for a long time. It's still here and it's still growing. Credit cards are generating much of the volume. The shift we're seeing in the marketplace has increased reliance on credit. Many people have two or three cards, each of which generates more mail going back and forth from company to customer. And every list you get on generates more mail as lists are traded and sold and merged and expanded.

The heavy hitter in mailboxes was and still is standard mail (third-class), especially regular rate or direct mail advertising, up .76 pieces a week to 8.61 pieces. Those most likely to be targeted recipients have higher incomes, higher education, and a household head between ages 39 and 69. Direct mail is still one of the most appealing ways to get a message to a buyer. Households and businesses still open, read, and respond to direct mail advertising at a steady rate.

The household study says the number of those who found direct mail advertising "useful" remained unchanged during the nine-year study period at 40.2 percent. While 14.6 percent said they would respond to mail containing advertising, another 60.9 percent said they would not. The more important statistic is the very high proportion who say they read advertising mail as compared to the small percentage that find it objectionable. The message to mailers is: the more information they provide to potential buyers in their promotions, the more likely those potential buyers are to read it.

That's especially true for nonprofit mail which rated a 58.9 percent read rate compared with 52.4 percent for regular bulk mail. Receptivity had a lot to do with the recipient's familiarity with the sending institution: 76.2 percent responded to direct mail from organizations they had done business with before, 43.3 percent from known organizations, and 37.3 percent from unknowns.

Charities, educational institutions, and churches accounted for most of the volume for nonprofits. Fundraising solicitations are on the increase, up from 36 percent in 1990 to 44 percent of nonprofit direct mail volume in 1998. Advertising mail in general continues to increase. Of seven major advertising categories, six registered growth over the past decade. Only direct mail requests dropped from 1988 levels. Bottom line: America's mailboxes contained 59 percent advertising. The rest was bills, financial statements and personal letters.

Periodicals (formerly classified as second-class mail) declined by 6.3 percent over the study period. The report suggests the drop is because publishers use mail for delivery in non-urban areas since urban dwellers rely more on newsstands.

Calculate the break-even point
Direct mail is a cost-effective way to reach prospects, and the outcome can be predicted. A direct mailer is generally able to quantify whether a campaign makes good business sense by simple mathematic equations and some inexpensive testing. What follows is a simple worksheet that will illustrate how to determine the response rate required to reach a "break-even" point. By knowing this, it is possible for a company to project the profitability of a specific direct mail campaign.

The following scenario illustrates how this works. Assume your initial calculations resulted in the following figures:

Direct mail expenses	$4,500
Total fixed expenses	$7,500
Selling price of product	$35
Variable costs	$17

$$\text{Break even point} = \frac{\$7,500 + \$4,500}{\$35 - \$17} = 667 \text{ Units}$$

Not all orders taken are actual "sales." There will almost always be returns and bad debt on a percentage of the initial orders taken. The number of these occurrences will largely be a function of the way you choose to receive payment. For the purposes of this illustration, assume that 12.5 percent (83 units) of the orders taken were either returned merchandise or bad debt. This increases your breakeven point to 750 units.

Under this scenario, 750 units would have to be sold as a result of a direct mail campaign to break even. By increasing or decreasing the variables, you can control the number of units that must be sold to reach the break-even point. To determine the response rate required to reach the break even point, use the following equation:

$$\text{Break even Response Rate} = \frac{\text{Break even orders needed}}{\text{Number of pieces mailed}}$$

If you mail 10,000 pieces, you need a response rate of 7.5%.

Break even Response Rate = 750 = 7.5% x 10,000

Testing is the key
The only way to get any idea of the response rate you might derive is to test various aspects of the mailing. Then create a database that tracks seven criteria:

1. names
2. addresses and phone numbers
3. the product or service acquired via the program
4. the date they ordered
5. the premium or other incentive they selected
6. how they responded (mail-in card, 800 number, etc.)
7. the value of the order

From this set of data you can compare response rates according to a test program. It is very important that you use a sample that is statistically the same as your target audience (and that you do not mail to them again with almost the same offer). The usual quantity for a test mailing can range from 500 to 5,000 names randomly selected from the list universe. Sampling from the main list is called *nth name sampling* because every nth name—that is, every 9th or 10th or *nth* name is selected.

Thus names are selected from across the entire list, not just one Zip code. Tests reveal many things. One brokerage company found that shading selected text with a blue tint increased response rates by three times. They found this out when the printer did not print the tints on one test mailing and its response rate was less. This is why someone in your organization should receive the mailings—to see what actually was mailed.

The better the test or tests, the greater the confidence level in the results. Also, two tests are better than one. Two separate *nth* mail samplings with slight changes and identifiable coding may make sense. It used to be that test mailings were expensive due to the economies of long run printing. But today, with digital printing technology, short runs are commonplace and economical. They also let you experiment more with color.

Focus groups
You can also test by bringing a sample group together in a room and asking them what they think about various offers. You would still need to produce even shorter runs of the mail pieces. You can also use telemarketing with a selected group. One might include people who do not mind being called.

Database marketing
Direct marketing is sometimes called database marketing because you are really directing the promotion to a set of individuals determined by a set of criteria. That means you need lists.

List brokers
List brokers are service providers who bring together the owners of lists and direct mailers looking for lists. This is what a list broker can do for you:

- Advise you on many aspects of a direct mail campaign.
- Find lists specific to your needs.
- Report on the past history of a given list.
- Review and critique a particular direct mail package.
- Help predict response rates.
- Assist in designing and implementing a test mailing.
- Help uncover new markets.
- Provide recommendations based on past experience.
- Help you develop a system to track responses.

List brokers typically work on a commission basis (generally around 20 percent of the list rental fee) which is paid by the list owner. The relationship between the list broker and the direct mailer is as important as the relationship between the buyer and seller. A good broker can suggest ways to make your mailing more profitable. Be open with brokers and provide them with all information available. If you do not tell your broker what kind of market you want to penetrate or the specifics of your offer, you may end up with a useless list. Treat your list broker(s) as part of your marketing team. The better the relationship between you and your broker is, the better your final direct mail list will be.

Do not be afraid to ask brokers to review your direct mail packages. They can provide valuable input about your efforts. The more brokers you work with, the better your list and resultant database will be. Using three or four reliable brokers may be better than relying on just one. Use your brokers' talents to their fullest potential.

List brokers will normally want to review the material you intend to mail. They are protecting the list owner, who may have limitations on competitors, or the nature of the product or service.

List exchanges

Many companies find that an excellent way to locate the best lists is to swap lists with other companies that may market similar products or services through the mail. These transactions are generally done on a name-to-name basis and can often be arranged by a list broker for a nominal fee. You also may know companies involved in direct mail that you can contact.

Some companies involved in list exchanges will hold back their most active buyers. Be sure to get the entire list (or let the price reflect the fact that certain active buyers have not been included in the list).

Postal mechanics

The U.S. Postal Service continually changes mail classifications for postage discounts. As it now stands, to get major discounts you must have your mailing checked with USPS-certified software that adds Zip + 4 codes. The USPS prefers all uppercase labels but this looks unprofessional. So there is also software that can change this format to upper and lowercase. Postal-related software includes:

- AddressPRO (Glick)
- Mailers+4 (Mailers Software)
- Right Fielder
- StyleList
- Personator

Every mailing list has the problem of mobility. People and business-es move. Unless you have a mechanism for verifying addresses, you will have about 15 percent of your list returned as undeliverable every year. You can have National Change of Address (NCOA) pro-cessing by authorized service bureaus that accept files on disk or via modem. They run your list against change of address data on file and record the changes. The Postal Service says that between 7 percent and 8 percent of all standard class (used to be third class and bulk mailings) business mailings are undeliverable, especially rental lists. These UAA (Undeliverable As Addressed) pieces are usually dis-carded unless you print "Address Service Requested" on the enve-lope. The cost at this writing is 33 cents for under one ounce and 50 cents for over one ounce pieces of mail. There is forwarding for stan-dard class mail at a special rates.

The USPS has an address change service (ACS) for big and small users who maintain databases. They will electronically deliver changes at 20 cents each if you have appropriate software. A special code must be printed on the mailing label.

What's in it for me?
Good mail advertising must overcome a natural skepticism and influence a person to take an action. Everyone, even upscale buyers, love a bargain. So do not start by appealing to logic; start by appeal-ing to emotion. Direct marketing is direct motivation.

Elements of good copy
No matter what approach your direct mail campaign takes—cata-logs, personal or nonpersonal letters, postcards, etc.—it will involve writing copy. All successful direct mailers agree that this is one of the most important features of any direct mail campaign. Writing effec-tive copy is something that can take years to master. If you are a first-time direct mailer, you may want to seek the counsel and assistance of an experienced professional. Consult your local business directory under "Advertising" or see the classified advertising in one of the

trade publications. What follows are some basic guidelines to consider when writing copy for direct mail:

Keep copy simple and easy to understand

Many readers will simply glance at your direct mail package and, unless the message can be understood immediately, there may be little chance of it grabbing their attention. Use the billboard approach. You are driving down the highway at 65 mph. You have about one quarter of a second to see, perceive, and understand the message on a billboard. Notice that there are very few words. Notice that every word counts. Notice that the words make a point or create an impression. There's another billboard. You did not even notice it but you just got a message.

Focus on the prospect. Who are they? What turns them on? What would motivate them? Will they understand a pun? You want to wind up with:

- a profile of the prime prospects
- description of the offer
- list of benefits
- list of unique advantages
- an action you want the prospect to take

Make effective use of headlines

Headlines break up long blocks of copy. This makes them more readable and allows recipients to get your message quickly. Headlines attract the attention of the reader and highlight key points. Rosser Reeves once described the concept of the *unique selling platform*. It essentially says that you must get as much about what you want to say about what you have into the copy, and especially into the headline, as early as possible and as succinctly as possible.

- State the strongest benefit in an interesting and direct manner.
- Write to one person. The most important word in direct marketing is *you*.
- Use puns and double meanings in your headlines with care. There is a danger that readers will not understand your intended meaning and will not invest the effort to figure it out. Puns and wordplay could distract from the selling message, so make sure the average person will get the joke. Headlines sell; sometimes they entertain.

- Communicate the benefit clearly and unambiguously.
  "Learn to speak French in two months or your money back."
  "Save 60% off your next rental car."
- Do not overuse bold and italic and underline. AND NO ALL CAPS! Especially with an exclamation point.
- Personalize your headlines. You will attract a greater number of qualified prospects if you address them by name, title, or area of interest in your headline. People scanning their direct mail will stop and read a piece if they know or sense that it contains information of specific interest to them.
- Use contractions and informal language.
- Use the "how to" approach.
  "How to save money on long distance calls."
- Include your product or company name in the headline. Since many people will read only the headline of your direct mail piece, you should take every opportunity to increase name recognition.
- Keep paragraphs to seven lines or so.
- Edit like crazy. Get the words down and then cut and slash and change. Nothing is sacred. Everything can be improved. Everything is longer than it should be, like this paragraph. Short sentences are better than long sentences.
- Make headlines stand out but not stand off. Use bold type or color, but do not use weird typefaces or all capital letters. Make sure that the type is legible and big enough for people to ready easily.
- Proofread with an eagle eye. Have the lawyers look it over. Have the lowest level assistant look it over.
- Use the verbalization test. Read your copy out loud. Does it flow "trippingly from the tongue?" Does it sound like natural conversation?

The classic form of direct mail advertising is the letter. That's right. A simple, personalized letter. Over half of all direct mailings consist of:

- an outer envelope
- a personalized letter
- an informational brochure
- an order blank as a self mailer
- an order blank and a reply envelope

The typical direct mail letter should:
- be personalized
- lead the reader through the copy
- explain benefits
- overcome objections
- engender action

It should look like a letter. Many use a typewriter type font. This is no longer as necessary as the number of typewriters declines. A good serif typeface is fine.

The first paragraph should be short and to the point. Think of it as your headline. If you can somehow link a piece of information in the database to the recipient, you will get and hold their attention, like:
> *Since you acquired your Ford pickup truck in 1996 . . .*
> *As a user of Microsoft Word . . .*

You can place a box around a paragraph that you want to emphasize. You should indent certain paragraphs to add some variety to the format. You might even want to add a postscript to throw in that last offer or premium.

Tell your customer how to respond

One way to get more prospects to respond to your direct mail piece is to tell them exactly what you want them to do. Be clear and precise in describing what has to be done to inquire about your product and when it should be done. Make the coupon easy to understand and use. Provide an envelope or instructions on how to fold the reply card or cut the reply card. Or just mail the reply card.

Tests have proven that providing both *yes* and *no* boxes on the reply form increases response rates. But they also reveal that more choices decreases response rates. It has been said that the reply form should look valuable. Examples: special review certificate, free reservation application, private trial certificate, and "valuable" coupon.

Business reply mail

Business reply mail is an essential part of direct marketing. The amount you pay depends on the volume. You can set up an advance deposit account and your reply pieces must be encoded so the Postal Service equipment can read and record charges automatically. To qualify for the Business Reply Mail Accounting System requires a sample card or envelope to be tested for mail processing. At 4.25x6 inches, a business reply card qualifies for the postcard rate. Over that size, it is charged at the first-class letter rate.

Warn of a limited supply or an impending price increase

Advise potential customers to take action immediately because delay could result in missing out on the offer entirely. Be sure to inform your prospects if your price represents a temporary reduction or if it is going to increase in the near future.

User testimonials

Testimonials are an effective sales method when writing copy. They lend credibility to the direct mail package by implying approval from a credible and respectable third party other than the actual seller. Make sure you have written permission before using a testimonial.

Use action devices or offer bonuses for action

Using a premium with a time limit or a bonus if action is taken before a certain date encourages immediate action from people who may put off responding to a direct mail solicitation.

Emphasize special prices

Bargain prices, discounts, new lower prices, and easy-payment terms should be emphasized. In addition, any special price reductions should be placed prominently on your direct mail package. Other tips that you should consider when writing advertising copy:

- Avoid using words like "official," "best" and "guaranteed." These words not only lack specificity, they may also raise potential legal issues. Remember, you must be prepared to back up any claim. If you say it's "the best" you will have to prove that comparison. "One of the best" may work better.
- Try reading your copy as if you were a pessimistic prospect who's looking for "the catch." Try to anticipate "this sounds too good to be true."
- "We" establishes your company's position; "I" makes a personal commitment. "You" is neutral. Trust us, use "you" instead of "we" and "I" whenever you can.
- Avoid overly aggressive or submissive openers. Present yourself at the same level as the prospect.

- The use of numbers and statistics can lend credibility to your message, especially if they are presented in easy-to-understand charts and graphs.
- Show it to informal focus groups, coworkers, and family friends.

Those companies who successfully use direct mail often experiment with a variety of direct mail approaches before selecting the one best suited to a specific situation.

Legal stuff

The Federal Trade Commission exists to promote free and fair trade. Its power has increased over the years to include "unfair and deceptive acts or practices in commerce." State and local governments have their own laws to protect consumers as well. We are not providing any legal advice, but we can say that common sense should prevail. Do not make statements or claims that cannot be backed up. Honesty is the best policy.

Envelope strategies

- Teasers
  Most of these merely alert the recipient that advertising lurks inside. They can also alert the recipient that something special is dying to get out.
- Mystery return address
  Nothing gets *me* to open a letter faster than a simple addressed envelope with a return address I do not recognize. If it looks like a mass market piece I treat it as such—it gets tossed in the dustbin with the mass of mail.
- Stamp or indicia
  The mailing approach is always a dead giveaway. I love those mailing that exclaim that they are priority or special and the indicia is for bulk rate.

Watch for oversized envelopes. Sizes over 6.12x11.50 inches are charged at a rate schedule called *flats*.

Even if you use a bar code, the postal service may slap a sticker on the envelope to correct it or add a reply code. The lower right of your envelope—.60x4.75 inches—may be covered, so consider this if you want to place copy there.

Personalizing direct mailings

There are three basic types of direct mail packages: personalized, semi-personal, and generic. Personalizing can be done through letters, addressing on envelopes, or even on inserts and catalogs.

Saluations. If you do not use the person's name in the salutation, use something you know about them:

> *Dear Harley-Davidson user*
> *Dear Prepress Professional*
> *Dear Public Television Supporter*
> *Dear Friend of the Museum*

One veterinarian writes letters to my cat. Now I know why all that catnip was ordered through the mail. You better know the gender. Unless your database has a specific field for gender, be careful about Mr., Mrs., and Ms. and do not forget Sister, Rabbi, Father, Brother, Dean, Dr., and more.

Personalization works

One of the most common methods of reaching prospective buyers is through personalized direct mail. When potential customers receive personalized mailings, they generally believe that the sender has used special thought and care in selecting their names. Recipients tend to think that not everyone on the block received the same letter. Many companies have found that by personalizing their mailings, the response rate has increased almost 50 percent.

Be careful, however, that your personalization does not sound too gimmicky. Readers might believe that if your direct mail package is a gimmick, your product must be as well. For example, by using a list based on Zip codes, it is possible to reach a neighborhood with similar characteristics, such as income and educational levels, housing preferences, or even automobiles purchased. Keep in mind that obtaining this type of information will cost more.

Whenever possible, it is a good idea to use an individual's title along with his or her name when mailing to businesses. This not only makes your package more personalized, but if the person to whom it is addressed has changed positions, you may still reach the new person holding the job. Using the name alone may result in your mail being returned or simply thrown away.

One of the easiest methods of personalizing your direct mail is by using a service bureau's mainframe computer to generate addresses. Service bureaus are companies that operate powerful computers, and often specialize in list maintenance and other direct mail support services. Manual typing of addresses can be expensive and time-consuming, while having a service bureau print labels for you may take only a fraction of the time and cost much less. Also, new computer software has made "mail merge" and address label printing much easier than in the past, in some cases giving you the ability to personalize your mailing inhouse using your own computer.

Other methods of personalizing your direct mail effort include:

- Attachments—these include personalized business reply cards and invitations.
- Illustrated letters—an illustration usually takes the place of the letterhead and can help set a personal tone for the letter to follow.
- Using computer-simulated handwriting to make it look as if you have personally addressed the direct mail package.
- Pre-printed signatures on letters.

Want to really get an envelope opened? Use a font that looks like handwriting and a real postage stamp in a #10 envelope.

Semi-personal approach. This is also known as the custom approach, and is generally used with in-house lists, where you know what previous customers have purchased. The salutation in a semi-personal letter usually reads something like "Dear International Business Entrepreneur" or "To a Valued [Product] Customer." This lets readers know that they are part of a select group. These pieces of mail can be effective and are, for obvious reasons, not as expensive to produce as personalized letters.

Generic approach. Approximately 65 percent of today's direct mail letters begin with a generic salutation like "Dear Friend." These kinds of letters are easy and inexpensive to produce, and can be used when personalization is not appropriate or cost-effective.

The goal of personalizing direct mail is to tailor your piece to the customer's habits, likes and dislikes—much of which can be determined based upon the list you use. Find out as much as you can about your customer and incorporate this information into any direct mail that you send. A good rule of thumb: the more personal you make your mail, the more likely you are to get a favorable response.

Paper
Paper is an important ingredient in the direct mail mix. It helps communicate a level of quality as the person opens the piece. In some cases you are limited by the digital printer because of the need to have paper that can hold an electrical charge to hold the toner, or special paper that works well with inkjet ink, or a special paper that is best suited for multiple color toners. The general choices are:
- uncoated bond
- newsprint
- coated stock
- textured stock
- tinted stock
- copier paper

Caliper and basis weight refer to the thickness and weight of the stock. Postcards must be .007 inch thick, for instance.

Paper weight is usually based on the weight of 500 sheets of a paper's basic size. This does not mean 8.5x11-inch—paper comes in larger sheets in most cases and is cut to size. You may have a ream of 500 sheets of 8.5x11 inch paper, but it does not weigh 20 pounds. That paper is based on a 17x22-inch sheet and 500 sheets of that size weigh twenty pounds.

The weight of the total package is the major consideration for many mailers. They often seek quality papers that are light in weight.

Inserts
Inserts range from folders and booklets to brochures and circulars and can be used effectively in a direct mail package. These inserts should differ from other package components in order to catch the reader's attention. Consider the following tips to help maximize profits and direct mail response when using inserts:
- The more creative (for instance, size, color, and content) your inserts are, the better. Your printer can help identify a few semi-standard formats that you can use to add interest to the mailing while keeping costs down.

- Consider adding inserts to your customers' packages when you fulfill their catalog orders, as well as in your direct mail pieces. You may find that additional inserts result in cost-effective orders you may not have otherwise received.
- To cut costs, you might consider grouping your inserts with those of other mailers who have non-competitive or complementary products or services. By combining resources and sharing mailing costs with the other mailers, you may be able to reach more potential consumers at a lower cost.

Additional techniques to consider when selecting a format:
- Using a brochure is an excellent way to provide potential customers full details of your product or service. Brochures are very versatile and can have a strong impact on your audience, especially if it is well done in terms of content and style.
- Avoid staples and paper clips. They only add weight to the mailing and are usually distracting to the eye. If there are too many things to look at, the reader may become frustrated and simply throw away your mail package. Such items can also hamper the processing of your mail.
- A common type of insert is a buckslip, usually a single sheet which which promotes a single product, feature, or benefit. Sometimes these inserts are included to place special emphasis on a previously mentioned product or to provide a more in-depth description of a new product.

Most brochures are based on standard sized sheets of paper:

8.5x11
    1 fold   5.5x8.5
    2 folds   3.66x8.5
8.5x14
    1 fold   7x8.5
    2 folds   3.5x8.5
11x17
    1 fold   8.5x11
    2 folds   5.5x8.5
    3 folds   3.66x8.5

What to put in the brochure
- testimonials
- list of benefits
- guarantees
- questions and answers
- tables, comparisons
- options
- highlights of features

Make sure the brochure is visually interesting and draws the reader into the copy.

Self-mailers
There is something about an envelope that engenders mystery. How often have you held one up before opening it? It is like a gift that sits wrapped under the Christmas tree. A self-mailer is an alternative mail advertising format, essentially a brochure that is folded and mailed without an envelope. It is written as any other direct advertising would be written. It is folded and either sealed or unsealed and opens to reveal a set of panels. It offers a higher level of personalization than any other direct mail since both sides can be personalized during the production process, and no collating is required.

Postcards
This is a minimalist self-mailer. You have two chances to get your message out: the front and the back of the card. Usually the side with an image is called the *billboard* side. Growing in use because no envelope has to be opened, and very inexpensive to produce and mail.

Card packs
This is a deck of cards, always in an envelope, sometimes in a plastic bag. Sometimes it is a set of coupons , or mixed coupons and cards.

Catalogs
Great covers command attention. Covers (both front and back) are the first things that buyers or prospects see. Front covers can make a 30 percent to 40 percent difference in revenue per catalog mailed. Using selective binding, larger catalog mailers pinpoint certain audiences with different covers and even center spreads. Why?
- Getting the customers' attention by using a hook based on their profile.

- Standing out in the crowded mailbox.
- Getting readers to open the catalog.
- Highlighting an offer that is irresistible.
- Giving customers a quick read about what is offering.

Great photography and image manipulation. If copy is king, the image is queen in the catalog environment. Unlike other types of direct mail where copy is often the "driver," a catalog is a visual medium and design and photography are the critical creative elements. In those catalogs that consistently stand out and produce great results, it is great photography and imagery that lead the way. There are lots of photo style options:

- bleed images
- silhouetted images
- fancy images or with no background
- highly accessorized, minimal accessories, or no accessories in the image
- with or without models
- on location or in a studio
- illustrative art rather than photos

Another aspect of photography is styling—how the image is set according to its background and surrounding items. Sometimes the item can stand on its own; other times it should be in a visually interesting environment.

Great copy. We have become a population of Attention Deficit Disorder individuals. We are scanners and "skimming readers." It is probably the impact of television, but today's readers concentrate on headlines, captions, and callouts to get the gist of an article. The importance of catalog copy has thereby been elevated to a new level. Headlines, subheads, charts, and captions all take on greater importance in assisting the skimming reader to the ordering process.

Whether one is telling the romantic narrative like J. Peterman or presenting the credibility of an L.L. Bean, the copy style must reinforce the brand. A copy breakthrough in catalogs is the use of "sidebar" or editorial information. Including background or editorial information is becoming more common to help the catalog build authority for its products. The concept of a "magalog" (half magazine/half catalog) is being tested.

Personalization. Direct marketers have long known that the use of personalization can dramatically improve response rates. Catalogers have been slow to adopt the available laser and inkjet technology. They are content with inkjet addressing the back cover and the order form along with an occasional, additional address panel message. With greater database segmentation and improved laser printing techniques, we will see more targeted, personalized messages being used as technology advances. Fingerhut has used large type personalization on covers for 20 years.

Another personalized technique in the food industry started by the Harry & David marketing company is the personalized giftgiver package in which the catalog is mailed in an envelope with a personalized letter to the gift giver and a personalized list of gift recipients from the previous year. Does it work? Like gangbusters! Digital or direct-to-plate printing, as well as selective binding, is making the cost and control of catalog versions much simpler.

Unique offers. Historically, catalogers have thought that presenting their merchandise in a well-designed, well-written, and well-photographed manner is all that it takes to get orders. And these elements are certainly the starting point. But with today's more fickle customers, we are seeing a greater use of offers to motivate targeted segments of customers to action. Database marketing and greater segmentation is driving such offers. Examples:

- Getting one time buyers to purchase a second time.
- Reactivating older year inactives.
- Increasing the average order value.
- "Early bird" offers to induce buyers to respond more rapidly.
- Positive offers to the very best customers to maintain their loyalty.
- Bundling of product or "twofor" or "threefor" offers to sell more items per order.

Testing an offer is a critical step in the direct mail process to really know if it is producing the gains that are needed.

Loyalty marketing. One of the creative thrusts of catalogers, and other marketing organizations, is relationship marketing or loyalty programs. It is driven by a better understanding of lifetime value, and how important it is to keep good customers. You can accomplish this by tying both retail and catalog sales into a loyalty reward program. One marketer built its program around its charge card and accumulated air miles. There are preferred buyer clubs as well.

Integrated marketing. Integrated marketing is based on three steps from a brand to the customer:

BRAND

Positioning
  Consists of a message directed at a defined audience.

Personality
  This consists of a strategy and a plan.

Proposition
  This consists of an offer and a call for action.

CUSTOMER

Linking the printed catalog to the Web. This is new creative ground for most catalogers. Dell and Gateway 2000's direct sales via the Internet are reportedly upwards to $5 million a day with as much as 30 percent of the sales coming from the consumer sector. These companies are the models to emulate. The creative challenge for both business and consumer catalogs is how to make the printed promotion and the Web site work together. As a start, every catalog needs to advertise its Web site in the catalog—at least on the back cover and order form. We will see an increasing relationship

Co-op advertising

"Co-op" can be defined as a marketing strategy designed to promote the manufacturer's brand name products on the local retail level. Co-op is a funding source allowance, for retailers, provided they meet the requirements of the manufacturers. These allowances are offered in many different forms and amount to tens of thousands of dollars in increased marketing budgets for retailers.

The co-op advertising strategy was first developed in the early 1900s. First used by the apparel industry in 1904, co-op allowances are now offered by most manufacturers to retailer and distributors in virtually all industries. The use of co-op funds has grown. U.S. manufacturers now offer a wide variety of complex promotional fund programs and are surprisingly well supported in the administration of them. Nearly 55 percent of manufacturers rely on consulting firms to assist with the database management and claim processes.

The retailer, on the other hand, has been ignored. Due to the overwhelming complexities of tracking and meeting program requirements, full participation in promotional programs is rare.

According to a top co-op consulting and administrative service company for manufacturers, 1997 promotional allowances increased by 5.6 percent to over $33 billion. Of these promotional dollars available to retailers and distributors, it has been conservatively estimated that $15 billion went unused, primarily because of the complexity of co-op funds management. Estimated figures for 1998 are even higher.

The root of the issue stems from the increasing variety of co-op programs available. A brief summary of available "soft fund programs" that need to be tracked includes:
- Co-op advertising programs
- MDF programs (market development funds)
- P-O-P display allowances (point of purchase)
- VIR programs (volume incentive rebates)
- Special promotional funds
- Pass-through dollars

In addition to the various co-op programs available, each vendor has their own particular claim requirements: allowable medium, particular logo use, claim submission frame and unique claim form layouts. Over time, the claim requirements have tightened, and the amount of time and paperwork associated with the process has simply been unmanageable. Other issues facing the management of co-op promotional funds include:
- Complexity of the process increases exponentially with the volume of business.
- As incentive, retailers are often offered multiple programs for multiple vendor products.
- Inter-departmental tracking (i.e. between Marketing, Advertising and Accounting).

Dealing with the USPS

Postage is reduced as you go from top to bottom in the two main classes of mail:

First Class
> Basic (full price)
> Presort (discount—must have a minimum of 500 pieces per mailing)
> Automated (Bar coded)
>> Basic
>> 3-digit Zip sort
>> 5-digit Zip sort
>> Carrier route (not in all Zips)

Standard Mail (was third class or bulk)
> Non-automated (no barcode)
> 3 and 5 digit Zip sort (must have a minimum of 200 pieces or 50 pounds per mailing)

Automated (Bar coded)
> Basic
> 3-digit Zip sort
> 5-digit Zip sort

Enhanced carrier route (not in all Zips)
> Basic letter
> Automatic basic
> High density
> Saturation

After you have addressed, bar coded, and sorted the mail, you must put it in trays (bags are rarely used today). These must be labeled in a certain way and delivered to the post office. The USPS has training programs that teach you how to do this. If you do it wrong, no matter who told you how to do it, you will have to take the mailing back and re-do it. There are many rules concerning size, thickness, address position and more. It is always best to check with a knowledgeable person before producing thousands of direct mail pieces.

Lettershops

This term refers to printing and mailing services that deal with direct mail of all kinds. Commercial printers usually specialize in printing direct mail but lettershops collate, insert, address, and mail. They are usually listed in the Yellow Pages under "Advertising—Direct Mail."

How to save money on postage
1. Clean your list regularly.
2. Focus on your market. Use smaller, targeted mailings.
3. Share mailings with other companies to get volume discounts.
4. Try smaller mailings using first class for better delivery and automatic forwarding.
5. Verify names and addresses through telemarketing.
6. Have all postal scales calibrated.
7. Use email or fax to communicate with special customers when appropriate.
8. Use "address service requested" to find customers who move.
9. Use Zip+4 and bar coding.

Fulfillment
Direct response is a two-way street. The mailee responds and so does the mailer. It is necessary to create a system to handle inquiries and orders and follow up and fulfill. An effective system should be planned before the initial mailing, such as:
- staff hours needed to handle responses
- effort that can be expended and still be profitable
- vehicle for following up that is the most effective

Never neglect a single response. Treat anyone who wants information the same as prospects who intend to buy. Many experienced direct mailers find that information seekers become important customers in the future, and you never know who they are.

Follow up each inquiry in a timely fashion. Regardless of the sales potential, each inquiry should be answered within two days of receipt. If you cannot immediately provide the inquirers with all the information requested, let them know their requests will be handled as soon as possible. Answer inquiries on a personal and friendly level. Organize your database so that "personal replies" can be automated. Give potential customers a complete answer to their questions. If you need additional time to find more specific answers, let them know.

Use your database to record responses. Information that should be recorded includes:

- who made the inquiry (with as much contact information as possible)
- who is responsible for the follow-up
- dates of inquiry—so you can track performance
- percentage converted into sales
- geographical location
- list of items sent to inquirer
- all data in separate fields to facilitate personalization

Prioritize the best leads. Keep track of these leads. Direct mailers may only send one letter to a prospect. Response rates often double the second, third, and fourth time the same prospect receives a mailing. Repetition and continuity are two important aspects in getting people to read what you have to say. Consider sending a series of letters a few days apart.

You can create a series highlighting different benefits in each letter, or you could send duplicates of the original. People may not even notice the mailing until the second or third letter, or piece, or package. Each unit should be a self-contained sales piece with all the information needed to sell your product or service. Treat each unit as the only one the prospect will ever see, even though it is part of a series.

As you can see, direct marketing is a complex area. It encompasses many sub-categories of activity that all involve relationship marketing: defining, contacting, communicating, and continually relating with customers—most often through highly personalized direct mail materials. Direct marketing is much more than what we think of as junk mail; it is one of the most effective promotion vehicles available to any company that wants to sell something to a defined audience. It is about finding and keeping customers.

This first chapter has attempted to give you an overview of many of the aspects of direct marketing. In later chapters we will show you how to create databases, how digital printing devices work, and how to create variable data printing materials, with lots of tips and tricks along the way.

What kind of work is applicable for direct marketing?
Here is a list of categories of material that lends itself to direct mail promotion:

Direct marketing categories:

Consumer Books/Records
Collection/Series—Books
Collection/Series—Audio; Video
Collection/Series—Cards; Misc.
Appointment Books

Clubs
Books
Food products
Records, CDs, Audios, Videos
Others

Collectibles
Lithographs
Prints
Posters
Artwork
Coins, Currency
Ingots
Precious Metals
Postage Stamps, First Day Covers
Stamps of Silver and Gold
Porcelain—Plates, Vases, Statuary
Sculpture—Silver, Pewter, Crystal
Jewelry
Others

Publications
General Interest Magazines
Special Interest Magazines
Women's, Home Magazines
Men's Magazines
Business/Financial Magazines
Regional Magazines
Computer Magazines
Newsletters
Newspapers
Investment, Financial Publications
Market Newsletters
Subscription Agencies—Consumer
Subscription Agencies—Library.

Catalogs
Consumer
Business
Computer
Food
Kitchenware
Consumer
Audios, Video
Gardening, Seeds
Shoes, Footwear
Forms, Binders
Imprinted Products
Children's Toys
Fine Arts, Crafts, Jewelry
Business Books, Audios, Videos
Seminars
College Courses
Home Study Courses

Merchandise
Cosmetics/Grooming
Clocks/Watches
Stereos/TV/VCRs
Cameras
Misc. Electronics
Health/Fitness
Housewares/Appliances
Luggage, Wallets
Tools
Do-It-Yourself
Optics
Shoes
Soft Goods (Rugs, Linens)
Food
Gardening
Photo Finishing
Crime, Protection
Heraldry, Ancestry
Horoscopes, Occult
Automotive
Telephone, Services
Wine/Liquor/Beer
Aircraft, Boats
Tableware

Animals/Pets
Sporting Goods
Men's Fashions
Women's Fashions
Men's/Women's Fashions
Tobacco Related
Furniture
Home Improvement
Cemetery Lots/Mausoleums
Other merchandise

Insurance
Accidental Death
Automobile
Homeowners
Condo/Apartment
Health/Hospitalization
Life
Travel
Other

Credit
Loans
Mortgages
Loans by Mail
Bank Services
Financial Services
Gasoline Credit Cards
Retail Credit Cards
Bank-Other Credit Cards
Affinity Cards
Secured Cards
Debit Cards
Corporate Cards
Credit Card Incentives
Add-On Services

Travel Promotions
State/City Promotions
Airlines
Timeshare
Hotel Promotions
Restaurants
Travel Clubs

Join, Attend, Be Listed
Clubs/Associations
Directories/Listing Forms
Seminars/Conferences
Cultural Organizations
Nominations/Awards

Arts
Performing Arts
Cable TV, Radio
Sporting Events

Health Related
Hospitals
HMOs
Medical Services

Lawyers, Legal Services

Child Oriented
Educational Services
Children's Books
Children's Magazines
Toys
School, College, Continuing Ed.
Baby Products

Fund Raising
Charitable
Social Action
Cultural
Environmental
Health/Handicapped
Minority Groups
Sports
Recreational/Environmental
Politics
Religion
Animals/Wildlife
Local Relief
Lobbying Efforts
Children
Education
Fund Raising Techniques

Communications
Renewals
Donor Efforts
Market Research
Military Recruitment

Academic Courses
Self-Study (Tapes, Tutors)
Distance Learning
Home Study

Financial/Investment
Commodities
Gold, Silver
Coins, Currency
Diamonds
Other Gems
Real Estate
Brokers—Stock/Bond
Funds—Mutual, Money Market

Business to Business
Business Books
Business Audios/Videos
Telephone Services
Business Services
Business Products

Imprinted, Monogrammed
Products
Printers/Copiers, Faxes
Business Forms
Office Supplies
Computer Hardware and Software
Online Services
CD-ROM
Annual Reports
Corporate Brochures
Franchise Offers
Auto/Equipment Leasing

Miscellaneous
Delivery Services
Coupons
Packaged Goods
Insert Programs
Retail Traffic Builders
Catalog Order Forms
Catalog House Solos
Sweepstakes
Card Decks
Printing
Stationery
Cards
Mailing Lists

An important aspect in the sale of these products and services is tracking customers and collecting information. To reduce input keying, information about the recipient is encoded in a barcode (on the right below) or in a data glyph (on the left). The glyph looks like a decorative element but contains more information than the barcode.

(420) SHIP TO POSTAL CODE

(420) 14450-8501

Personalized direct mail can be categorized in a number of ways. The chart on the next page summarizes one approach.

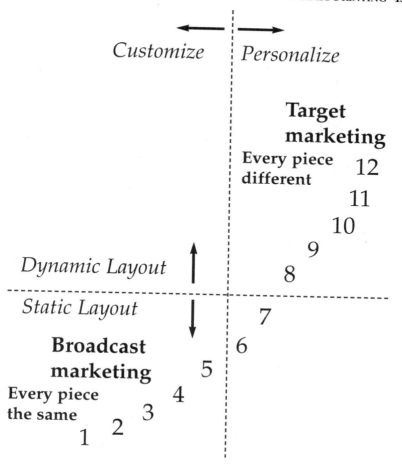

Customize | *Personalize*

Target marketing
Every piece different 12
11
10
9

Dynamic Layout 8

Static Layout 7

6

Broadcast marketing 5
Every piece 4
the same 3
1 2

12. Every pixel on every part of a piece or mailing personalized
11. Rules-based database and image merge, plus dynamic layout
10. Database and image merge (link to database and images)
 9. Hybrid documents (personalized pages with static pages)
 8. Database merge (link to all fields in database)
 7. Data merge (name/address, salutation, plus other data in text)
 6. Document assembly (assemble pre-written paragraphs)
 5. Mail merge (name and address and salutation)
 4. Address merge (name and address on letter and mail piece)
 3. Name and address on envelope or mail piece; sorted by state or Zip
 2. "Resident"—sort by state/Zip, contents via selective bindery
 1. "Resident"—same contents—every piece the same

These levels range from mass marketing where every piece is the same to target marketing where every piece is totally different.

1. "Resident"—same contents—every piece the same
You have received envelopes chock full of coupons and ad flyers for companies that are national in nature and every package is the same to every resident in every Zip code.

2. "Resident"—sort by state/Zip, contents via selective bindery
Envelopes chock full of coupons and ad flyers for companies that are local, with some national ad flyers—inserted via selective bindery. Pockets in the bindery system contain various pieces and, based on Zip code, which is inkjetted on the envelope, only pieces from certain pockets are inserted in the envelope.

3. Name and address on envelope or mail piece; sorted by state, Zip
At this level only the envelope is personalized, usually via inkjet and then sorted by state and Zip code. A message may also be printed on the envelope for each recipient.

4. Address merge (name and address on letter and mail piece)
Once you decide to place the name and address on a letter or promotion piece, you have three choices:
- a. Personalize the letter and the envelope and then hope you get the right piece in the right envelope.
- b. Personalize the letter and use a window envelope—the most common approach.
- c. Personalize a self-mailer so the address area and the promotion are part of the same piece.

5. Mail merge (name and address and salutation)
The letter has the name and address and a salutation area—"Dear So-and-So . . . "—make sure you get the gender right.

6. Document assembly (assemble pre-written paragraphs)
Sometimes called "boilerplate," because like a plate, it was unchanging and the document is assembled from these pre-written text units that are selected according to data in fields in the database.

7. Data merge (name/address, salutation, plus other data in text)
We have moved beyond addressing and have developed a set of pre-

written paragraphs with places to insert a limited amount of data, which has been output from the database

8. Database merge (link to all fields in database)
We are dealing with the database directly and every field is fair game.

9. Hybrid documents (personalized and static pages mixed)
This has been a major area for a long time. The static material is printed, usually by offset, and then the sheets or roll are run through a black-and-white digital printer or inkjet printer for personalization.

10. Database and image merge (link to database and images)
At this level, both text and images are integrated into the document based on the personalization program.

11. Rules-based database and image merge, plus dynamic layout
This level includes Level 10 with the use of dynamic layout, where the arrangement of the information varies according to the size and appearance of the material.

12. Every pixel on every part of a piece or mailing personalized
This is only possible with digital color printing. Images, text, and data are applied in a totally dynamic layout. Sophisticated programming.

All of these levels have one thing in common, they are a little bit different. There is no single approach. The term "personalization" may muddy the water, because much of personalization isn't so much "personal" as it is plain variable data. Black-and-white "personalization" has been going on for years: your credit card statement or phone bill is a variable-data printout. A phone bill is not a marketing campaign; but what's the production difference?

The waters are also muddied because some of our bills are becoming marketing campaigns. Your American Express statement comes with extra pages of variable-data promotional offers—some are based on your Zip code, some based on products that they know you've bought in the past (using the credit card). A driving factor for putting offers in your bill is postage. Forty five percent of the cost of any promotional mailing is postage. If you can suddenly stick personalized sales offers into an envelope, at almost no extra postage cost, it changes the economic profile of the whole deal.

Anyone who's done mail-merge has been doing Variable Data Printing Two VDP programs (Fiery Freeform and Splash DiamondMerge) are based on ordinary mail merge. You give the print shop a background page created in any program and a mail merge file. The VDP program overlays the mail merge on top of the base page, and presto: variable data. This is not the slickest or fastest kind of VDP, but it works and it's easy and there's a lot to be said for that.

- Just data: phone bills, etc. (no "publishing," really?)
- mail merge letters—vary the name and address—use pre-printed letterhead
- Vary the text, too: mail merge on pre-printed pages—store the letterhead in the system, vary the data.

In all of the above, the VDP product is making no decisions. It's only printing what you send it—and you have to send it everything ready-to-print. This doesn't mean it has to be a small or simple application—mail merge can be very sophisticated. But the VDP tool isn't doing anything fancy—the mail merger is doing the fancy stuff. Now we might move into a next tier, where the VDP products (or the prepress specialist) play a more active role, for instance:

- Refine the data: use a spreadsheet or VDP tool to fix capitalization, combine data fields, etc.
- Conditionals: use the "IF" feature of a spreadsheet or a VDP tool to create a new variable, based on another variable in the data file: gender, age, Zip code, etc.
- Auto-import graphics: a product photo, a sales rep's photo, an EPS file for a coupon, a map.

Beyond this you move eventually to the super-fancy systems like Bitstream's PageFlex, that can automatically vary the page layout to adjust for things like the size of the imported pictures, the length of the imported text, etc. None of the above addresses what will be a major stumbling block for the early pioneers: production speed. There are very big differences in how long it takes to produce some jobs, depending on what RIP technology and printing engine you use: some systems (for instance, the mail merge ones) have no time-saving features at all—you RIP every mail merge page entirely, even if it uses a photo you've used on 1,000 other pages. But, we got to draw the line somewhere, right? Maybe there's "levels of VDP for editors" and another chart someday on "levels of VDP cleverness in the RIP."

Glossary

Barcode Sorter (BCS) A mail processing machine that reads barcodes on mail and automatically sorts the pieces.

Break-Even Point The minimum number of sales a direct mail campaign must generate in order for the direct mailer to recover associated costs of the campaign.

Business Reply Mail (BRM) A service that enables mailers to receive first-class mail back from customers or prospects by paying postage only on the mail actually returned to them from the recipients.

Bulk Mailing Allows you to present large quantities of mail to a particular post office for mailing at lower rates.

Collect on Delivery (COD) A service whereby payment for a purchase is collected by the deliverer of the goods, who in turn pays the sender.

Data Glyph A barcode-like element that contains name, address, and other information about the recipient and may be scanned upon receipt to eliminate re-entering data about the sender.

Flat A piece of mail that exceeds the dimensions for letter-size mail, but not certain maximum dimensions.

Fulfillment A company's following through with its promise to a customer, usually by sending them the item purchased or information offered.

Fulfillment House A company specializing in, responding to, and tracking orders sold through direct mail.

Generic Describing a trait common to all items in a class; lacking personalization.

In-House List A list of names, addresses, and/or telephone numbers of customers compiled by a company.

Indicia A preprinted marking on each piece of a bulk mailing that shows payment of postage by the sender.

Insert Any item, such as a brochure or pamphlet, that is placed in a direct mail package.

Lettershop A company that personalizes, labels, sorts, and stuffs envelopes in preparation for bulk mailings.

List Potential customers for your product or service comprised of, at a minimum, their street address, city, state, and Zip code. It may also contain their name and/or title.

List Broker An individual or company that brings together owners of lists and the direct mailers who use them.

List Compiler An individual or company that specializes in gathering names, addresses and information from a variety of sources to produce a customized list of prospective customers.

Merge/Purge The process of combining two or more mailing lists into a single list. Duplicate names and/or addresses are deleted.

OCR (optical character reader) A computerized mail processing machine that scans addresses on mail and applies the proper barcode.

Overs (or Overruns) The portion of a print run that exceeds the quantity specified in the purchase order.

Premium A free gift sent to a potential customer either with the mailpiece (front-end) or after the prospect has responded (back-end).

Psychographic Refers to qualities defined by a person's habits, hobbies, occupation, and/or socioeconomic status.

Response Rate Measurable account of people or businesses who respond to a mail campaign. Equals total number of respondents divided by total quantity mailed and multiplied by one hundred. For instance, if you mail one hundred letters and six people respond, the rate response is six percent.

Saturation A complete or maximum penetration of your market, usually by geographic or demographic area.

Shelf Life The length of time before an item (such as a catalog) becomes obsolete.

Sorting In direct mail, the arrangement of pieces in a bulk mailing by Zip code to facilitate processing and more reliable delivery.

SIC (Standard Industrial Classification) The statistical classification standard underlying all establishment-based federal economic statistics classified by industry. The SIC is used to promote and compare the compatibility of establishment data describing various facets of the U.S. economy.

Tracking The maintenance of records concerning various aspects of mailings, for instance, response rate, date mailed, location of respondents, etc.

Unders The number of pieces by which a printing run is short of the quantity specified in the purchase order.

Window Envelopes Envelopes having an opening through which an address, or other information, printed on an insert is visible.

2

Digital Printing is Dynamic Printing

All printing today is digital, no matter how you do it. But digital printing as we will discuss it falls into these categories:

Monochrome			Color			
Electro-photography	Inkjet		Electro-photography	Inkjet	Thermal Wax	Dye Sub

The defining devices of paper-based replication are:
- printer
- copier
- press

A printer uses inkjet, wax-transfer, or toner technology to make marks on paper from data, resulting in the production of first generation originals where every one can be different, thus allowing the production of a collated document.

A copier uses inkjet or toner technology to make marks on paper from an original, resulting in the production of a second-generation copy, which, when copying multiple originals in an automatic document handler can also produce a collated document.

A press typically means a mechanical device that uses an image carrier to replicate the same image on paper, over and over again, resulting in a large quantity of the same images. A press may also handle larger sheets, resulting in multiple pages on one large sheet of paper used in a binding/finishing operation.

International Data Corporation reported that the number of pages printed on printers in 1995 for the first time exceeded pages printed on all models of copying machines. This led Hewlett-Packard to coin a new buzzword: *mopier*—a multiple original printer. If you make multiple original prints from an original-producing printer instead of an original-copying copier, it is a mopier. Since copiers are evolving to digital approaches—scanners on the top and printers on the bottom—they become de facto printers.

Printers at the high end, like the Xerox Docutech, are challenging offset duplication at the low end of the black-and-white printing world. Low-end printers are absorbing some of the work of both offset duplicators and mid-level copiers. The copier is pretty much a dead duck over the next decade. As scanners become cheaper and wind up on virtually every desktop, we can easily scan hard copy and print when we want to actually make a copy of something. But in most cases we are already preparing the information in computers and will probably print that information on a printer, rather than make one print and then copy it.

The last nail in the copier coffin is the fact that most files that would have been printed out and then copied are now just printed out in the required quantity. So over time we arrive at the following levels of replication device:

- printer
- printer-press
- scanner-printer (copier)
- press
- press-printer

A printer is easy to fathom. It hooks up to a computer, big or small, and prints stuff on paper at speeds from 1 to 50 pages per minute, simplex (that is, printing one side of the sheet). They range from desktop printers to production printers, increasing in the volume they can produce in a month (duty cycle) and usually in quality.

A printer-press is the way we presently describe a high-end black-and-white or color printer. Operating speed would be 50 pages per minute or more. In order to provide the production speed, these devices have had to find innovative methods for moving paper. Using rollers may provide opportunities for jams, so belts are used which hold the paper on them with static electricity. Or, webs (rolls) of paper are used. It may be that instead of re-imaging the photo conductive drum or belt for each copy, we image it once for some number of copies or even for all copies. Lastly, we are seeing the sheet size increase so that more pages are imaged at one time. These devices then become high-speed, high-capability printers and usually integrate some level of on-line bindery and finishing.

A scanner-printer is a printer with a scanner somewhere in the system, usually built into the device. These devices most often have plugs for network connectivity through an optional raster image processor (RIP). Calling them copiers makes no sense, but the term will persist for a long time.

A press is just what it is now, with plates and ink, printing a number of pages of the same information, on a large sheet of paper. Press refers to a device that makes an image carrier and then replicates images from that carrier. Every image is the same (hopefully). Think *printing* press when you think press.

A press-printer is a printing press with automated on-press image carrier generation and some level of variable printing integrated into the process, usually an inkjet system at the back-end of the device.

The objective of replication technology over the next decade will be to build into the printing press the kind of automation that is now built into copiers and printers. By de-skilling the process and automating it to a high level, the cost of paper-based communication comes down. Cycle time is reduced which leads to all the current buzzwords: short run, on-demand, just-in-time, distributed printing and more. Maintenance of graphic arts quality levels is assumed. The majority of digital printing technologies are based on:
- ink
- toner
- inkjet
- other (wax)

The table below categorizes digital printers by speed and other characteristics. When you say "digital printer" you are covering a great deal of ground, from very low-end desktop devices to color-based devices that compete with printing presses.

But why even consider a digital printer or printer/press? Ink-on-paper printing has been around for over 500 years. Why change? Let's get some background.

The complete spectrum of digital color printers/presses

Pages per minute

300+ / 250 / 200 / 150 / 125 / 100 / 75 / 50 / 25

Look for this area to keep growing. A $1,000 toner-based desktop printer possible	There are now over 20 models of color copier and RIP that can be acquired. Look for great deals	We think that a number of systems will be introduced into this category	We think that Xerox and other companies will enter this category	Canon has done a great job in this category. Surely, they are being challenged from below and above	The Indigos get their own category because of the resolution leve. The Pro is the low-cost version	There is the Docucolor 40 and there is the more expansive Docucolor Pro
<5ppm	7–12ppm	13–19ppm	20–29ppm	30–34ppm	35–39ppm	40–49ppm
400dpi	400dpi	400dpi	400dpi	400dpi	800dpi	400dpi
$4,000	$10,000	$20,000	$45,000	$100,000	$300,000	$135,000
Desktop laser printers	Color copiers w/RIPs	To come	Canon CLC2400	Canon CLC1000	Indigo E-Print Pro, E-Print 1000+	Xerox Docucolor 40

Price is the average for devices in category

T/R Systems MicroPress cluster printers at 48 ppm

The reproduction of information on paper falls into two categories:
- static printing
- dynamic printing

Static printing refers to traditional ink-on-paper approaches, offset lithography being the most common, where each and every sheet is reproduced from the same image carrier which is fixed with the same image. The copies look exactly the same. Toner-based printers, con-

<–Sheet-fed : **Web-fed–>**

					Certainly web-fed, absolutely 600dpi or better	
We will see devices in this category by 2000, and the resolution will jump to 600	Look for significant competition here by 2000 in quality, speed and productivity	There will be other web-fed digital printers by 2000	To be a true digital press, we expect 4-up signatures or better	Perhaps the next generation of Xeikons?	120+ppm 600dpi+ $1,000,000	500–1000ppm 1000dpi+ $500,000–$2 million+
50–60ppm	60–70ppm	70–80ppm	80–100ppm 600dpi $500,000	100–120ppm 600dpi+ $800,000		
400dpi+	800dpi	600dpi				
$180,000	$700,000	$400,000				

The dotted lines are for devices that are yet to come

The upper limit on the rule is the speed in simplex or one pass 4-color through the marking engine; the lower limit is the duplexed speed—8.5x11 standard sheets

To come	Indigo UltraStream, others	Xeikon 32cm versions	Xeikon 50cm versions	To come	To come 2-up sheet-fed to 4-up web-fed 4-color offset press
		Agfa, IBM, Xeikon, Xerox			

versely, use an image carrier that is imaged each time a sheet comes in contact with it, re-imaging for each copy. The copies look the same, but each is generated individually. Dynamic printing means that the printer must re-generate the image for every page; thus, every page can be different: variable data printing.

Process differences

	Static (offset printing)	Dynamic (digital printing)
Image Carrier	Fixed	Variable
Material	Ink	Toner, Inkjet
Quality	High	Moderate+
Variability	None	High
Quantities	Moderate to high >2000	Low to moderate <2000
Paper selection	High	Limited
Sheet size	Small to large	Small*
Documents	Moderate to long runs	Short runs

*except for 50 cm (20-inch) Xeikon engines

The advantage to static printing is the cost effectiveness of long runs.

The conceptual chart on the facing page shows the relationship between offset color printing and digital color printing by comparing run length and cost per unit. Our numbers have always shown that offset printing has a high up-front cost based on makeready and that each additional unit printed absorbs a part of that cost. The more units, the less cost per unit. Digital printing on the other hand has no real makeready as such so each unit costs the same.

You can create an artificial system that either reduces or increases cost based on volume. "Click" charges can either reward a user for higher volumes or penalize them. The direct imaging color presses still have makeready so they fall into offset printing. The gray area is the opportunity area for digital printing.

We think that the crossover point is about 2,000 copies but this is a moving target as both technologies continually tweak their cost structure and productivity.

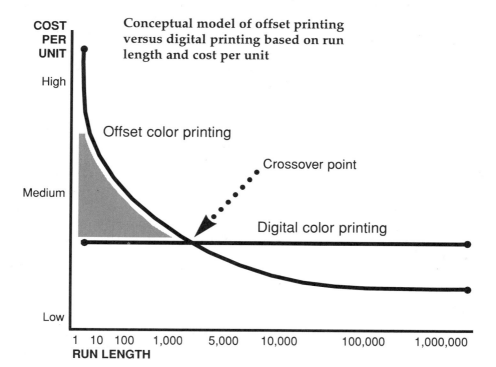

Conceptual model of offset printing versus digital printing based on run length and cost per unit

The advantage of dynamic printing is that the re-imaging for each sheet lets you do two things you cannot do with a printing press:
- each sheet personalized to a person or company
- one multi-page document at a time

You can only do these things on a digital printer.

There are some other advantages but, in some cases, newer printing presses with built-in automation compete in the areas of:
- very short runs
- very fast turnaround
- distributed printing

Thus, printing presses are still in the equation as viable reproduction systems.

Digital printing

Digital printing is any reproduction technology that receives electronic files and uses spots (or dots) for replication. Ink, toner, inkjet, or any other dye- or pigment-based transfer system may be used. This covers almost every present system for outputting graphic information to film, plate, or to paper.

Totally electronic printing (TEP) refers to the use of a re-imageable image carrier or no image carrier for the transfer of toner or inkjet ink to paper. TEP often uses pixels—spots with gray levels. Inkjet is a direct-to-paper technology with no intermediate image carrier. Toner-based reproduction requires a photo-conductive drum or belt to create the toned image and then transfer it to paper. In essence it is an image carrier, like a printing plate, except that the printing plate is fixed and does not change during reproduction. The toner-based image carrier must create a new image for every reproduction and is thus re-imageable.

This means that toner-based systems are inherently slower than fixed-plate ink-based systems, since re-imaging in zero time is not really a possibility. The downside to re-imageability becomes the upside in the ability to produce variable printing. The term "digital printing" is often used to mean "totally electronic printing."

Direct imaging

Direct imaging replaces the term "hybrid press" which refers to the imaging of *fixed* image carriers (plates) on the press, rather than offline. On-press platemaking refers to the use of a one-time use plate; on-press image carrier creation may allow the re-use of the image carrier after cleaning. Developmental systems may image the plate cylinder directly and then clean it for another imaging. The advantage to on-press platemaking is that makeready is reduced substantially, especially if plates are loaded, imaged, registered, printed, and unloaded automatically.

Variable printing

Variable printing means that each printed piece can be different and that customized and personalized printing can be produced for target marketing purposes. Customized means that documents can be assembled particular to selected audiences. Personalized means that each unit is particular to a specific person or other entity.

On-demand printing

On-demand printing is a euphemism for short run, distributed, just-in-time printing, no matter how it is produced, but many consider it as totally electronic printing. The term is so fraught with misunderstanding that it will hang on for a long time because it can mean anything to anyone who wants to exploit its ambiguity. Just remember than printers and prepress services have always produced work on demand—the customer demands, printers deliver.

Distributed printing

This aspect of printing is often lost in the on-demand rush. It essentially says that the print-and-distribute model is not always valid. With distribute-and-print we can send digital files anywhere and print the quantity required proximate to the point of distribution. As large printing companies acquire medium-sized printers in different geographic regions they are establishing the network for distributed printing. Loose affiliation between other printers is related. But keep in mind that not all printing can or will be distributed. The economics for centralized reproduction are still strong for many types of printing. The printing that is distributed may be either ink or toner or inkjet on paper. A digital file can be sent to a remote location to make a plate as easily as it can charge a drum with toner.

Digital prepress and workflow

Prepress is now over 85 percent digital. Its major connotation has to do with preparing material for the press. Today, printers are also preparing information for recorded disks and for the World Wide Web. Is it still prepress? Or is it pre-publishing? Or pre-media? We will probably say prepress when we are talking about the preparation of information for distribution in any form. Moving files around on a network is only a part of digital workflow. It refers to the processing of those files as well. We prepare PostScript files, swap low-res for high-res images, interpret, trap, impose, rasterize, screen, and output. All of that and more is digital workflow.

Print, the final frontier

In the last few years print has gotten a negative rap. Many people outside the industry do not understand that this is not your father's printing industry anymore. It is high tech and high time. Some companies and even some institutions of higher learning have been dropping the word *printing* in favor of *imaging* or *graphic communications*.

Like all terms we can make print mean what we want. So let us all make it mean the communication of information via spots on paper, pits on discs, or pixels on video screens, produced with digital technology. Print is communication of information to an audience.

One way of categorizing printing approaches is by their run length.

Run length vs. reproduction approach

	Digital Printing	Direct Imaging	Offset Litho	Flexo	Gravure
Ultra Short Run (1) (12% of all volume)	100%	—	—	—	—
Very Short Run (2-500) (15% of all volume)	85%	10%	5%	—	—
Short Run (501-2,000) (14% of all volume)	19%	35%	43%	2%	1%
Moderate-Short Run (2,001-5,000) (13% of all volume)	2%	39%	55%	2%	2%
Moderate Run (5001-10,000) (10% of all volume)	—	23%	65%	9%	3%
Average Run (10,001-50,000) (9% of all volume)	—	15%	70%	11%	4%
Moderate-Long Run (50,001-250,000) (11% of volume)	—	2%	80%	12%	6%
Long Run (250,001-750,000) (7% of all volume)	—	—	76%	14%	10%
Very Long Run (>750,001) (9% of all volume)	—	—	50%	15%	35%

(Does not total 100%)

Non-impact printing

With a non-impact printer there is, theoretically, no contact between the printer and substrate, except for drums and or belts that carry the computer-generated image and transfer it to the substrate and must of necessity touch one another. Most non-impact printers use toner that is attracted to the substrate by an electric charge rather than an impact mechanism that pounds out every character that the printer can create. Non-impact printers developed because users wanted faster printout and larger character sets and more fonts than the original impact typewriters and dot matrix devices that were attached to early computers.

Impact printers that housed characters on belts and wheels were too slow, broke down often, and could not produce high enough resolution. There are basically five main categories of non-impact printers:

- inkjet
- thermal (thermal transfer, dye sublimation)
- electrophotographic
- ion deposition
- magnetographic

The dot matrix printer, invented by Centronics and mass-marketed by Epson and other companies, showed that characters could be reduced to dots. The push to develop non-impact printers began in 1978 with the introduction of Xerox's 9700 Electronic Printing System, a fully capable typesetter, plateless printing press, and automatic printer, all combined in one machine. The 9700 worked like one of Xerox's copier/duplicators, but without the need for an original image because pages were created by the Xerox Integrated Composition System (XICS) software. This was also one of the very first on-demand printers. Xerox tried to expand on the 9700 by developing the 8700, a lesser version; the 5700, designed for the network market; and the 2700, a much smaller version of the 9700.

There were many competitors joining the market when Xerox introduced the 9700. There was the IBM 3800, Xerox's biggest competitor, the Agfa P400, and an ion deposition printer from Delphax.

The impact printer market has all but disappeared with users preferring the ease, speed, and quality found in non-impact printers, mainly laser printers. Xerox's DocuTech has wiped out much of the offset duplicator business, and electronic printers like the Xeikon and Indigo are making inroads to the color on-demand printing market. Critics have predicted that this technology will eliminate traditional printing, but that prediction is still far too early to worry about.

Bits are building blocks
Another word for "digits" in digital printing is the word "bits," or binary digits. Imagine a piece of grid paper forming a mosaic of empty boxes in rows and columns. Fill in some squares and leave others blank. By choosing some and leaving others, you create a crude letter "A." If you had enough patience, you could create a pattern of squares that looked like the Mona Lisa.

```
0 0 0 1 0 0 0              X
0 0 1 0 1 0 0           X     X
0 1 1 1 1 1 0         X  X  X  X
1 0 0 0 0 0 1      X                 X
```

The number one tells the computer to fill a location with black and the number zero tells the computer to leave it blank. The digital revolution is all about making images from numbers. And digital printing is taking those numbers and imaging spots onto a substrate—paper, plate, film, whatever. Each location of the grid above is technically called a picture element. Each element or tile of the grid is called a *pixel* (short for "picture element"). The finer the grid (meaning the higher the resolution of the output imager), the more pixels that you'll need to fill, and the finer and more detailed the patterns rendered. The more pixels that you have to fill, the better your image can look. But, pixels have a meaning that goes way beyond on and off, zero and one.

Gray levels

Binary *bits* have two "levels." In order to create images of all types, we will need more. In drawing, there are two ways to do this. First, the illusion of gray value can be created with a black pen on paper by varying amounts of cross hatching or stippling. This varies the amount of white paper which remains visible, and thus creates an illusion of gray. Second, different shades of gray are created in conventional printing by varying the sizes of small "halftone dots" even though a press can only print black spots on white paper. Halftoning means taking a cluster of the output device spots—the unit that the device actually images (its resolution unit) and clustering some number together to create the illusion of gray.

By assigning different numbers (other than 1 or 0) to a pixel, it can represent varying levels of gray without halftoning. Exactly which trick is used to fool your eye depends on whether the image is rendered on the computer screen, on a printer, or on a press via an imagesetter or a platesetter. It is as if each pixel can be shaded with a pencil that has a different number indicating the shade that it can put down on paper (or the monitor screen.) Pixels that are not just binary bits are stored in the computer as *bytes*, usually a number from zero to 255. An image made up of pixels stored as *bits* is sometimes called a *bitmapped* image. However, an image with pixels made of bytes is *not* a bytemap. It is sometimes called a grayscale image, if it is a single color. It has greater *bit depth* than a bitmapped image, which just means it has gray values. Color images are stored in computers in various ways, but terms like "24-bit" or "36-bit" refer to color images with intermediate tones (that is, "gray" levels.)

Contone means continuous tone

Contone and continuous-tone refer to the same thing. When the tonal gradation of an image is continuous from white to black, we call it a contone image. This also means that we have several intermediate levels of gray between white and black. These varying gray levels give a feel of the image being continuous in its tones between white and black. Examples of continuous-tone images are photographs. The words grayscale, graylevels, bitdepth, and tone are very close. When shading is used in an image as in a contone image, depending on the levels of gray required, there will be a bitdepth higher than 1.

Raster file and bitmap file

A bitmap is a map of bits—by definition a one-bit-deep raster file. We often think of bitmaps as the things that RIPs generate from raster and other data to send to printers, platesetters, and imagesetters. A bitmap is an array of pixels—each pixel defined by its bit depth. It can be one bit deep (bilevel)—what Photoshop calls bitmap mode. This used to be called line art—it may or may not be in black-and-white (it could have been colored in QuarkXPress/PageMaker), and may or may not be at 100% (could have been screened). It can be 8 bits deep (grayscale, aka monotone or index color). It can be 24 bits deep (RGB). It can be 32 bits deep (CMYK). A CMYK image, for example, has four channels, each of which is eight bits deep.

A bitmap is a type of graphics file in which a separate value for each pixel of an image is stored in a bit or group of bits. Scanned images are stored as bitmaps. Adding more depth to raster files, we arrive at what we describe as a contone or continuous-tone image. How can something broken up into little squares be continuous-tone? Contone and continuous-tone actually refer to the type of original image that we are attempting to digitize, and do not describe the data itself—after all, individual pixels are squares of uniform color; the tones do not actually flow continuously from one area of an image to the next, but the squares create the illusion of continuous-tone when viewed from a reasonable distance. In prepress we use the term contone for a non-screened (non-halftoned) image. Thus, some digital printers are capable of outputting pixels—bitdepth—and are often called continuous-tone printers, where printing presses must, of necessity, output screened halftones for images. Printers can also do halftones, but why? Because many of us are accustomed to them.

Electrophotography

The first attempts at developing the process of electrophotography are explained in a patent in 1922. These attempts were directed toward the utilization of photocurrents to activate electrosensitive papers, which were sandwiched between a photoconductive layer and a conductive plate. A Belgian engineer came closer to Chester Carlson's discovery of xerography with his patent in 1932. This invention involved the use of a selenium plate and a Leyden jar to form an image as a powder pattern on another plate placed close to the selenium surface. This never developed into a practical process. Pursuit of these experiments may have led to Carlson's inventions. The active history of electrophotography, most commonly known as xerography, begins with Carlson's invention in 1938.

Carlson's first electrostatic image was produced on a photoconductive surface, developed with powder, and transferred to a piece of paper. The sensitive plate consisted of a layer of sulphur on a metal plate. The plate was then charged by rubbing the surface with a cloth, and the electrostatic image was produced by contact exposure to a hand-prepared transparency. His historical patent was filed on April 4, 1939, and was first issued on Oct. 6, 1942, as number 2,297,691.

No further experiments were performed until autumn, 1944, when the Battelle Memorial Institute in Columbus, Ohio, began its laboratory investigations. Between 1944 and 1948, the experimental effort at the Institute produced many important discoveries, improvements, inventions, and developments that made Carlson's invention feasible, and eventually made xerography a commercial success. Major discoveries included E. N. Wise's cascade development and the two-component triboelectric developer; J. J. Rheinfrank and L. E. Walk's contributions to corona charging; C. D. Oghton's introduction of vacuum evaporation as a means of making xerographic plates; R. M. Schaffert's introduction of electrostatic transfer; and W. E. Bixby's discovery of amorphous selenium electrophotographic plates.

An important event occurred in 1947 when the Battelle Memorial Institute began to receive additional funding for research and development from The Haloid Company, now Xerox Corporation, of Rochester, NY. The lab work became oriented in the direction of photocopy applications—the prime interest of The Haloid Company. In 1948, The Haloid Company won the interest of the U.S. Army Signal Corps and in mid-1948, the Signal Corps began sponsoring a project on electrophotography.

Beginning in 1950, Xerox's first copier consisted of units for charging xerographic plates, a camera for exposing the plate, a device for developing with powder, and a unit for heat fixing the image. In 1954, Young and Grieg of the Radio Corporation of America (RCA) announced a modified form of xerography, known as Electrofax. In 1958 3M Company introduced an electrophotographic process utilizing persistent conductivity (a concept first reported by H. P. Kallman of the Signal Corps.) in combination with electrolytic development. The process was first used in a microfilm reader-printer. But, in 1960 Xerox introduced its 914 copier. Its successors, the 720 and 1000, were similar but faster. Then, in 1963, Xerox introduced its 813 copier, a smaller desktop copier.

Just one year later, Xerox introduced the 2400, a copier-duplicator. The word duplicator described a faster copier. This was followed by the 3600, which operated at a speed of 60 copies per minute, and the 4000, which was capable of copying on both sides of a piece of paper. In 1970, IBM came on the scene with its Copier I, which used an organic photoconductor. Two years later, IBM came out with the Copier II. And after 1972, Japanese copiers came on the market. Companies have continued to come out with new and improved electrophotographic products; however, the basic technology of xerography has remained the same.

In the late 1960s and early 1970s the first color copier entered the market such as 3M's Color in Color copier. 3M's release was followed by competitive products which established the aspect of color within the former black-and-white market. Xerox introduced its color copier, the 6500 in 1973, and Canon announced its Canon T machine in 1978. All color copier approaches had two things in common. The mentioned color copiers were based on a three-color concept and, therefore, used three toners. And they were all analog light lens copiers.

As late as 1988, when Kodak released its ColorEdge copier, manufacturers used three toners and a light/lens system. Color copier technology, however, changed dramatically in the same year with Canon's introduction of the CLC-1. The CLC-1 was further developed to become the CLC-500, which used four toners (including black) and, in addition, relied on laser imaging technology. Most importantly, the device was a combined scanner and printer.

Xerox entered the market as the first vendor with a 300 dpi laser printer in 1978. The 9700 laser printer was based on the electrophotographic process, was priced at $400,000, and output 90 ppm. However, the landmark in the history of laser printers is the year 1983. Canon introduced the LBP-CX which was a 300 dpi laser printer that was priced under $5,000 and output 8 ppm. Canon's inventions were adopted by Hewlett-Packard and sold as the H-P LaserJet. With Apple's 1985 introduction of its Laserwriter, also based on the Canon engine, another important step in the history of output devices was made. Apple did not add significant changes to the printing process, but Apple's Laserwriter was the first PostScript printer. Laser printing advanced rapidly from that point.

Some results of the competitive atmosphere are cheaper prices, improvements in performance and speed. While PostScript established itself as a de facto standard since the mid-1980s, manufacturers accomplished significant improvements in terms of output addressability. Within 10 years the standard output addressability of 300 dpi increased to 600 dpi. Lexmark's Optra series, however, released in 1995, offered an output addressability of 1200 dpi. As far as the number of copies is concerned, Xerox's Docutech set the benchmark. Released in 1990 with an output speed of 135 pages per minute, Xerox's DocuTech was up to 10 times faster than previous output devices—a true production-based system.

The achievements in electrophotography not only have improved the performance of laser printers, but also have added color. Due to technological advances, laser printers were able to provide the user with the four process colors of cyan, magenta, yellow, and black. While Apple's Laserwriter, or Hewlett Packard's Laserjet are black-and-white output devices, Indigo's E-Print 1000 utilizes the four process colors with output at speeds above 30 ppm—such output devices are referred to as digital color presses.

Color copiers

Color copiers are essentially a scanner at the top and a digital printer at the bottom. They are designed for making one or several copies of spot- or four-color process pages. When controlled by computers they can be used for very short-run color printing (1–500). The first color copier used for digital color printing was the Canon CLC in 1987. It was also the first copier device to integrate a PostScript controller (from EFI). The Canon Color Laser Copier is a digital printer with a scanner that color-separates the color original into the four separation colors (CMYK), each with 400dpi resolution and 256 levels of gray per channel.

The CLC produced the four composite toned images on the paper mounted on a drum, as a result of four revolutions of the drum, after which the images were fused on the paper using a special fusing oil and heat. A RIP was used to produce images digitally from PostScript files. Today's color copiers also use the same digital technology as scanners and printers, but face greater issues as they are integrated into one unit. Early color copiers made copies that were inherently more expensive because the images were "built up" during each pass with the color toner.

All color copiers use black, cyan, magenta, and yellow toners. Theoretically, only three colors are required to print. However in traditional printing and color copying, adding a fourth color, black, improves picture quality and decreases cost for printed text. Color copiers often use successive scans to estimate the amount of toner of each color to apply. This adds complexity to the printing because each pass must maintain tight register. Another issue with color copying is the ability to mimic shading.

This is not as much of an issue with black-and-white copiers because people don't expect the picture to copy that well. Generally, the darker the text the more the customer is satisfied. With color copiers, lightness is a critical issue in the reproduction of color images. Correct lightness depends not only on the copier's scanning or optical systems to capture the correct color, but also the copier's print engine. Image processing becomes an important factor.

Optical copiers flash light and record light as it is reflected from the original through three or four color filters onto a photosensitive drum. Although not as flexible as digital copiers, optical copiers are generally less expensive and have the advantage of copying three-dimensional objects, a feature important to the jewelry industry. Connectivity, or the ability to connect your computer to the copier, is more formally called a color copier interface, or printer controller.

The first Canon color copier users were able to price their 8.5x11-inch color copies at $3.00 each, or more, and the 11x17-inch copies at $6.00. Today, the standard page is going for under a dollar (mostly about 75 cents), and the double-page sheet is going for $1.50 to $2.00. The introduction of the EFI Fiery PostScript RIP increased the per-copy price by increasing the value. Thus, customers could go directly from electronic files to good quality color pages.

Canon's newer copiers feature a new laser engine with duplexing (two-sided printing) capabilities and output speeds of seven pages per minute, 40 percent faster than the previous generation. The copiers also have numerous features designed to enhance image quality, including a smaller laser beam spot, a new method for sending charges to the transfer drum, and an anti-moiré filter. These copiers use a new, larger drum that yields of 40,000 copies before replacement as opposed to 20,000 from the old drum. They also feature a 50-sheet bypass tray that allows transparencies and paper stocks up to 90-lb. (163 gsm) index or 60-lb. (162 gsm) cover.

Both Indigo's E-Print and Xeikon's DCP-1 were announced in 1993. Whereas the Indigo provides the operator with an addressability of 800dpi and liquid toner, the DCP-1 (now the DCP-32D) is 600dpi and uses dry toner. It should be noted that the Indigo is a combination of electrophotographic and traditional printing technology because of its use of an offsetting blanket. The high demand for color output put pressure on competing manufacturers. Canon reacted to the market needs with its CLC-2400 and CLC-1000 at 24 and 31 pages per minute in full color respectively. In the meantime, Xerox entered the arena with the DocuColor at 40 pages per minute based on alliances with Fuji and Scitex. A 30-page per minute version is announced.

Recent products indicate that the trend is to merge copier and printer technologies. This trend is supported by the close relation of the technologies and it was the answer to the demands of the market for affordable, flexible, yet high-quality color output.

Technology

Copiers and laser printers use a similar technology to reproduce images. Because of the close relation and the number of similarities, it becomes more and more difficult to differentiate properly. However, there are distinct differences and some limitations that might apply to one, but not to the other technology. A copier will reproduce an original (whether or not it is a halftone) to the best of its capabilities. A laser printer, on the contrary must rasterize the image. Consequently, the source for a laser printer is a digital file. Although both technologies are combined into copier/printer in recent products such as Canon's CLC 900, this discussion divides the toner-based output devices strictly into four categories:

- laser printer, black-and-white
- laser printer, color
- copier, black-and-white
- copier, color

Laser printer, black-and-white

Toner-based laser printers use electrophotography, often referred to as xerography. The core of this process is a revolving drum or belt which is coated with a photoconductive material such as selenium. This photoconductor drum is uniformly charged prior to its exposure by a laser or light emitting diodes. During the exposure, the laser either charges the image areas or eliminates the charge in the non-image areas. In other words, the laser transfers the image information onto the photoconductive drum. For this purpose, the laser needs the appropriate data to decide which part must be exposed and which part must not. This is the job of the rasterizer or RIP—the raster image processor.

The required information for controlling the laser is provided by a print controller that interprets image information in PostScript format, rasterizes it, and sends it to the print engine. After exposure, an electrical charge attracts toner, which has an opposite charge. At this point the drum carries a copy of the image. Paper, which has an opposite charge from the toner, then attracts the toner which is transferred. Finally the image is fused onto the paper with heat and pressure. After the transfer process, the drum is cleaned and recharged.

A typical imaging workflow would involve scanning the original artwork, processing the scanned image with image manipulation or page layout software and outputting to a laser printer. Like any traditional printing process, a laser printer has only two possibilities, either it applies toner to the paper or it does not. Therefore, originals have to be converted into image data prior to their reproduction with a laser printer. The quality of the printed result depends on the number of gray levels that can be reproduced, the chosen screen frequency and the output addressability of the laser printer.

The higher the screen frequency, the fewer levels of gray one will get with a given output addressability. Consequently, the two possibilities to work around this obstacle are to either increase the output addressability or decrease the screen frequency. Recalling the fact that the number of gray levels is determined by the number of dots in a halftone cell, one can see the relation between screen frequency and levels of gray. The finer the screen ruling, the fewer number of dots reside in each halftone cell. Resulting from this ratio, fewer levels of gray can be rendered.

By applying the above equation, the limitations of an output device can be calculated. If a laser printer with an addressability of 600dpi has to handle 256 levels of gray, the screen ruling is limited to 38 lines per inch (lpi). One might be surprised by the low screen ruling, but the key is that 256 levels of gray are not always necessary. Often fewer levels of gray are enough to render an image. Even more important is a limitation given by PostScript. PostScript can only create 256 levels of gray and ignores everything that exceeds this number. Even with an output addressability of 2400dpi, a PostScript 1 or 2 level device will only render 256 levels of gray.

The same is valid in terms of screen frequency. If the screen frequency is reduced to a coarse pattern, the number of gray levels that can be achieved is limited to 256. Two unwanted effects tend to appear if not enough levels of gray can be reproduced. These are known as posterization and banding. Both occur if the output device cannot render sufficient levels of gray to ensure a smooth transition from one gray level to another. Banding, however, might also be caused by the deficiencies of the motor that operates the print engine.

Focusing on output quality, one will be confronted with the term "resolution." Resolution is the ability of an output device to render detail. Although resolution mainly depends upon the sampling rate of the scanner used and the chosen reproduction size, the laser print-er becomes involved if it comes down to output. The gain of a high-resolution scan might be lost because the amount of information exceeds the rendering capabilities of the RIP used with the printer.

At this point the screen frequency plays an important role. If one makes a high-resolution scan to enlarge an original but still wants to keep a high screen frequency, the RIP and marking engine will ren-der the image to the best of its capabilities. In other words, a high-res-olution scan might result in a large file that slows down the output process but does not necessarily enhance the image quality.

Output addressability has an important impact on how well images can be rendered. The output addressability, which is a measure of how many marks an output device can make within a linear inch, is determined by the spot size the laser beam can create and the size of the toner particles.

After receiving the necessary commands from the control unit, the laser exposes the photoconductive drum and light energy is trans-formed into electrical energy. If the laser spot has a large diameter, the addressability will decrease. If the laser spot's diameter is small, the addressability increases. A 20-micron spot, for example, equals a two-percent dot at a screen ruling of 200 lpi or a one-percent dot at a screen ruling of 150 lpi.

Conversely, a three-percent dot at 200 lpi has a size of 25 microns and at 150 lpi, 33 microns. However, the smallest laser spot size is not always the better choice. To create a solid black, the neighboring spots need to overlap. For that purpose a specific size is required.

But the appropriate spot size has to be chosen carefully. If the spot size is too small, one will not achieve solid blacks; however, if the spot size is too large, the resulting overlap might cause a loss of gray values. Unfortunately, there are no rules for the "right" spot size, and each manufacturer has its own philosophy about the optimum spot size. Some recommend the inverse of the addressability, others tend to a value between two times the inverse of the addressability and the square root of two times the inverse of the addressability. Laser imaging with toner is an evolving science. Quality and reliability are increasing at a rapid rate.

Nevertheless, the most important part is still the mark on the paper, which is caused by the toner. It is basically the size of the toner and the control over the toner spread that determines how many marks within a linear inch a laser printer can create. To achieve an output addressability of 1200dpi, Lexmark decreased the particle size of the used toner to 8 microns. These particles are a fraction of the size of previous toner. Assuming that a 600dpi laser printer has a toner particle size of 16–24 microns, one can see that the particle size limits the output addressability as well. Moreover, at higher screen frequencies single toner particles might account for variations in tone value.

Closely related to the size of the toner particle is the control of the toner transfer. In order to achieve good halftones, the toner spread has to be kept in narrow tolerances, and the thickness of the toner layer should be stable. The finer the toner particles are, the more difficult it is to control their spread. As a result of uncontrolled toner spread, the image might look grainy.

Toner is attracted to the imaged photoconductor drum, utilizing the fact that opposite charges attract each other. In addition to the problems already mentioned, charge voltage decay can affect the output. Due to the time delay between charging and exposing the photoconductor drum as well as between exposure and toning, the electrical charge might not be consistent. These inconsistencies in the electrical charge might lead to drop-outs which affect the image quality.

Laser printer, color
Color laser printers face the same problems as black-and-white output devices. Additionally, with the addition of color, the reproduction of halftones becomes more difficult. A decrease in output speed is based on the fact that for each process color, one revolution of the photoconductor drum is necessary. Consequently, a four-color image used to require four revolutions, whereas a black-and-white reproduction is printed in a single pass. New color systems use four drums to transfer the process colors in one pass.

The imaging process is the same as for black-and-white laser printers. However, each color is "painted" on the photoconductor drum separately. In the next process step, the appropriate toner is applied and transferred. The photoconductor drum is cleaned, recharged, and exposed to the next color separation of this particular image.

As far as the transfer process of the toner is concerned, two concepts are available. Either the single colors are sampled on an intermediate drum or belt and transferred to the paper all together, or each color is transferred directly to the paper which remains in a fixed position until the imaging process is completed.

The additional problems that occur within the imaging process are similar to those of the lithographic printing process. In addition to the issues of addressability and screen ruling, the imaging process requires the highest accuracy in terms of registration and screen angles. If a proper registration cannot be maintained or if the screen angles of the process colors are not correct, the printed image will feature obvious misregistrations and an unwanted moiré pattern.

Furthermore, the toner used will have a major influence on the image quality. The toner particle size affects the graininess of the image. In addition, the toner and its distribution determine the color gamut that can be covered. Color toners are translucent and act as filters. Often, those translucent color toners are based on polyester particles which are mixed with iron-bearing carrier particles. The iron-bearing carrier particles are necessary to maintain the toner quality and electrical charge.

Colored toner particles vary in size, but an average size is approximately 12 microns. High-quality images require small particle sizes to increase the resolution and to decrease the graininess. Small particles, however, are difficult to control. If the amount of toner cannot be kept stable, varying toner film thicknesses will occur which results in variable color reproduction from one print to the next. A gloss enhancement approach is sometimes used to "crush" the toner to smooth it evenly on the paper. This changes its optical appearance and improves its quality.

Moreover, light-scattering effects that are caused by the particles as well as toner surface modifications due to the fusing process make the color output difficult to predict. One approach to minimizing the problems of colored toner particles is the use of liquid toners. The drawback of this technology is the handling of the liquid carrier component which has to be recovered somehow. To avoid misregistration or an uneven distribution of toner, all mechanical components should be adjusted with high precision.

Copier, black-and-white

Today's copiers are both scanner and printer. Therefore, most copiers utilize electrophotography, although, some Hewlett-Packard printers use inkjet. Copiers have to struggle with the same restrictions as laser printers. Earlier models did not rely on a laser but used a light/lens system to expose and charge the photoconductor drum. An original was placed on a glass plate and exposed to light. The reflecting light was projected on the photoconductor drum by a system of lenses. Similarly to the laser printer concept, the toner was applied to the photoconductor drum and the image finally fused onto the paper.

Some manufacturers used a technology known as electrostatic technology, which is based on charging the paper stock directly. To ensure a secure imaging process, specially coated paper was necessary. Both concepts have unique drawbacks that add to those already described. One depends upon the quality of the optical system using light and optical means to copy an original.

If the lens system is not able to resolve the image detail sufficiently, the copy of the original will lack important detail. In addition, the original's substrate absorbs light, which leads to darker copies. Copies of continuous-tone originals produced by the optical system result in poor output because the copier either applies toner or does not apply toner, and cannot make halftones. As far as the electrostatic process is involved, certain areas of the stock may not accept the charge properly, which might cause drop-outs and less-than-solid fills in some parts of the image. The paper must hold an electrical charge to attract toner, and its charging properties as well as its smoothness are important attributes.

Copier, color

By incorporating appropriate color filters into the light/lens system, manufacturers achieved the color separation of the original's color into the process colors of cyan, magenta, and yellow. Three successive exposures through the filters exposed three images—one for each color—onto the photoconductor drum. Initially black was created by overprinting all three all toners. Modern color systems now add black. To transfer the image from the drum to the paper, the right toner is applied. The transfer of the image to the paper takes place either directly to the paper, or by using an intermediate belt or drum prior to transfer to the paper.

It was the missing fourth color that accounted for the major disadvantage of this concept. Black areas of the original were reproduced as muddy brown, and shadow lines tended to loose their sharpness. It was the Canon Color Laser Copier in 1987–88 that added the black toner, made copying into scanning and printing, and ushered in the new age of digital color.

Toner-based printing

The toner chemist must consider the entire electrophotographic cycle when designing a high-performance toner, based on process speed, media, and marking engine. The most common laser toner is an insulative magnetic toner. The toner should be a matrix of resin and pigment where the pigment in the case of a magnetic toner is iron oxide powder. The external shell of the toner particle should be resin, rendering it non conductive. Toner physical properties:

- Particle size: The size and distribution of toner particles are specified for the expected resolution of the images produced. Properly manufactured materials will control the fine particles that can cause background.
- Inherent strength: The resin/pigment matrix must be able to retain its form as a finished product. If the toner continues to process inside the printer, the resulting images will not be consistent.
- Dry powder flow: Most toner cartridges have some form of agitator bar to help overcome the poor flow characteristics of microfine toners. The smaller the particle's size, the more difficult it is for dry powders to flow.

The electrical charge on laser printer toners is derived from triboelectric (static) properties. The chargability of individual toners is related to the particle size. Smaller than average particles tend to charge to a higher value within a given charge time. A laser printer the developer system may agitate the toner for a minute or less during the printer's warm-up cycle. It is useful to understand completely why toner from various manufacturers function differently within the same laser engine family. The initial toner design, which will fix basic physical characteristics, contributes a portion to the price and performance of a toner. The manufacturer's process technique and process control will contribute the remainder to the price and performance. The cost to the remanufacturer for a toner is not just the price. The customer's satisfaction with the final product must be factored.

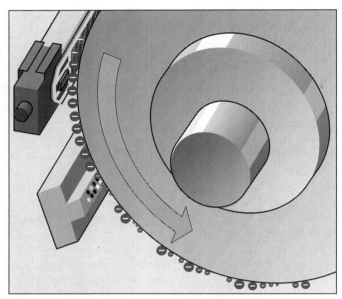

Traditional electrophotography involves cleaning, charging, imaging, toning, transferring steps in order to put information on paper.

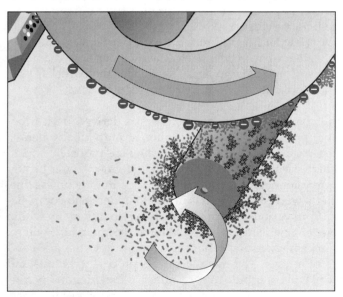

The illustration above shows toner and developer particles attracted to the charged areas of the organic photo conductor (OPC) drum.

The toner has stable triboelectrical characteristics for extended time periods for dispersion of the resin and wax. There are three major groups of toners

- dual component
- mono component
- liquid

Think of toner as a very small capsule that can hold an electrical charge with a pigment inside. Toner is 3 to 30 microns in size, depending on the desired resolution of the printed image.

Dual-component toners are made up of toner and carrier beads. Cascade development is the most common method. It is based on triboelectrification, which is the process of exciting toner particles by causing an electrical charge through the use of friction. The triboelectrification process causes excited toner particles to cling to a beaded carrier. The higher the resolution, the smaller the toner particles needed.

Carrier beads are about 70 to 400 microns in diameter and usually are a metallic or magnetic compound. Carrier beads consist of a blend of organically treated inorganic fine powder which acts as a developer and lubricant, while providing releasability. Because the toner particles are insulative, toner images on the photoreceptor are easily transferred electrostatically to plain paper. These particles are small, charged, pigment particles, which attach themselves to much larger carrier beads. A single carrier bead can hold multiple toner particles. The name "carrier bead" comes from the idea of "carrying" the fine toner particles to the latent electrostatic image where the toner is stripped from the carrier, thereby developing the image.

Dual component toner is used in over 90 percent of the current xerographic copiers and digital printers. Printers such as the Xeikon and Xerox Docutech use dual component toners.

Carrier beads are magnetic materials, which are specially coated with a polymeric film to provide the proper triboelectric properties for attracting toner. The magnetic material can then be transported from one location to another through the use of magnetic fields. Methods are used to adhere dual-component toner particles to a charged material, until it is torn away from that material, primarily by the competing electrostatic force exerted by the electrostatic latent image.

Cascade development is the method most widely used for document copying. It is commonly called cascade developer, because in use the mixture is poured or "cascaded" over the inclined surface bearing an electrostatic latent image.

With magnetic brush developer, the carrier is approximately the same size as the toner, rather than being much larger. High-quality lineart can be produced by this development method.

Continuous-tone development

In the case of continuous-tone development, the charged density within the electrostatic image varies from point to point. The density of the developed image is a result of the amount of charge at each point on the surface to be printed. The material most commonly used for this process is ball-milled charcoal (carbon black). Ball-milled charcoal cannot be fixed by heat or by solvents. Such toners are described as powder-cloud toners and they are generally charged by turbulent impact of the particles with some conducting wall or nozzle through which the powder-cloud is blown on its way to the development zone and fixed by pressure in some cases.

Mono component toners differ from dual component toners in that they do not require the use of carrier beads for development. There are several ways to charge mono component toners—induction, contacting, corona charging, ion beam, and traveling electric fields. The easiest and most commonly used of these is induction charging. Through induction charging, a conducting particle sitting on a negative surface becomes negatively charged. Once toner particles become charged they can be transferred to the substrate. This change in charge causes toner to move in an opposite direction of a magnetic roller forming a conductive path. It is then attracted to the latent image and adhered to the substrate by a photoreceptor and Coulomb force. The name Océ comes from "one component."

Liquid toner

Liquid toners comprise toner and solvent. The use of solvent instead of developer caused them to be liquid instead of solid. Liquid toner solvents are non-conductive and primarily made up of thermoplastic resin particles, which are suspended in a saturated hydrocarbon. In many respects liquid development is related to or considered with powder-cloud development. In both cases, freely moving charged toner moves under the action of the electrostatic field of the image. Currently Indigo is the only major user of liquid toners. Their printing devices account for over 90 percent of the liquid toner currently being used. Indigo's liquid toner consists of 1 to 2 micron toner particles suspended in a highly refined kerosene known as isopar. The isopar acts as the controlling agent of the solution, by carrying the charge placed on it.

Toner charge
The magnitude and polarity of toner charge is critical. The charge on the toner must have the correct polarity or no development will occur. The magnitude of the charge is also critical because the development force is directly proportional to toner charge. Development will occur only when the electrostatic development force exceeds the adhesive force. In many cases, the carrier beads are coated with a polymer that transfers the amount of charge to the toner. Carrier coatings and toner materials can be selected from a tribo series, which is a listing of polymers in order of charging polarity. The tribo series lists polymers according to charge, polymers appearing higher on the list will charge positively with respect to any polymer lower on the list. The total amount of charge exchange between the toner and the carrier is a function of the total number of toner particles contained on each carrier bead.

Toner concentration
The image density is highly dependent on the concentration of toner within a given area. Image density is not completely determined by charge because the developablity of a given developer is dependent on environmental conditions such as humidity, and temperature. Toner concentration may vary from .5 percent to approximately 2 percent by weight, depending upon a number of chemical and reproduction variables. The toner transfer efficiency of printers and copiers is 85 percent. The 15 percent scraped off the photoreceptor is waste. In the U.S., around 21 million pounds of waste toner is disposed of annually. It is non-toxic and inert, so it is deposited into landfills. It resists ultraviolet light, and, being black, is unsightly. Economic incentive to recycle toner is minimal; due to this, under 1 percent of U.S. waste toner is recycled.

A triboelectric charge is a friction induced static charge between two dissimilar materials. When toner is rubbed across a developer roller it builds up a static charge similar to running a comb through dry hair, or even petting your long-haired cat during the winter. Static electricity is a triboelectric charge and an indication of the charge acceptance of toner. It is measured by Q divided by M or charge divided by the mass that was transferred. A toner with a higher triboelectric charge will transfer a smaller amount of mass than a toner with a lower charge.

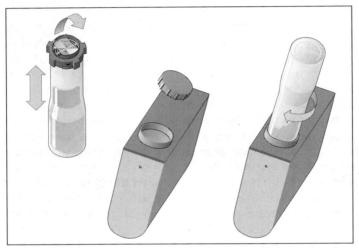

Toner bottles have special adapters so that the toner only flows when the bottle is seated in the receptacle in the imaging engine.

When an OPC drum is charged by the corona wire and is then discharged by the laser, a charge difference is created on the spots where the laser light hits the drum. This charge usually maintains a lower voltage than the rest of the OPC drum and represents a reverse image of what will be printed on the paper. Since no toner is yet distributed to the drum, it is a latent, or potential, image. Only after the developer roller transfers the toner to the OPC drum does it become an visible image. After the toner is transferred to the paper and the nontransferred toner is removed by the wiper blade, the latent image remains on the OPC drum. To remove latent images, erasure lamps in older printers and the corona wire in current printers must recharge the drum. If the corona wire fails to completely recharge the drum, portions of the latent image could remain. This results in positive image ghosting, which is caused by toner transferring to those portions of the latent image remaining on the OPC drum.

Fusing is the process which causes toner to adhere to itself and to the paper. This is accomplished by the fuser, or fixing assembly, in the printer. The fuser's main components are the heating element (lamp), upper roller (optional, since radiant fusing is an alternative), lower roller (optional), a thermistor (heat sensor), and a thermoswitch (safety circuit). The thermistor will continuously regulate the operation of the heating element to keep the temperature within range. Problems may interfere with the fusing process: a worn upper roller (which causes toner build-up), worn pressure springs (which fail to press the lower roller against the upper roller), or a damaged gear.

The Agfa Chromapress uses the Xeikon engine.

New digital color systems

Agfa announced Chromapress in September, 1993. It was the Xeikon DCP-1 which became the DCP-32D, an integrated computer-to-paper system for on-demand, high-quality toner-based color printing. Chromapress is said to be a complete solution, incorporating prepress through reprographic technologies to support the production of timely, cost-effective color documents. This "systems" philosophy extends from the creative concept to PostScript files and all the way to printed and finished documents, and it embraces the critical ownership issues of training, service and long term support.

Xeikon

Xeikon was founded in 1988 as a spinoff from work done at Agfa on digital printing. The initial funding came from the Agfa Gevaert Investment Fund. In the early 1980s Agfa marketed the first high-speed laser printer—the P400. It was the first laser printer with a resolution of 400dpi and was rated at 28 ppm. Xeikon was founded by Lucien de Schamphelaere and the DCP-1 was announced at a press conference on June 21, 1993. It was first introduced as the Agfa Chromapress and was shown in September, 1993 at the IPEX exhibition in Birmingham, England. The first production units were shipped in April, 1994. Xeikon announced the Xeikon DCP/32D, its second-generation digital short-run color printing system, in 1995*The*

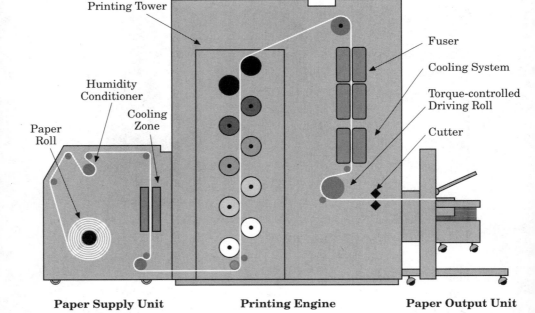

Paper Supply Unit   **Printing Engine**   **Paper Output Unit**

The Xeikon digital color press is web-fed. It consists of one large tower with a paper feeder on one end and a paper handler on the other.

Xeikon offered an upgrade package to users of the DCP-1, its first-generation system. The Xeikon DCP/32D had numerous engineering changes to increase reliability and cut cost; in addition, it uses a Gloss Enhancement Module, called the GEM, to print images with glossy finish and better color saturation said to be equivalent to off-set printing. The system uses Xeikon's One-Pass Duplex Color tech-nology, which enables its systems to print full color simultaneously on both sides of the paper. The Xeikon DCP/32D is able to process nearly twice as many jobs as many other commercial digital color presses and significantly more short-run jobs than the most ad-vanced offset presses in a given amount of time.

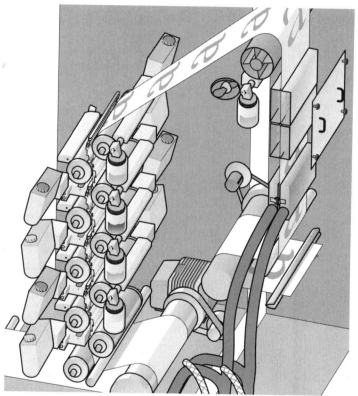

The paper passes by four sets of organic photo conductors that transfer toner onto the sheets. There is a fifth set of drums for the packaging version.

The electrophotographic process is a well-established process used in a variety of laser printing and copying devices. There are four basic steps: In the print tower, the engine is made of ten print units, eight of which are used to print four-color images on both the front and back of each side of the web. The others are for packaging models.

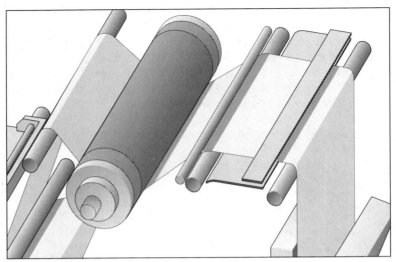

(Above) The torque control keeps an even and consistent tension on the paper.
(Below) The illustration shows the light-emitting diode module.

The building block of the technology is the organic photoconductor (OPC) drum, which consists of an aluminum core covered with a light-sensitive material that converts light energy into an electrical charge. In the first step, the drum is charged with static electricity.

The corona, a wire within a metal enclosure, sits very close to the drum and is attached to a high-voltage power supply. When the corona is charged, the air becomes charged with ions and/or electrons. These particles charge the drum surface. Another device called a corotron, a special kind of corona, is responsible for controlling the electrostatic charge.

In the second step, a light-emitting diode (LED) exposes the drum to precise levels of light, generally from a laser beam. On the Xeikon, a fixed bank of 7,424 LEDs expose the drum to varying amounts of light.

When the light hits the drum the OPC layer becomes conductive, and the exposed areas lose their charge.

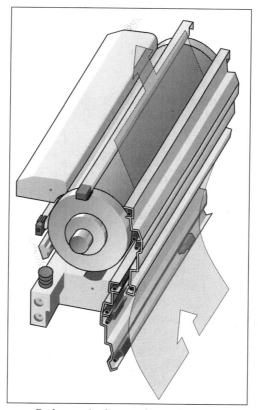

Each organic photoconductor drum is a complete unit for cleaning, changing, imaging, toning, and transferring the image.

Precisely controlled amounts of light from the LED array build the image on the photoconductive drum.

In the third step, the toner particles are electrically attracted to the drum. As the web of paper passes the OPC, the toner cartridge releases the toner and the magnetized carrier particles from a magnetic brush pass down the drum, transferring toner particles that adhere to the latent electrostatic image on the drum. Most toner-based systems are all about electrical charges.

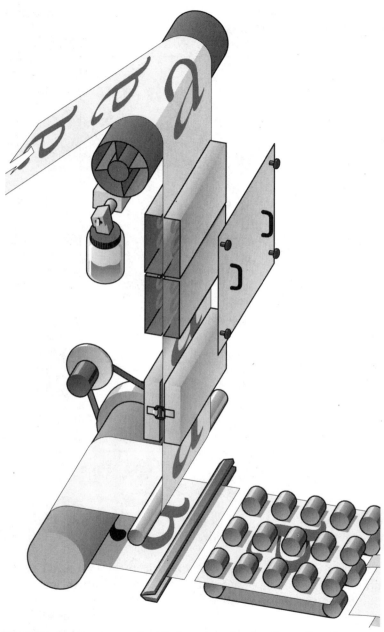

The Xeikon engine uses a radiant fusing approach rather than rollers. Paper then goes through the GEM unit for gloss enhancement.

In the fourth and final step, the image is transferred to the paper. The developed image is transferred to the web of paper, then bonded to the paper with heat. The Xeikon engine is contained in multiple cabinets. The first cabinet contains the paper supply. The second and largest cabinet contains the imaging units, which are stacked one on top of another, and the fuser. A third unit collects and stacks paper as it exits the machine. There are optional finishing devices as well.

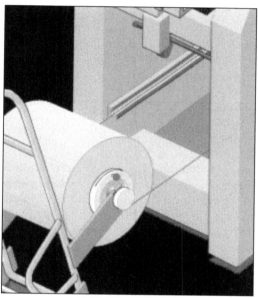

Paper is loaded as rolls with a special roll dolly.

In the second cabinet, the drums are imaged, and the toner comes in contact with the paper. The web of paper is transported between eight color rollers, two for each color. It has eight identical printing units, five on each side of the paper, corresponding to the cyan, magenta, yellow, and black units of a conventional four-color press. The fifth allows for future expansion and is now used in the packaging version of the machine to put white toner on clear films. The fusing of the toner to the paper occurs in the second cabinet. The DCP-32D uses a non-contact radiant fusing system. The advantage of this system is the wide range of papers that can be used. The press is rated for paper weights from 80 to 200 gsm, which translates to 54- to 135-lb. stock.

Depending on the paper stock, the roll can range between 2,000 and 4,000 ft. (610–1220 m) in length. With 100-gsm paper, one roll allows for over two hours of printing. After imaging, the paper is passed into the third unit, which contains a built-in sheeter and stacker assembly. The sheeter cuts the paper and deposits it into a removable output bin. Also included are an automatic job separator and a special tray for unprinted and test sheets. An optional in-line finisher allows sheets to be collated and folded into booklets.

In terms of speed, the DCP prints 35 letter-sized sheets/minute. Because the press images both sides of the web simultaneously, there is no speed penalty for duplex printing, meaning the Xeikon can really print 70 ppm or 4200 letter-sized pages an hour.

Unlike sheetfed devices, which are restricted in size in two dimensions, the Xeikon is only restricted in the width of the roll; you can output an image 9 meters long.

Using copier-based technology after imaging, the toner is applied and permanently fixed to the paper by a noncontact, heat fusing system. The system is capable of printing a fifth color, but this capability is only available for the packaging version for printing white toner. The registration system is based on Xeikon proprietary technology and is so good that many users claim they do not need to trap color in their files.

Like the Indigo, no plates are used in imaging, but unlike the Indigo, there is no ink to adjust. The cabinet only needs to be opened for maintenance, loading toner, changing OPC drums, or re-threading paper. Usually, paper is not re-threaded, but rather spliced to the paper still threaded in the machine.

Resolution for copier-based technologies is different than traditional four-color process. In traditional four-color printing, film is created with a resolution of approximately 1000 or 2000dpi. The dots are fixed in size but "clumped" together to create different size "spots." In this system, the maximum levels of gray depend on the resolution and line screen. The Xeikon prints at 600dpi for color, but incorporates a variable spot function that allows each 600dpi spot to print with any of 64 levels of gray by applying different amounts of toner. Spatial resolution is 600dpi for each color.

With Xeikon's DCP, the screening is made up of four lines of continuously varying width, each at a different angle. Under a loupe, some areas look like small diamond-shaped cells, while others look like a number of intersecting lines. However, none of this is obvious to the unaided eye. Xeikon also offers traditional screening with a clear-center rosette at 170 lpi.

The Xeikon uses light emitting diode (LED) imaging technology. Light-emitting diodes, like laser diodes, generate light by passing a current through a silicon crystal that has been "doped" with selected impurities. Unlike lasers, though, the light from an LED is not coherent, and is thus harder to collimate and focus. Rather than sweeping a single light beam across the image from a distance, LED printers use arrays of tiny LEDs placed very close to the image. Each LED is responsible for forming a single dot of the output. The DCP uses standard LED wafers, assembled into arrays of over 7,000 diodes, spaced at 600 per inch. Xeikon's printing process requires that each diode provide a variable amount of output. Xeikon also uses a proprietary method to normalize individual LED exposure to ensure consistent image density across the LED array.

The standard Xeikon print engine is driven by PostScript code. It uses Harlequin's interpreter, supplemented by Xeikon's EISA-bus screening card. The controller creates four bitmaps, one for each color. Output from the RIP is buffered to disk. Bitmaps are stored on up to 12 GB of disk space and then transferred to the page buffers. Each color printing unit has its own image-buffer memory. A computer chip with a maximum data transfer rate of 192 Mbits/second feeds data from memory to the LED imaging array. All of the separate processes in the machine are handled by a set of distributed microcontrollers that are connected to a supervising controller by means of an optical network.

Barco Graphics introduced its PrintStreamer with a large and very fast buffer for storing ripped pages between the Barco Graphics FastRIP/X and the Xeikon DCP/32D or 50D. PrintStreamer enables digital presses to be used for sophisticated applications by allowing collated printing of variable information. Concurrent input and output streams permit the PrintStreamer to simultaneously accept data coming from the FastRIP/X and send previously stored data to the press, improving its capacity utilization.

An instant job switching feature is standard on all Xeikon systems, including entry-level versions, and was provided to all existing users as a free upgrade. It allows one job to follow another job without stopping the print engine. All jobs that are in the print queue will be printed nonstop.

One of the most significant of the enhancements to the print engine is a new toner-fusing mechanism intended to give the output a higher gloss and closer resemblance to offset printing. Xeikon calls this optional enhancement GEM—Gloss Enhancement Unit; Agfa calls it OmniGloss. It consists of a new, two-part fuser and finishing system as a replacement for the original toner fuser in the engine. With the new capability, the output medium is heated and toner is partially fused at the first station; the medium then passes to the second fusing station of pressurized rollers, which results in a calendering effect on the media and a glossier appearance from the fused toner. A new, heavier-duty web puller motor is also part of the option.

As a byproduct of the two-part fusing process, the fusing temperature in the engine can be lower, thus allowing the use of a broader range of stocks, including coated and heavier substrates. The new fusing technique also makes the toner less susceptible to scratching. The stronger web puller motor helps accommodate heavier stocks, so the machine is better able to print covers, business cards, display materials, and the like. The engine can now accommodate stocks from 40 to 170 lb. (60–250 gsm). It is possible to tune or turn off the second fusing station under operator control.

New "second-generation" microtoners and developers enable lower toner consumption by up to 15–20% per page, Xeikon says, a longer developer life of more than 150,000 sheets (up to three times the life of the previous developer); and enhanced toner coverage. This last factor, coupled with the ability to run more media types, greatly increases in number the kinds of jobs that can be printed on the press. Agfa states that the enhanced consumables reduce the variable costs associated with printing by one-third, which undoubtedly will have an effect on the economic model and ROI for the devices.

The new toner and developer is now available and in use by users of the Xeikon engine. Related to the lower cost of ownership are new preventive-maintenance tools and procedures for the upgraded engine, which result in substantially longer lives for parts and other consumables. For example, the OPC (organic photoconductor) drum will be able to achieve a useful life of 200,000–300,000 sheets. Likewise, the longer developer life means less preventive mainte-nance from fewer developer changes (a change takes about 4–5 hours); thus, less downtime.

Xeikon 4-up digital color printing system
Xeikon announced the Xeikon DCP/50D, the world's fastest and widest heavy-duty digital color printing system and the only one able to print an eight-page signature, the common format produced by traditional offset presses. The Xeikon DCP/50D offers commercial printers a digital color printing solution that combines offset-quality results with faster turnaround times and lower costs for short runs.

The Xeikon DCP/50D prints on a sheet 20 inches/50cm wide.

The Xeikon DCP/50D is targeted at the commercial printing and in-plant marketplace, the largest segment of users within the U.S. print-ing industry. Commercial shipments of the Xeikon DCP/ 50D began in November, 1997. Price will range from $450,000 to $600,000. The DCP-50D offers a 20" paper width and a print width of 18.7" (versus the 12.6" paper width and print width of 12.1" of the Xeikon DCP-32D). The unit works with the same 600dpi, variable-spot-size, LED-imaging technology used in the Xeikon DCP-32D press, with screen values of up to 170 lpi. The DCP-50D can be driven by either a Harlequin ScriptWorks RIP or a Barco FastRIP/X. An enhanced Barco PrintStreamer with 64 GB of storage, about 20,000 pages, can also be used.

The press delivers cut, but not trimmed, sheets into a 500-sheet capacity jogger designed to fit existing printing production work-flows. There is also an optional electronic collation facility for pro-ducing completed booklets or brochures in one pass. Xeikon says the press can handle twenty four 500-page, A3-size jobs in an eight-hour shift. The Xeikon DCP/50D, with either of its RIPs, including the control console and a jogger for finished cut sheets.

The Xeikon DCP/50D will be able to print eight-page, or B2 size (20"x 24"), signatures at the rate of 750 sheets per hour. This is equiv-alent to 6,000 8.5x11-inch full-color impressions per hour, or 100 per minute. This means that the Xeikon DCP/50D can produce 24 aver-age jobs of 500 duplex 11x17-inch sheets per eight hour shift—a pro-duction level that is more than double the level achievable by any other digital or computer-to-press system available today. Moreover, the Xeikon DCP/50D's web configuration allows users to print jobs in a variety of sheeted lengths, even up to 24 feet.

Among the applications made more practical with the Xeikon DCP/50D are customized, commercial print quality, 8-, 16-, or 24-page catalogs or brochures. Posters and other large-sized printed products (up to 24 feet in length) are also feasible. Xeikon also announced new enhancements to its DCP family of digital color presses. PrintSync is a new registration control system that enables the DCP/32D to overprint on preprinted stock with highly accurate registration. A series of hardware enhancements will deliver two-to-three times higher image data throughput for full-page variable data printing on the DCP/32D.

Xeikon N.V. announced that it has entered into a strategic partner-ship with U.S.-based Varis Corporation. The alliance plans to devel-op products which significantly advance the degree to which vari-able content can be employed in heavy duty full color digital print applications. Initial product introductions resulting from this part-nership are expected to occur in the first quarter of 1999. Xeikon will have exclusive worldwide marketing rights to any products resulting from this partnership. Under the agreement, Xeikon's digital presses will be combined with Varis' VariScript technology, enabling the creation of massively variable targeted documents in full color. VariScript, first released in September, 1997, is a technology for sophisticated one-to-one printing applications for black-and-white and spot color production.

With VariScript, every piece of text, graphic, and image in a document can be customized, using over 17,000 different combinations of formats, lengths, images, text and graphics on a page. In combination with Xeikon, it will be possible to offer 100% variable, full color production printing, thereby enhancing one-to-one marketing applications. VariScript's raster image processor (RIP) technology with no spooling enables Xeikon's presses to produce large production variable data jobs such as individual financial statements in a virtually continuous mode. In addition, VariScript's software incorporates features performing physical page verification and auditing of the entire print job from data collection through finishing to ensure correct production of one-to-one marketing materials. The combined cost of a printer and the front end would be about $700,000.

Xerox DocuColor 70
The DocuColor 70 uses the Xeikon DCP/32D engine and supports two RIP servers, one from Scitex and one from EFI. The Scitex-based RIP is targeted at the high-quality color offset printing market, where the EFI-based RIP is targeted for distributed printing. The DocuColor 70 will be shipped in September. The list price for the EFI-based system is $375,000. The system with a Scitex RIP is $390,000.

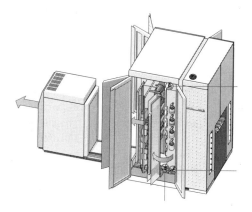

The Scitex RIP server uses the latest Scitex IBM PowerPC platform, referred to by Scitex as the SX3000, running under AIX. It has Scitex color management and provides what Xerox claims is a better quality image from the Xeikon engine, plus very efficient prepress workflow, probably to compete with Agfa's Chromapress workflow. The EFI Fiery RIP server is a new EFI engine using the DEC Alpha processor running under Windows NT. EFI claims it is 4-5 times faster than the Fiery XJ Plus and will run Adobe's Extreme technology utilizing multiple processors running PostScript 3. The Xerox DocuColor 40 is targeted at environments printing less than 100,000 prints per month. DocuColor 70 is targeted at higher-quality work in excess of 100,000 prints per month.

Xerox DocuColor 100 Digital Color Press
The DocuColor 100 Digital Color Press has an 18.7-inch-wide image area that can print two letter-sized images side by side—generating 100 impressions per minute (ipm) in two-sided mode. The Docu-Color 100 is as much as 50 percent more productive than the Xerox DocuColor 70 Digital Color Press. The DocuColor 100 is expected to accelerate the migration from offset to digital printing among commercial and in-plant printers because it delivers greater productivity and offers capabilities that enable creation of individually customized materials—enhancing the effectiveness of documents ranging from marketing brochures to catalogs. The new model claims costs of less than 20 cents per impression, two to five times less than offset run lengths of less than 500 impressions, according to Xerox.

The new DocuColor 100 is based upon the DCP/50D engine from Xeikon N.V. and uses the same imaging technology as the Xerox DocuColor 70. It features Xerox-exclusive digital front-end (DFE) controllers from Scitex Corp. and Electronics for Imaging (EFI). Pricing for the base configuration begins at $550,000.

IBM launches InfoPrint and InfoColor products
IBM has announced several new products in its InfoPrint (black-and-white) and InfoColor (color printing) line that offer more printing options, including the ability to deliver printed output to devices anywhere on a network. The new products include the IBM InfoPrint Manager 3.1, InfoColor 100 (based on the wider Xeikon engine), InfoColor Off-Line RIP and the InfoPrint 4000 high-resolution IR3/IR4 print engines.

InfoPrint Manager 3.1 can manage workgroup, print-on-demand and production printing, locally and globally. InfoPrint Manager submits, controls, archives, and retrieves print jobs. New features include clustering, support for workgroup and color print-on-demand environments as well as Enterprise Resource Planning (ERP) applications, including SAP/R3, and a new Java-based user interface. Beyond printing, InfoPrint Manager can intelligently direct information across the Internet, e-mail, fax machines, scanners, servers and electronic archives.

Building upon the InfoColor 70, IBM is adding the InfoColor 100, at 20 inches wide, capable of outputting up to 105 full-color pages per minute (50 duplex pages). The printable area is 18.7 inches on a 20-inch web. Personalization is supported by a range of variable-content offerings, including IBM's MergeDoc and Content Adder, Barco's VIPDesigner, and customized solutions from FAIR Information Services.

Bitstream's PageFlex, which is designed for the InfoColor 70, will also run on the InfoColor 100. Increased RIP speeds (a 40 percent increase, to be exact) are achieved through the use of a dual 400MHz Pentium II processor. Standard features include a 64 GB Collator, which provides a high-speed variable-data system that can handle the most complex requirements. The additional support of a new InfoPrint color off-line RIP gives the InfoColor 70 increased performance and more scalable throughput. When more than one job is in a queue, InfoPrint Manager automatically spreads the workload across RIP resources. IBM intends to offer similar off-line RIP capabilities on the InfoColor 100.

Agfa high-speed Chromapress
For the Chromapress, Agfa has developed its own RIP using Adobe PostScript 3. Also new is the option of a fifth color (white) for packaging, labeling, and other applications. The single-sided model can print on a range of substrates, such as foils (polyester, plastics, and transfer foils), adhesive, cover stock up to 250 gsm^2, canvas, transparencies and polyester (for special applications), as well as paper. Agfa featured a new line of polyester media, known as Agfa DigiFoil, optimized for a higher fusing temperature to achieve better toner adhesion, higher-quality color reproduction, increased durability, and greater ease of use.

The Chromapress 32Si digital color printing system, a single-sided (simplex) four-color printing system operates at twice the run speed of the Chromapress 32 duplex model, upon which its design and front-end architecture are based. With a rated speed of 14.7 meters per minute (the equivalent of 70 single-sided A4 pages), the 32Si is highly productive. It can handle a wide range of substrates including foils (polyester, plastics, and transfer foils), adhesive (for labeling), cover stock up to 250 gsm (for packaging, posters, and point of purchase materials), transparencies, and polyester (for special applications), as well as paper. This makes it an ideal alternative to conventional print technologies for the packaging industry, especially label printing. Similar versions, without Agfa's front end, are sold by Xeikon and its dealers, and certain Xeikon OEMs.

The Agfa IntelliStream front-end architecture combines hardware, software, and patented Agfa compression technology to offer an innovative solution to the processing demands inherent in digital printing. IntelliStream enables such advanced digital print capabilities as electronic collation of long documents, unlimited page lengths, and powerful variable data processing.

Indigo
Indigo was founded in 1977 by Benzion "Benny" Landa, the company's chairman and CEO. In 1992 Indigo went public. Landa creates as much press as his Indigo E-Print 1000+ Digital Offset Color press. He holds over 100 patents, including those for ElectroInk, Indigo's unique ink technology. "Indigo," says Landa, "has invested 16 years pursuing a single goal: merging the quality, economy, and performance of printing ink with the power of electronic printing."

Landa claims that the Indigo's Digital Offset Color is "the only process that combines the unique qualities of liquid ink with the durability of the offset process." The technology utilized in the Indigo printer was under final development for at least three years before it was first introduced on June 20, 1993.

The E-Print is a sheetfed digital offset press that prints four to six colors on most of the popular paper stocks at 800dpi, 11x17-inch in size (A3), at 4,000 sheets per hour, at one color on one side, or 67 per minute. Thus, for black-and-white work, it is just about the same speed as a Xerox DocuTech (135 8.5x11-inch pages per minute).

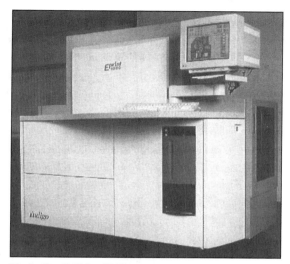

The Indigo E-Print 1000.

Paper substrates for Indigo presses can be coated or uncoated, varying in thickness from very light sheets to card stocks. The E-Print 1000+ can print 4-color work at thirty five 8.5x11-inch pages per minute. Up to 3,000 sheets can be loaded in the feeder, though single sheets are handled separately. It uses the same principles as traditional offset printing, with plates (OPCs actually), blankets, impression cylinders, and liquid ink (toner actually).

The image on the plate cylinder is transferred to the blanket surface and then is "offset" to the paper held on the impression cylinder. However, in other ways, the Indigo digital press works like a copy machine or laser printer by charging a cylinder using a laser beam to create an electrophotographic image.

To image 8,000 A4 pages per hour, the Indigo's print controller must produce 200 Mbits/sec. The process is divided between the workstation, which performs the loading and rasterizing, and a dedicated controller. If the print job exceeds the RAM buffer, the E-Print 1000+ stops and waits until the next page is ripped and the memory is flushed. If the print job does not exceed the RAM buffer, additional jobs can be held in the print queue. The TurboStream version, introduced in 1998, improves the front end and thus speeds up the overall imaging system.

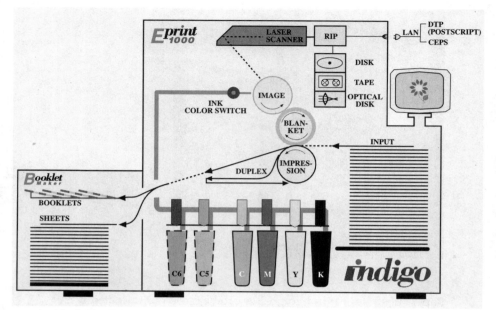

The Indigo E-Print 1000 can have four to six colors—CMYK plus two spot colors. It can also be set up for Indigo's version of Pantone "Hexachrome" printing.

The printing function starts imaging the reusable digital electrophotographic offset plate. The plate called ElectroPlate and it is the equivalent of an OPC drum. Indigo, which calls the electrophotographic plates "dynamic," says they last tens of thousands of impressions each. The plate cylinder is electrostatically charged and exposed with the laser as it rotates at a speed of 4,000 impressions per hour. Next, the cylinder rotates and is exposed to toner spray of one color (cyan, magenta, yellow, or black) from the ink nozzles called the Ink Color Switch. Toner adheres to the imaged area. As the plate cylinder continues to revolve, the ink is transferred to the blanket and then all of the ink is transferred to the paper.

ElectroInk. Besides being able to expose and image on the fly, a completely different image is created with each revolution. This is enabled by the reusable plates and by the toners. The 100 percent toner transfer and reusable plates allows each image to be different. In color printing, it could be the next color separation, while in database printing it could be the personalization of text and images on each page. In four-color printing, it is the Ink Color Switch that changes the toner color. The ability to transfer 100 percent of the toner from blanket to substrate is unusual in offset printing.

This is made possible with the E-Print because of Indigo's patented liquid ElectroInk, which uses pigments similar to those in regular offset inks but with two dramatic differences. First, it acts electrostatically, meaning it can be charged, and second, it dries very quickly. Contained in the toners is a dispersion of pigmented polymer particles ranging in size from 1 to 2 microns. In contrast, the dry toner particles used in copy machines have an average size of 8–15 microns. When transferred to the blanket and heated, these polymers turn into a tacky polymeric "film."

When the ink film polymer comes in contact with the substrate, it hardens instantly and peels away from the blanket. There are two interesting contrasts with traditional printing. First, with the E-Print 1000+, the toner does not bind with the substrate paper as in traditional printing but laminates or coats the substrate. Second, with the E-Print 1000+ press, 100 percent of the toner is removed with each revolution, while in the conventional offset printing process, half of the toner is transferred to the paper and the balance stays on the blanket, to be re-toned on the next revolution.

It is difficult to compare E-Print 1000+ speeds to conventional press speeds. Conventional presses print one, two, three or four colors at the same speed (on a multicolor press). In contrast, the E-Print 1000+ prints one color pages faster than two, two colors faster than three, etc. This ability is due to the very tight press registration. The paper is held in place on the impression cylinder throughout the imaging process for each side of the paper. Once all of the colors have been printed on the first side of the page, the sheet is transferred from the cylinder into the duplex buffer. Next the trailing edge of the paper is picked up and pulled back to the impression cylinder such that the other side is presented to and retained on the impression cylinder. At this point the colors can be applied to the reverse side of the sheet.

To duplex-print, the sheet is released by the impression cylinder after it is printed into a duplex buffer. The trailing edge of the paper is clamped back onto the impression cylinder and the second side is printed. Each side can be printed with as many or as few colors as desired. The printed sheet is then ejected. An optional Booklet Maker retains the printed sheets (up to 100 pages) and then releases them to an on-line folder/stapler. There is no trimming. At the delivery end of the press, the finished pieces come off either as sheets or as folded and stitched books containing a maximum 100 pages each. This is different from sheetfed or web presses, which print the same image over and over in succession. In the conventional sheetfed press work-flow, collation is performed in the bindery.

Advances in image quality for the E-Print 1000+ are provided by High Definition Imaging, an option that provides an effective line screen of 200 lines per inch, substantially enhancing fine details and overall image sharpness. Sequin Digital Screening can produce high-quality images without large volumes of data. Sequin produces a sharper apparent resolution and finer color detail. Other advantages include an expansion of the number of gray levels up to 256 per sep-aration and the elimination of moiré.

"Yours Truly," Indigo's trademarked personalization option, not only makes real-time personalization an affordable reality but is being used increasingly for a variety of precision-targeted full-color prod-ucts. The company has upgraded its entire worldwide installed based of E-Print 1000s to the new E-Print 1000+ machines. They also introduced an enhanced line of imaging products including newly designed ink cans that increase yield by 30 percent and a new Photo Imaging Plate.

Indigo adds new digital presses
At Ipex '93, Indigo's launch of the world's first digital offset color press, the E-Print 1000, heralded the dawn of the digital printing era. At Ipex '98, with the introduction of the E-Print Pro, the UltraStream, and lower cost-per-page showed that Indigo continues to innovate. Indigo launched two new digital presses, one at a ower price point and the other at faster print speeds. The new E-Print Pro is priced at $249,000 and is the lowest-cost digital color press on the market, according to Indigo. The new UltraStream is claimed the fastest dig-ital color press available, although Xeikon disagrees. It is the fastest sheet-fed four-color digital printer.

The E-Print Pro is claimed to be the world's lowest cost digital color press if you do not consider Canon CLC-1000 or Xerox DocuColor. Simultaneously, the company unveiled the Indigo UltraStream, claimed the world's fastest digital color press, if you do not consider Xeikon or its ilk. In addition to the presses, Indigo also announced new consumables plans offering the industry's lowest cost per page; however, no numbers were provided to support this claim.

The two new digital presses "produce the same high quality, vibrant, glossy color printing, on the same limitless range of substrates, as Indigo's flagship TurboStream Digital Offset Color press." Mr. Landa pointed out that the new E-Print Pro is an entry level product, offering budget-conscious users easy entry into the lucrative world of digital printing. He said Indigo's UltraStream, scheduled for shipment during the second half of 1999, is ideal for high volume production environments, complementing the TurboStream, Indigo's high-productivity mid-range product.

The four-color E-Print Pro enables newcomers to digital color printing to enter the market with a modest capital investment and achieve profitability from relatively low volumes of short run jobs. As their businesses grow in volume or migrate to higher value digital printing work, E-Print Pro customers can trade up to the fully-featured TurboStream, making a seamless transition to the highest margin markets. E-Print Pro uses TurboStream digital front-end technology, but will not support options such as auto-duplexing, electronic collation, high definition imaging (HDI), fifth and sixth colors, personalization, and extended 36 GB page memory. This may be a strategic error in that personalization, at least, is one of the driving forces behind digital printing.

Because it is a simplex device, the E-Print Pro will compete as an alternative to short-run color offset printing, especially the Heidelberg Quickmaster DI. Indigo's entry-level price point can now compete with the Canon CLC-1000 and the Xerox DocuColor 40. The lack of auto-duplexing and electronic collation could be a limitation. The E-Print Pro is really aimed at the QuickMaster-DI. Indigo Turbo-Stream customers can trade up to the new UltraStream. Engineered for high volume users, with its seven-color capability and 240 feet-per-minute process speed, the UltraStream is the most powerful, highest productivity digital press in the Indigo product family. TurboStream (the upgraded E-Print 1000) is the fastest of its kind for simplex printing and second only to the Xeikon DCP/50D for duplex printing. (The DCP/50D is capable of printing one hundred 8.5x11-

inch duplex color impressions per minute.) In addition, at these speeds the UltraStream is unique in its seven-color printing capability, which opens new quality levels for matching colors. We estimate its pricing at $550,000 for a four-color base machine, but over $600,000 with all the bells and whistles.

The sheet-fed UltraStream, scheduled for shipment in 1999, is designed for high-volume production. It can print with up to seven-colors and is double the speed of the E-Print 1000 via a new double-size impression cylinder. Indigo America also has two new programs with cost reduction incentives with discounts ranging from 5 percent to 10 percent for orders above a certain value: A 5 percent discount on consumable (blanket, PIP, Electroink, fuser oil) for orders over $6,900; and a 10 percent discount on consumable orders over $15,000.

Xerox DocuColor, Scitex Spontane, and the Canon CLC-1000
Introduced in Japan in 1995 as the 4040, introduced in May, 1995 at Drupa as the Scitex Spontane, and introduced in May, 1996 as the Xerox DocuColor 40, this digital printing system incorporates a high-speed full-color print engine designed for high-quality color reproduction of flyers, brochures, pamphlets, comprehensive proofs, and short-run, print-on-demand applications. A feature for variable information that allows printing localized inserts, mailers and flyers, and customized catalogs, tailored to interests of targeted readers is optional with most RIPs.

The Canon CLC-1000 was secretly shown in 1993 and shipments started during the first quarter of 1997. The major difference between the Canon and the Xerox is speed: 31 ppm vs. 40 ppm. But when it comes to duplexing, they are very close. Canon uses a duplex tray to hold copies and then feeds them back through; the DocuColor 40 flips each sheet and duplexes one at a time. The result is 12–15 ppm.

With a small footprint and a speed of up to 40 full-color simplex A4 pages per minute, the Xerox DocuColor provides an entry-level solution for printers, repro houses, and digital service bureaus interested in making the evolutionary shift to digital printing.

Both accept files in PostScript, Scitex, and other digital prepress formats, process them, and print them in CMYK, in A6 to A3 formats, including automatic duplex printing. Special features include electronic collation of documents, and three different paper trays that can be loaded with various stock types and other materials (like overhead transparencies) and integrated automatically into the final documents. The printing priority queue can be altered for rush jobs or quick proofing.

The DocuColor results from a strategic alliance with Fuji Xerox and Xerox Corporation, Scitex and other RIP suppliers to jointly develop a series of highly productive solutions for integrated color document reproduction, bringing together their accumulated expertise in the relevant technologies and markets. The companies joined efforts in the development and distribution of products for the on-demand digital printing market. Shipments began near the end of 1995.

Scitex demonstrated a Fuji-Xerox printer-copier connected to a Scitex RIP-server at Drupa in May, 1995. The engine was manufactured by Fuji-Xerox in Japan and sold by both Scitex and Xerox. The device

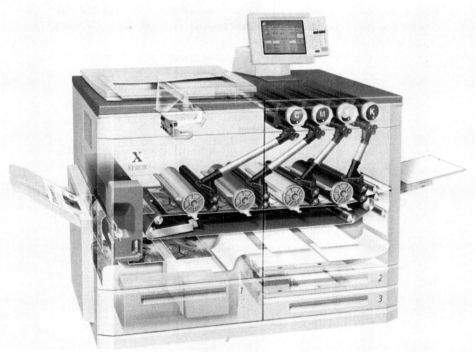

The DocuColor 40 digital color printer/copier

was a developmental extension of the Majestik print engine with four imaging and toning stations in a row. It was first prototyped back in 1993–1994, but Xerox decided not to go forward with it as a product. The folks at Fuji persevered and that led first to the Scitex relationship and the Spontane and then to a Xerox version. Resolution is 400dpi with 8 bits per pixel.

For both the DocuColor 40 and the Canon CLC-1000, paper is moved via a plastic belt that holds it with static electricity as the paper passes beneath four laser and toning heads. For the DocuColor 40, a unique "flipper" mechanism turns the paper over so it can then make its way back through the printing path to print the flip side. Duplex printing cuts the speed to 15 pages per minute. To maintain this speed, the system prints the first side of a sheet as the previous sheet is being flipped and re-printed.

DocuColor 40 advances
Xerox Corporation expanded its DocuColor 40 color copier/printer line, solidifying its leadership in the fast-growing market for color digital copying and printing in offices and the production environment with:

- The DocuColor 40 CP, a new model that delivers high-speed, networked copying and printing to lower-volume production environments at a much lower cost.
- Enhanced digital controllers for network connectivity
- A less expensive unit called DocuColor 30 CP or Pro.

Models operate at 30 to 40 prints per minute (ppm) and include a new feature that can produce acetate transparencies at higher speed. The DocuColor CP is a network-connected color copier/printer equipped with a newly designed digital controller manufactured to Xerox specifications by Electronics For Imaging (EFI). It is designed to provide digital walk-up copying as well as network printing for lower-volume production environments such as entry-level centralized reprographics departments, color-intensive offices, and price-sensitive print-for-pay businesses that produce an average monthly page volume of up to 30,000 prints. It is priced less than the previous generation of network-connected DocuColor models.

The Xerox DocuColor 40 Pro improves the price-performance of the color copier/printer with a variety of newly updated digital controllers designed for sophisticated color document production environments where speed, color quality and workflow are paramount and print volumes range to 100,000 pages per month. The Xerox DocuColor 40 CP with front-end controller carries a manufacturer's suggested U.S. list price of $135,000. The standalone Xerox DocuColor 40 Pro copier carries a manufacturer's suggested list price of $117,000. Controllers for the Pro, which enable network print capabilities, are available from Scitex, EFI, and Splash and range in price from $42,500 to $52,000.

So, Xerox uses the "Pro" to mean the higher end member of the family and Indigo uses it to mean the lower end member of the family.

Canon pioneers mid high-speed color segment
Canon U.S.A., Inc. continues its 10-year-plus history of innovation in the color copier market with the introduction of the 24 page per minute CLC-2400 Color Laser Copier/Printer. The CLC-2400 features a full-color copy speed of 24 pages per minute, 400 dots-per-inch image quality with 256 gradations, a four-drum imaging engine, the ability to run 110-lb. index stock through the bypass, automatic duplexing, plus plug and play connectivity with the addition of an optional ColorPASS controller.

A 5,250-sheet standard paper supply, first copy time of 16 seconds and the capability to produce 11x17-inch full bleed further enhances performance. The paper supply includes two front-loading, user-adjustable paper drawers that accommodate paper sizes ranging from statement through ledger. Each drawer holds 500 sheets, and there is a 250-sheet stack bypass for copying onto paper stocks ranging from 20-lb bond to 110-lb index for covers, labels, and transparencies, as well as letterhead. The standard 4,000 sheet paper deck for letter size media increases on-line paper capacity to 5,250 sheets.

T/R Systems connectivity for multiple Minolta CF900s
T/R Systems announced connectivity of multiple Minolta CF900 Color Copier/Printers with the MicroPress Cluster Printing System. The MicroPress is a scalable, short-run, on-demand, digital printing system designed for production printing of both black/white and color documents. With a single MicroPress PressDirector Cluster-Server, one to four color copiers can print a document up to 6 to 24 pages per minute (ppm).

By connecting multiple different output devices to a single Cluster-Server, users are able to leverage a consistent operating environment and user interface for different types of output. The same Cluster-Server can simultaneously drive four additional black/white PrintStations delivering up to 96 ppm for black/white output. This MultiBurst capability to simultaneously drive more than two different types of printing devices as an integrated printing system is exclusive to the MicroPress Growth Optimized Architecture. The controller is a multiplexer that allows multiple print engines to be driven simultaneously.

NexPress Solutions LLC

Heidelberger Druckmaschinen AG (Heidelberg) and Eastman Kodak Company have completed an agreement first disclosed in September, 1997 and created NexPress Solutions LLC as a joint venture. The new limited liability company, headquartered in Rochester, NY and Kiel, Germany, will develop, manufacture and market non-impact digital printing solutions. "Kodak and Heidelberg agree that it makes strategic business sense to combine Heidelberg's great strengths in commercial printing with Kodak's preeminence in digital color into a single company focused on digital color printing," said Patrick Siewert, president, Kodak Professional Division, and vice president, Eastman Kodak Company. "Together we have the resources, the management, and the vision to be a leader in this new industry," said Siewert, a member of the NexPress board of directors.

"Furthermore, we believe that *plateless digital printing* will leap into increasing importance in the printing and publishing industry," said Wolfgang Pfizenmaier, chairman of NexPress' board and a member of Heidelberg's board. "And, we believe NexPress will be significant in developing the technology to make that industry leap."

The two companies have assembled a management team to lead the new joint venture. In addition to Pfizenmaier and Siewert, the board of directors comprises Dr. Herbert Meyer, member of Heidelberg's board and Chief Financial Officer; Bernhard Schreier, member of Heidelberg's board and Pre-Press Business Unit General Manager; Hans Peetz-Larsen, President and CEO, Heidelberg Americas; David Beck, Chief Financial Officer of Kodak Professional; and Dr. Carl Kohrt, Executive Vice President & Assistant Chief Operating Officer of Eastman Kodak.

"Although we are officially a new company as of today, that's not the whole picture," said Venkat Purushotham, president of NexPress. "In fact, Heidelberg and Kodak have been independently building applicable technologies, long before last fall when we announced our intent to form a joint venture. Now, with the combined resources of our parent companies and more than 400 dedicated employees in our centers in Rochester and Kiel, we are committed to introducing our first important product to the market in May, 2000 at the world's largest printing exhibition, Drupa, in Dusseldorf, Germany."

"NexPress marries Heidelberg's preeminence in commercial offset printing with Kodak's expertise in digital color technology to focus squarely on the future of digital printing. In addition to sharing equally in ownership, the partners share a vision and a unwavering commitment to make that vision a reality," said Wolfgang Pfizenmaier, chairman of NexPress' board of directors and a member of Heidelberg Druckmaschinen AG's board.

Appointed as NexPress senior management are Venkat Purushotham, President, and Udo Draeger, Executive Vice President. Purushotham brings to NexPress over 25 years of experience in all aspects of printing and publishing, including 17 years in Kodak R&D and business management. Draeger has successfully managed large, multinational joint ventures for over 20 years. The goal of the company is to provide solutions to enable value delivery in One-to-One Marketing. Products will include plateless, digital color printing systems for new markets like Personalized and Customized Printing, On-Demand Printing, Short Run and Fast Turnaround Color, and Distribute-Then-Print applications. Experts see these markets as the next growth wave in the printing and publishing industry. The name NexPress reflects the goal of the new company.

"We will literally be designing and marketing the next generation press—actually *beyond what the printing press* will be in the future. NexPress will allow print users to express their message in new ways and to drive value through the use of targeted information. Print providers will reap corresponding rewards," said Purushotham.

The new company, however, will not limit itself to a single product. NexPress intends to develop, manufacture, and market a continuing stream of products and services for *non-impact digital color printing applications.* "Our intention is to be on the leading edge of the new and rapidly growing digital printing industry," said Draeger. "We will always offer the best digital press, to enable and drive profitable growth in this new and energized industry."

NexPress products will complement Heidelberg's existing Speedmaster, Quickmaster, and Printmaster lines of digital, automated, and traditional printing presses. Heidelberg's contribution to NexPress is integral to its long-term strategy to remain the preeminent supplier of commercial printing solutions. The Heidelberg Group, based in Heidelberg, Germany, with approximately 18,000 employees and agencies in over 160 countries, is the leading supplier of printing systems. And, as we went to press, it was reported that Heidelberg was negotiating to take over Kodak's office copying and printing systems division.

Well, there you have it—the official announcement that this joint venture will develop the printing press of the future. Non-impact. Variable data. A printer, but also a press. They will meet competition from Xerox and Scitex, one with toner and the other with inkjet. The prototype of the Scitex press is built and it is expected to double its resolution. Xerox has stated that it intends to be a force in the printing industry. It is all quite exciting. Drupa 2000 will come almost 550 years from the invention of the press.

Almost all the digital color press and printer suppliers were developing lower cost per page approaches. Xeikon, for instance, states that the cost per page today was a quarter of what it was in 1993. As we count them, here are the worldwide digital color printing units projected to be shipped through the end of 1999:

By year

	1993	1994	1995	1996	1997	1998	1999
Units shipped	31	295	674	1,782	6,187	9,602	14,000

Thus, a market that did not exist as of 1993, now has over 30,000 users around the world.

Our table on the next page is an ever-changing list of digital color printers. Please check will all vendors to assure accuracy.

High-level digital color printers

	Res. dpi	4C ppm Simplex/Duplex	Price
Agfa			
Chromapress 70	600	35/70	$420,000
Chromapress 100	600	50/100	$550,000
Canon			
CLC 2100	600	6/2	$ 7,000
CLC 950	400	8/3	$ 19,000
CLC Z	600	11/4	$ 28,000
CLC Expected	600	15	$ 40,000
CLC 2400	400	24/10	$ 85,000
CLC 1000	400	31/11	$100,000
IBM			
InfoColor 70	600	35/70	$420,000
InfoColor 100	600	50/100	$550,000
Indigo			
E-Print 1000+	800	70/35	$380,000
TurboStream	800	70/35	$420,000
E-Print Pro	800	70/35	$249,000
UltraStream	800	80/40	$550,000
Xeikon			
DCP 32/D	600	35/70	$420,000
DCP 50/D	600	50/100	$550,000
Xerox			
Office 5	400	6	$ 16,000
5750 (Majestik)	400	6	$ 26,000
5799 (Regal)	400	9	$ 50,000
Expected	400	12-14	$ 60,000?
DocuColor 30 CP	400	30/10	$ 99,000
DocuColor 40 CP	400	40/15	$135,000
DocuColor 40 Pro	400	40/15	$167,000
ExpectedColor	400	50-60/?	$200,000?
DocuColor 70	600	35/70	$420,000
DocuColor 100	600	50/100	$550,000

Under speed, the first number is the simplex speed and the second number is the duplex speed. RIP configurations are a determining factor. Also, there are many options as well.

Xerox DocuTech

Black-and-white laser printers play an important role in personalized printing. Most often, color and certain images are printed by offset and then imprinted by running the sheets (or web) through monochrome printers. This is hybrid printing and the pre-printed sheets are called "shells." Also some black-and-white printers have software and functionality specifically for personalized printing.

The DocuTech Publishing Series is a group of 600dpi output products: the DocuTech 6135 and 6180. There are two basic engines: the 6135 operates at 135 pages per minute (ppm), and the 6180 operates at 180 pages per minute. Both accept electronic files and is designed to operate as a high-speed printer, with the formatting of pages being performed upstream and then sent to the printer. All three models can accept PostScript formats. All models of the DocuTech can also be in a networked environment. A customer can "print" to these machines via a network.

Two-sided originals can be run as either two-sided or single-sided copies. Likewise single-sided originals can be turned into two-sided copies. A job may be rotated on the sheet. The image or part of it can be shifted, which is important for some bindery considerations. If the job will be saddle-stitched, the individual pages will be automatically rearranged, shifted if necessary, and blank pages will be added to properly produce a saddle-stitched booklet.

The engine uses a revolving electrophotographic belt whose surface is charged as it revolves. The belt is large enough to hold seven 8.5x11-inch page images. The image source is a helium-neon laser that is split into two beams to lay down two raster lines at a time on the belt, spaced to achieve 600dpi resolution. A spinning polygon mirror focuses the beams on the belt. The beam erases the charge in each spot it hits, which prevents toner from adhering to the belt in that spot. The toner is supplied from a cartridge, like all copy technologies, except that it uses a dual-component toner. The other component for the dual-component system is the carrier beads that attach to the toner until the charged belt attracts the toner.

One way the DocuTech achieves its fast speed is in the duplexed printing. Instead of flipping pages, the DocuTech uses software to determine the fastest way to accomplish the two-sided printing. It might for example, follow the printing of side one immediately with the printing of the other. In other cases, it could interleave the printing of the second side of one sheet with the printing of the first side of the next sheet.

Designed for long periods of uninterrupted service, the DocuTech is rated at one million impressions per month. During peak periods some report printing 2.5–3 million impressions per month. A wide variety of paper stocks can be used. Paper weight can vary from 16-lb. (60 gsm) bond through 110-lb. (199 gsm) index. Transparency material, carbonless paper, both precut and full-cut tab stock, and recycled paper can be printed. Preprinted stock can be sent through the DocuTech if laser-approved, wax-free inks are used on the lithographic press. Before printing, the DocuTech checks to see whether the stock loaded in the trays matches the requirement specified on the job ticket. If the job ticket doesn't match, the system refuses to print the job. A unique solution for paper supply is available from Roll Systems Corporation, whose DocuSheeter allows a DocuTech to operate off of a roll of paper. The 17-inch-wide (432-mm-wide) roll of paper is cut into sheets as it enters the printer, allowing for 12 hours of continuous operation at rated speed.

All models of the DocuTech have stapling and two adjustable side stitches. This is performed in-line and has a maximum capacity of 70 sheets of 20-lb. (80gsm) bond. The Model 6135 and 6180 also have the capability of applying a heat-activated tape binding strip to the side of a book. The number of pages can be between 15 and 125, and can only be applied to 11-inch-long (279-mm-long) paper. The binding tape is supplied on a reel that contains 425 binds. The tape is available in black, blue, brown, gray, and white.

An important advance with the DocuTech 6180 is the Interposer, which allows sheets that have already been printed with toner to be collated with sheets run through the laser printer, without themselves going through the printer unit. Covers can be done on color laser printers and then merged with text pages to make finished documents. The DocuTech is already used in many "imprinting" applications—that is, sheets that have been printed on offset printing presses (called shells) are run through the DocuTech and the variable data is laser printed. If the sheet has lots of static color, this is a very cost-effective way of imprinting black-and-white text.

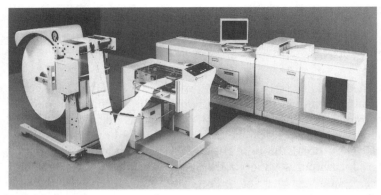

Roll-fed adapters are very popular.

Xerox announced new additions to its DocuTech product line. The DocuTech 180 hits a 180-page-per-minute print speed. The 6180 is the fastest cut-sheet printer with a print speed of 180 letter pages per minute (90 ppm duplex), and runs at a comparable speed to a small offset press at 10,000+ impressions per hour. The unit also has a new variable-pitch option that allows for gradual speed reduction as the sheet size increases. This means that printing smaller format documents, on pages larger than A4 size, the unit does not slow to half speed as happens with the DocuTech 135. The new 6180 slows only slightly.

The 6180 has five paper trays, which can feed 11x17-inch pre-printed sheets. The DocuTech 6180 has a new imaging system that is still 600dpi, but the imaging technology works in quarter-pixel increments horizontally to provide more accurate tints and shades but this technology cannot yet be used for increasing the screen value of halftone images. Xerox has also improved the DocuTech's darkness range control for eliminating gray cast in backgrounds at darker settings and to adjust text, line art and halftones through ImageSense, which automatically calibrates the print engine to a standard, freeing the operator from adjusting toner levels.

Digital printing to the max
A new IBM printer using Adobe Extreme technology will print 464 pages per minute—pages, not phone bills. As the first product to implement Adobe's Extreme multiprocessor RIP architecture, IBM introduced at the XPLOR Conference and Exhibition in Orlando a RISC

6000 processor driving the InfoPrint 4000, a 600dpi, 464 pages per minute (8.5x11-inch, 2-up) monochrome printer that can rip and print documents with both PostScript and IBM's data processing architecture, AFP (Advanced Function Presentation). The combination enables the printer to use variable information in tandem with the graphics capabilities of PostScript to allow customized applications for complex documents such as textbooks, operating guides, academic materials, manuals and other publications. The printer was available in the first half of 1997 with a list price of $780,000 for the 600dpi duplex model.

IBM's InfoPrint 4000 uses the new InfoPrint Manager which includes electronic job ticketing and a server-based printing scheduler. The system automates and tracks print jobs through three components: *InfoPrint Operations* creates customer-specific electronic job tickets that are stored in a central file storage directory. *Print* requests can be received via cartridge, Internet, Intranet, or scanned copy. *InfoPrint Scheduler* takes print requests and queues them for printing on any of the network attached printers whether IBM-only devices or other vendors. *InfoPrint Library* provides storage capability of job tickets and their print files.

McGraw-Hill is now using the IBM 3900 600dpi digital printer to print customized and other textbooks, reference books and technical books in short runs, on demand.

Delphax tried for the honor of fastest digital printer on earth at 800+ pages per minute but at a piddly 300dpi. What was most evident at XPLOR was that digital printers are starting to achieve speeds more like printing presses with the added dimension of customization and personalization.

Considered the fastest book printing solution in the industry, the InfoPrint 4000 High Resolution Printing System, model IR3/IR4, is nearly 50% faster than the existing high-resolution model and enables statement printing at a higher quality. The system outputs documents at speeds up to 708 impressions per minute (ipm) at 480dpi or 600dpi selectable resolutions. InfoPrint Manager's base license fee is $15,000 and attachment fees will be based on the speed and quantities of printers. The InfoPrint Color 100 has a list price of $590,000. The IBM InfoPrint 4000 IR3/IR4 is priced at $920,000.

At the XPLOR event in 1997, Xerox announced a family of webfed printers with speeds of up to 300 feet per minute, the first results of its acquisition of high-speed printer maker Delphax. The fast webfed product line has three models: the DocuPrint 330, DocuPrint 900 and DocuPrint 1300 with speeds of 330, 900 and 1,300 letter-size pages per minute in the two-up duplex configuration, respectively (equal to 5.5, 15, and 21.7 letter-size images per second.)

The machines are targeted primarily at statement printing and similar applications. The 330 supports PostScript, but the resolution is only 300dpi. The other two machines support 600dpi output, but they do not support PostScript (only Xerox, LCDS and IBM APDF print streams).

Ion deposition
As the 1980s approached, impact printers were causing data processing logjams at mainframe sites everywhere. The situation inspired research and development of imaging companies to bring faster, more reliable and higher-quality printing technologies to the market. These corporations responded with commercially available non-impact technologies—Xerox Corporation and Océ with laser electrophotography, Bull Printing Systems with magnetography, and Delphax Systems with ion deposition.

In 1980, the Dennison Corporation and the Canadian Development Corporation formed Delphax (initially to explore methods of improving photocopier performance), to further develop the budding ion deposition technology. Three years later, Dennison created Presidax, a service bureau which used ion deposition technology for printing in the tag and label manufacturing business. With a slight modification to the original technology, Presidax successfully established itself as a printer of bar-coded tags and labels.

In 1984, the Canadian Development Corporation, having made a significant return on its investment, sold its interest in Delphax to Xerox. In 1987, Delphax began marketing a press-integrated, ion deposition print station—but only for sale outside of North America, so as not to compete with its service bureau operation. When Avery merged with Dennison, the imaging systems division of Dennison was sold to Delphax. Finally, in 1990, Olympus Optical became a third partner in Delphax. And in 1997 Xerox Corporation acquired Delphax.

Ion deposition principles

There are four basic steps in ion deposition printing:

- imaging
- developing
- transferring
- cleaning

A stream of electrons is projected from a print cartridge containing a matrix of holes. Under computer control, the stream of electrons is selectively projected onto the rotating imaging cylinder, called a dielectric cylinder. A dielectric cylinder has a special coating allowing it to become selectively charged. (This surface is also extremely durable, having a print life of over two million feet.) The electrostatic image projected onto the cylinder is still a latent image—it is not yet visible to the naked eye.

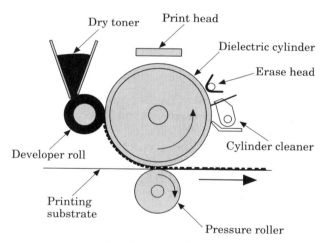

Dry toner   Print head

Dielectric cylinder

Erase head

Developer roll

Cylinder cleaner

Printing substrate

Pressure roller

Ion deposition is an effective imaging process for electronic data.

As the dielectric cylinder continues to rotate, the latent image comes into close proximity of a supply of single-component toner held in place by a rotating magnetic toner brush called a developer roll. (According to proponents of the technology, it is the use of the single-component toner which give ion deposition printing the ability to better cover large areas of a substrate.) In a manner similar to development in electrophotographic systems, an electrical field created by a voltage differential between the cylinder and the developer roll causes the toner to move to the image areas of the cylinder.

The newly-toned image on the dielectric cylinder continues to rotate to a point where the substrate and toner pass through a nip created by the dielectric cylinder and a pressure roller underneath. The toner is then actually squeezed onto the substrate as it is passing by. This method of transferring and fusing of toner in one operation is known as *transfixing*.

Lastly, there is the erasing process. The toner is scraped off the cylinder with a scraper blade and any residual latent image is neutralized by an electrically-charged "erase head." After the erasing process is complete, the imaging process is set to begin again.

There are three electrodes, called respectively the drive electrode, control electrode and screen electrode. These units, isolated from each other, consist of thin metal layers which resemble printed circuit board elements. In operation, bursts of high-frequency electric current, applied to the drive and control electrodes, generate a stream of charged-air molecules—the ions. The control electrode imposes the image signal on the ion stream, allowing ions to pass when an image element is to be created.

To develop a high pixel resolution, the print head is arranged for multiplexing, a technique of staggering multiple arrays of electrode strips and actuating them in synchronism with the cylinder rotation so that several rows of ion-emitting sources form image pixels as the cylinder elements pass underneath the print head. The screen electrode focuses the ion stream and prevents reverse ion flow in the multiplexed arrangement.

Since ionography does not use any effect of light in creating the latent image on the intermediate image carrier, neither selenium nor any other photoconductor is used. Like such a photoconductor, however, the ionographic cylinder must accept and hold a charge without leakage to surrounding areas. A hard aluminum surface is usually used. An environmentally controlled cylinder and print head surface temperature of about 180°F keeps airborne chemical effects of ionization from affecting the critical cylinder surface property.

Resolution of ion deposition printing is rated at 240 pixels per inch; however, this is misleading because the actual dots per inch resolvable is higher than the number would indicate. Essentially, real resolution may be gauged at 300dpi. In terms of speed, ion deposition, web printing devices can reach 400 feet per minute. For today's use, an inherent advantage of ion deposition technology is that it can be readily integrated into a web press. Since this system fuses toner by transfixing, heat is of no concern—allowing for printing on a wide variety of substrates. Because of this, ion deposition is commonly found integrated into flexographic systems.

With its modular design, substrate flexibility, print quality and speed, ion deposition has transcended its original intention of supplementing the photocopier and "data processing" industries. In fact, ion deposition has found quite a niche market with the tag and label industry. Ion deposition is especially suited for high-quality, short runs on jobs that require variable data on each page. Examples of this are customer statements and bills from banks, utilities and service companies. A new ion deposition device from Xerox has 600dpi capability and very high speed. It was shown as a technology in 1998 and we expect that it will be a product very soon.

Continuous inkjet printing

Inkjet printing is a form of non-impact printing. The first inkjets were created in the 1970s by Dr. C. Hellmuth Hertz, a physics researcher at the Lund Institute in Sweden. Inkjet printers have become increasingly essential in the wake of desktop publishing because of the great demand for the high-quality printers for character printing and color printing, especially when associated with digital photography.

There are two kinds of inkjet printing: Drop-on-demand (DOD) and continuous inkjet printing. Continuous inkjet printers have a significant advantage over DOD because of their ability to produce high-quality images that closely resemble those of a photograph.

The fact that it is a non-impact printer makes it excellent for printing on surfaces which are difficult or uneven. Continuous inkjet printers are capable of matching speeds similar to speeds in automated factories. Inkjet printers have a wide range of applications in the printing and packaging industries.

Inkjet printers can be used for marking products with dates, such as "best before," as well as coding information like prices and product tracking. There are hundreds of different products which can be coded through the use of inkjet printers: food and beverage containers, cosmetics, pharmaceuticals, electronic components, cable and wiring, pipes, glass and some bottles and and industrial components. Ticket numbering and high-speed addressing for magazines and mail are just some of the applications in the printing industry.

There are several steps in the process of continuous inkjet:

- The formation and electronic control of micron-sized droplets starts when a highly liquid ink is forced through small nozzles at high pressure, producing a stream of ink that is invisible to the naked eye.
- Surface tension causes the ink stream to break up into small, relatively uniform droplets of about 8-10 microns in diameter.
- By applying voltage to an electrode surrounding the nozzle orifice, it is possible to mark and place a charge on the droplets.
- The flight path of these charged droplets can thereby be controlled as they pass through an electrical field.
- This technique applies charges to the droplets if they are not to be used to form an image.
- When they are charged, they are deflected downward by an electric field created by a deflection electrode.
- The deflected droplets are caught in a gutter structure and siphoned away.
- Uncharged droplets, unaffected by the strong electric field in the control structure, pass through and are deposited on the paper.
- Approximately one million droplets per second are produced by a single nozzle.
- A single "off" pulse permits some droplets to remain uncharged and to reach the paper, which is mounted on a rotating drum.
- The resulting tiny dot will be one of millions required to produce a full-color high resolution image.
- The high rate of droplet formation permits very high rates of information transfer and correspondingly fast print times, even for large formats.

Continuous printing speed is approximately 45 square inches per minute or even higher.

The Hertz technology that created inkjet printing is known for the high quality images it can create. The main reason that the quality is so high is because the inkjet can produce true halftones, such as different gray levels, or color tones, which can be generated with every single pixel. This true halftone printing is achieved by varying the number of drops in each pixel. The number of drops can vary from 0 to about 30 for each color, which means you can get a number of different density levels for each pixel and each color. It is possible to increase the number of density levels per pixel from 0 to 200 for each color.

Another key point to keep in mind when discussing continuous inkjet printers is that they use a recirculated ink system in which evaporation of ink can cause changes in ink composition. The physical properties of inkjet ink such as viscosity, conductivity, and density depend on its composition.

Serious printing problems can be caused by changes in these physical properties. Changes in stream velocity, drop charge, and drop mass can lead to the problem of drop misplacement or a variation in character size, while levels of solvent in ink can alter its drying time. Ink control systems must be added to the recirculation of the ink in order to compensate for any evaporation loss that will occur over time. The system is quite sophisticated.

Since the time of the creation of the continuous inkjet printer, there have been several modifications and improvements to the system. There were two main concerns of the early inkjet printers: nozzle clogging and uncontrolled ink mist. Since then, the creation of the Iris continuous inkjet printer has addressed these problems. After each cycle is complete and the nozzle has stopped firing, the nozzle tips are vacuumed to remove any residue ink.

An automatic nozzle maintenance cycle is built into each system. When the printer is not in the print mode, the system powers up on timed cycle and fires ink through the nozzles for a few seconds, shuts down, and vacuums the tips again. Uncontrolled ink mist is a result of the reaction between the dropping ink and the printing surface. Ink droplets are forced out of the nozzle at about 650 pounds per square inch of pressure. This means that the droplets travel about 30 millimeters from the nozzle tip to the print surface at a speed of 20 meters per second, or 50 miles per hour. The mist develops from the millions of drops that are hitting the paper every minute. A mist shield was created to to control these random ink spots. The mist shield consists of an absorbent material which is positioned near the printing surface which catches the ink as it bounces back toward the ink nozzle. This allows for a clean print surface with fewer random background spots, as well as clean internal surfaces.

Scitex Digital Printing has a digital printing system for books capable of 3,800 book pages per minute at 300x600dpi called VersaMark. It uses continuous inkjet on a web printer at three times the resolution of the 240dpi earlier models, The speed is achieved by printing three 6x9-inch pages side by side on a 20-inch web. For 8.5x11-inch pages, the rated speed is 2,100 ppm.

There are two nine-inch imaging heads, each with 2,600 ink-jet nozzles for monochrome printing, but it is also applicable for spot-color applications. Binding is a separate step. Scitex isn't attempting to RIP incoming jobs at the speed of the imager. The RIP supplier is Varis and PDF is the standard format for input to the RIP. The cost per page is less than half a cent, or about $1.30 to print a 300-page, 8.5x11-inch book. The VersaMark is priced at $800,000 to $2 million, based on configuration, with the first customer site in place. Thus, inkjet has a viable future in digital printing, as we look at page reproduction:

Page counts

	1996	2001	2006
Percent of 1996 page volume	100%	105%	110%
Pages reproduced on paper	85%	70%	55%
Pages totally electronic	10%	20%	30%
Pages both digital and print	5%	10%	15%
Total pages on paper	90%	80%	70%

Where reproduced?

	1996	2001	2006
Home (including SOHO)	4%	7%	12%
Office	15%	23%	24%
Plant	81%	70%	64%
Total	100%	100%	100%

Copies, pages, sheets & images per minute

The time has come to get our terminology to be consistent and correct. As with spots, dots, pixels and pels, which has never been truly resolved, we have an opportunity to define the speed of replicating devices and systems in a manner that allows honest comparison.

Copies per minute (cpm) is commonly used to rate the speed of copying machines in standard single-sided pages per minute. In fact, copiers are categorized by their cpm speeds.

Sheets per minute (spm) is used in some cases by printer suppliers who feel uncomfortable with copies per minute. Since a printer technically makes originals and not copies, cpm is an iffy term to them. spm seems to be a more honest way of describing the number of sheets of paper that go through a device in a unit of time. If we stay with standard 8.5x11-inch sheets, then we can all understand what the device is really doing.

Pages per minute (ppm) sounds easy but it is not. If the device can print or copy both sides at one time, one could claim two pages per minute for each sheet per minute. A device that prints both sides of the sheet simultaneously may run at a lower sheets per minute but at a higher pages per minute (double, actually). If you have to re-run the sheets for the second side you still run at the the same SPM but the ppm is cut in half. For instance:

10 spm single sided (simplex) = 10 ppm
10 spm simultaneously duplexed = 20 ppm
10 spm re-run duplexed = 5 ppm

Thus we have three machines with the same Sheets Per Minute speed for single sided printing but three different speeds for duplexed printing. You also get in trouble if the spm is based on something less than or greater than a standard page. If the spm were in 11x17-inch sheets, then each spm equals two ppm simplex and four ppm duplex. Images per minute (ipm) is used as a euphemism for pages per minute, since some digital printing will not use what we may call a page. An image is therefore some level of printing on a sheet of paper. This term gets really esoteric when you consider that variable printing can vary images as well as text and one could confuse the "page image" with the images on the page. If there were three images on a page, this number would be incomprehensible.

Impressions per hour (iph) is used in the printing industry. It is somewhat misleading in that it can refer to a large sheet of paper or to the number of images on that paper, since printers gain significant productivity by printing multiple units on a signature.

Feet per minute (fpm) is used by some suppliers, but this is completely meaningless to users. It really comes down to clearly defining the unit of printing and the unit of time. Most devices use "per minute" and some use "per hour." Printing press people usually think in terms of hours and copier/printer people think in terms of minutes. So let's all get together and get this all ironed out in dpm: Decisions per minute.

Are you really confused by the terminology used to define the speed of digital printers? So are we. We pretty well know what sheets per minute is—an actual sheet of paper. In the case above there are two sheets: 8.5x11 and 11x17 inches. The sheet in question has toner on one side (simplex). Now, put toner or inkjet ink on the other side of the same sheet (duplex). The speed normally is cut in half when printing duplex; but it does not work that way on some devices.

The DocuTech belt can have seven 8.5x11-inch toner or inkjet ink images on it (pitch), but for duplexing it has less. Sheet-based systems require a second pass in order to print the flip side; web-based systems can print both sides at virtually the same time; thus giving them a production advantage, although, sheet-fed printers provide more flexibility for online finishing.

The Xeikon engine (Agfa, IBM, Xeikon, and Xerox) puts toner on both sides of the sheet (web) at almost the same time. So we tried to figure out what the net output was for each of the terms used to characterize what digital printers produce. All of those terms have to do with what is on the sheet, but they are often confused with the sheet itself. Remember, there is the sheet of paper and there is the toner or ink that is on it.

The table on the next page tries to probe this area of output productivity and offer some food for thought:

Per minute	Simplex Unperfected Single-sided 1-sided		Duplex Perfected Double-sided 2-sided	
	8.5x11	*11x17*	*8.5x11*	*11x17*

1. Sheet — the actual piece of paper that will be imaged

DocuTech 135	135	57	67.5	28.5
Xeikon engine	35	17.5	35	17.5
DocuColor 40	40	20	15	15

2. Impression — the toner or ink that is deposited on the paper

DocuTech 135	135	57	135	57
Xeikon engine	35	17.5	70	35
DocuColor 40	40	20	30	15

3. Print — the toner or ink that is deposited on the paper

DocuTech 135	135	57	135	57
Xeikon engine	35	17.5	70	35
DocuColor 40	40	20	30	15

4. Click — registers each time toner is imaged onto the paper

Docutech 135	135	57	135	57
Xeikon engine	35	17.5	70	35
DocuColor 40	40	20	30	15

5. Image — the final printed unit — may be smaller than
the sheet of paper

DocuTech 135	Depends on size of finished piece. How
DocuTech 180	many up are you positioning on the sheet.
Xeikon engine	Multiply that number-up by the impress-
DocuColor 40	ions/prints/clicks/images/pages

6. Page — sometimes used synonymously with sheet,
more likely the toner or ink on the sheet

Docutech 135	135	57	135	57
Xeikon engine	35	17.5	70	35
DocuColor 40	40	20	30	15

7. Unit — can mean anything you want it to mean: the paper
itself or the toner or ink on the paper

Docutech 135	
Xeikon engine	Can mean sheets — or impressions/
DocuColor 40	prints/clicks/images/pages

Digital color printing: too early or on time?

Major players in digital color printing have stated that there was slower than expected development of the digital color market than expected. Let's recall what has happened so far.

- September 1991: Heidelberg announced GTO-DI at Print '91. This ushers in the first approach to digital color.
- January, 1992: Heidelberg installed GTO-DI at Sir Speedy in Los Angeles.
- June 1993: Indigo announced E-Print 1000.
- July 1993: Xeikon announced DCP-1.
- September, 1993: Both Indigo and Agfa showed systems at Ipex 93 in Birmingham, England.
- Mid 1994: Less than 20 Indigo and AM Multigraphics (Xeikon) units in the U.S.
- Early 1995: 400 Indigo units and 400 Xeikon units installed worldwide.
- May, 1995: Drupa showcased digital printing as working technology.
- August, 1995: Indigo upgraded all systems to improve reliability.
- Scitex introduced the Spontane, a Fuji-Xerox scanner/copier/printer with a RIP, later called the DocuColor.
- January, 1996: About 1,000 digital color printers and 110 hybrid platemaker/presses installed worldwide—less than 400 U.S. sites.
- March, 1997: Xerox introduced the DocuColor 40 and a year later Canon had the CLC-1000
- December, 1998: Almost 19,000 digital color printers are shipped worldwide.
- December, 1999: Over 30,000 digital color printers, and possibly 40,000 will be installed worldwide.
- May, 2000: A number of advanced digital color printing systems will be introduced that will compete with offset lithography.

In other words this market is still very young—only a few years old. The gap between the announcements and the installations has certainly been a factor in the development of this market. There are two requirements for a market to develop:

1. a large base of buyers
2. a reasonably large base of sellers

For buyers of digital color there is the need for digital document preparation, which means they must be users of desktop or other digital technology. Fortunately, 70% to 80% of all pages now printed are prepared digitally, so the base is large and growing. Unfortunately there were not that many sellers for some time, and the early adopters lived with reliability and quality problems that have since been pretty well corrected. You must draw parallels from the development of color copying. From virtually zero in 1987 until today, color copying grew because there were many users and they were all promoting their services. The EFI Fiery RIP made color copiers de facto digital printers and today over 50% of all color copies go through the RIP, so there definitely is a digital printing market.

There is a pent-up demand for digital color printing. It is based on three major factors:

- *The number of pages in electronic form.* Counting both PostScript and pages produced on color prepress systems, well over half of all pages are now in digital form and thus ripe for electronic printout.
- *The preponderance of color printers and copiers.* As a result of their popularity, many buyers have been exposed to color reproduction. They have also developed an acceptance for color printer and copier quality levels.
- *The cost pressures on American business.* With or without an expanding economy, business maintains profit levels by cutting cost. Just-in-time (JIT) approaches help. But for JIT to work, it must also offer a time advantage as well as a cost advantage. Digital printing is a faster process than traditional printing.

We estimate that almost 1.14 trillion pages worldwide are available for digital printing. This volume will come from:

- Volume that would have gone to low-level color printers and color copiers—19%
- Volume that would have gone to conventional offset color printing—45%
- Volume that would have been black-and-white copies off of copying/printing systems—15%
- New volume developed for digital color printing—21%

Because the bulk of volume will initially come from commercial printing, commercial printers have become the first users.

Variability

PERSONALIZED
CUSTOMIZED
MASS MARKET

Variable Data/Images Short Run	**Variable Data/Images Long Run**
Canon CLC-1000 Indigo E-Print 1000+ Scitex Spontane T/R Systems Micropress Xerox Docucolor 40 Agfa Chromapress IBM InfoColor 70-100 Xeikon DCP32-50D Xerox Docucolor 70-100 Mitsubishi? Ricoh?	Kodak/Heidelberg Thing NexPress Solutions LLC Scitex Ink Jet systems Xerox Future Things
Fixed Data/Images Short Run	**Fixed Data/Images Long Run**
Heidelberg GTO-DI Heidelberg Quickmaster-DI Heidelberg Speedmaster 74-DI Omni-Adast-DI Scitex/KBA 74 Karat Heath/Presstek-DI Goss ADOPT press Creo/Ryobi Thing MAN-Roland DICO press Barco? Komori? Others?	Flexographic presses CTFP Gravure presses CTGC Toray (Sony) Gravure Thing Offset presses CTOP

Run Length

1   500   2000   5000

We categorize color reproduction systems by run length and variability. The lower right includes the traditional printing processes of flexo, gravure and offset litho, all of which are seeing the impact of computer-to-plate. Toray acquired the Sony computer-to-plastic gravure sleeve technology and Creo recently announced a computer-to-flexo system. Ohio Engraving has computer-to-gravure cylinder, among others. CTP allows traditional printing processes to handle shorter runs.

These are all presses that utilize a fixed image plate and operate best at 2,000 or more impressions, usually of a signature-sized sheet. To the left we find the systems that either make an image carrier on press or are new concept presses. The Heath/Presstek is our guess of a possible link between Presstek technology and the Heath Custom Press company which Presstek acquired. Heath was actually shown with on-press imaging at an event a few years ago. There is probably a market for an under-$300,000 4-color DI. We would expect that future DI presses will use processless thermal printing plates. DI approaches are extremely productive for a multitude of short-run jobs, and also provide benefits for longer runs as well. We would guess that every press manufacturer on earth is working on a version that makes plates on press—or image carriers on press. They are applicable for short runs, but cannot handle variable data printing.

The box in the upper left lists the toner-based digital printers. The sheet-based systems are towards the top and the web-based versions are flush right towards the bottom. All of the web-based versions are Xeikon engines. Mitsubishi once showed a web-based color printer but it has never been introduced as a product.

The last box includes the yet-to-come long run printers that provide press-like productivity with printer-like variability. We are not sure of these but it is assumed that Kodak and Heidelberg would not come together to introduce just another laser printer. We would expect that Xerox will continue to push the envelope at the upper end of the industry and that Scitex Digital will continue to advance inkjet.

As companies enter this market they will have to pick one of the four quadrants. We are not covering copiers or desktop digital printers here, nor have we included the black-and-white printers, especially those at the high end of the industry. Color is where the action will be over the next decade. Spot color is good, but full color is better.

Why do you want variability?
1. Personalized printing: If customized and personalized color printing are important new markets, digital technology is essential.
2. Short runs: Very short runs. Under 2,000. Like one.
3. Publications: Documents with lots of pages with page numbers organized into a set—books, etc. on demand.
4. Quick turnaround: Very fast turnaround. Like now.
5. Distribute and print: Files sent to remote locations for print production.

The concept of digital color coverage

If you took black toner (or ink for that matter) and covered a page completely you would have 100% coverage. The higher the resolution, the more pixels there would be on the page. For instance, and 8.5x11-inch page at 600dpi has 33.7 million possible pixels. If you made every pixel black, this to us would be 100% coverage. But we do use tints and you could have a 50% tint of black, which means that only half the pixels are "on" or only half the density of individual pixels is printing. What is difficult to understand concerns the other three colors. In a CMYK world, any time you have to print something out, you must use the subtractive colors of C, M, Y, K. That means that you could theoretically have 100% of Cyan, 100% of Magenta, 100% of Yellow, and 100% of Black on a page at one time. Technically, you would have 400% coverage.

We created a page in QuarkXPress with a full-color image, some black type and a 50% yellow tint. We then converted the page to an EPS file. We opened the EPS file in Photoshop, went to Mode and made it CMYK. We went to Image and Histogram. The Histogram function gives you an indication of the number of pixels affected by each color out of the total. This is the "Mean" and it is available for each color. For our test page we recorded the following values: C = 211.52, M = 213.41, Y = 202.52. and K = 221.84. We then apply these numbers in a formula:

$$\text{Coverage} = \frac{255 - \text{Mean}}{255} \times 100$$

The four values that result from the formula are: C = 17.05%, M = 16.30%, Y = 20.58%, and K = 13.0%. They total 66.93%—which we consider the coverage. Many printer vendors use an average of 30% to 60% when trying to provide a reasonable estimate of toner use. The assumption is that many pages have type on them, with margins and gutters of white space. If you had a page with all black text, then the coverage is 22.51%. The purpose of this investigation is to arrive at some fair method for evaluating coverage. Toner is more expensive than ink and constitutes between one third and one half of the cost per printed unit in digital printing. All suppliers are working very hard to extend the coverage of their toner and other consumables in order to make digital printing more competitive with lithography and at longer runs.

3

Database
Basics

A database is a collection of data that is organized so that its contents can easily be accessed, managed, and updated. There are three types of database:

- relational database, a tabular database in which data is defined so that it can be reorganized and accessed in a number of different ways
- distributed database, one that can be dispersed or replicated among different points in a network
- object-oriented database, with data defined in object classifications and subclasses

Databases contain collections of data records or files, such as sales transactions, product information and inventories, and customer profiles. Database management provides users with the capabilities of controlling read/write access, specifying report generation, and analyzing usage.

Databases and database management is prevalent in large mainframe systems, and also present in smaller distributed workstation and mid-range systems, and on personal computers. SQL is a standard language for making interactive queries from and updating a database such as IBM's DB2, Microsoft's Access, and database products from Oracle, Sybase, and Computer Associates.

Data

- In computing, data is information that has been translated into a form that is more convenient to move or process. Relative to today's computers and transmission media, data is information converted into binary or digital form.
- In computer component interconnection and network communication, data is often distinguished from "control information," "control bits," and similar terms to identify the main content of a transmission unit.
- In telecommunications, data sometimes means digitally-encoded information to distinguish it from analog-encoded information such as conventional telephone voice calls. In general, "analog" or voice transmission requires a dedicated continual connection for the duration of a related series of transmissions. Data transmission can often be sent with intermittent connections in packets.

Some of us, cognizant of the word's Latin origin and as the plural form of *datum*, use plural verb forms with *data*. Since *datum* is rarely used, most treat data as a singular form. A database is made up of:

- tables
- records
- fields

Tables. A table stores information about one subject. For example, if you created a database to store information about all of your friends, the details would be stored in a table.

Records. A record stores information about one entry in a table. If you had stored details of five friends in a table then the table would contain five records—one for each of your friends.

Fields. A field stores one piece of information within a record. Below is an example of a table:

First name	Last name	SS number	Date of birth
John	Caslon	123456789	1/1/61
Beatrice	Warde	987654321	2/2/62
Steve	Davis	020234562	12/06/58
Angela	Webster	112234109	12/12/65
Jack	Fisher	223309812	05/01/55

This database contains five records and four fields.

Types of database

There are two types of database, flat file and relational. A flat file database contains details about one subject as in the example above. A relational database contains details about two or more related subjects, with each of these subjects having its own table. An example of this would be an invoicing system, where there would be separate tables for customers, invoices, invoice lines, and goods. The process of taking all the information required for a database and breaking it down into separate tables is called normalization. The information in these separate tables can be brought together by the structured query language (SQL).

Relational databases

In 1970, a new model for database structure and design appeared when E. F. Codd laid out the basics of relational database systems in his article "A Relational Model of Data for Large Shared Data Banks." The main principle of the relational model is the absolute separation of the logical view and the physical view of data. The physical view is implementation-dependent and not further defined. The logical view of the data is set-oriented. A relational set is an unordered group of items, sub-divided into fields. In a given set, all items have the same structure—the same number of fields and the same data type for corresponding fields. Only the field values are different from item to item in a set.

A relational database is a collection of data items organized as a set of formally-described tables from which data can be accessed or reassembled in many different ways without having to reorganize the database tables. The relational database was invented by E. F. Codd at IBM in 1970. The current standard user and application program interface to a relational database is the structured query language. SQL statements are used both for interactive queries for information from a relational database and for gathering data for reports. In addition to being relatively easy to create and access, a relational database has the important advantage of being easy to extend. After the original database creation, a new data category can be added without requiring that all existing applications be modified.

A relational set is often modeled as a table with the items of a set as the rows of the table. The fields in the items are the columns and these can have names, but the rows are unordered and unnamed. A database consists of one or more tables, plus a catalog (also represented by tables) describing the database. The relational model defines a set of mathematical operations and constraints that can be applied to tables in databases. Relational operations and constraints are used to define rules (user defined constraints). A database management system provides mechanisms to support relational operations and constraints for user defined databases and rules.

A relational language like SQL is descriptive, specifying the results desired rather than how to obtain the results (procedural). Using mathematical theorems, requested relational operations can be divided into components that can be processed by independent tasks running on one or more CPUs, even distributed machines. Relational models offer parallel processing. Other database approaches include:

- the hierarchical database model
- the network database model
- the inverted file model
- the object-oriented database model

In 1985, Codd published a series of articles that outlined the basic requirements of a relational system. He also provided a scorecard to measure the relational compliance of a DBMS. It is claimed that no existing relational database management system is close to full compliance. Oracle would be close. The relational model is an integrated whole. Missing support for a given feature weakens the effectiveness of supported features. The relational model is really about practical solutions for real world problems.

For example, a typical business order entry database would include a table that described a customer with columns for name, address, phone number, and so forth. Another table would describe an order: product, customer, date, sales price, and so forth. A user of the database could obtain a view of the database that fitted the user's needs. For example, a branch office manager might like a view or report on all customers that had bought products after a certain date. A financial services manager in the same company could, from the same tables, obtain a report on accounts that needed to be paid.

When creating a relational database, you can define the domain of possible values in a data column and further constraints that may apply to that data value. For example, a domain of possible customers could allow up to ten possible customer names but be constrained in one table to allowing only three of these customer names to be specifiable. The definition of a relational database results in a table of metadata, or formal descriptions of the tables, columns, domains, and constraints.

Object-oriented programming (OOP)
A concept that changed the rules in computer program development, object-oriented programming (OOP) is organized around objects rather than actions, data rather than logic. Historically, a program has been viewed as a logical procedure that takes input data, processes it, and produces output data. The programming challenge was seen as how to write the logic, not how to define the data. Object-oriented programming takes the view that what we really care about are the objects we want to manipulate rather than the logic required to manipulate them.

Examples of objects range from human beings (described by name, address, and so forth) to buildings and floors (whose properties can be described and managed) down to the little widgets on your computer desktop (such as buttons and scroll bars).

The first step in OOP is to identify all the objects you want to manipulate and how they relate to each other, an exercise often known as data modeling. Once you've identified an object, you generalize it as a class of objects (think of Plato's concept of the ideal chair that stands for all chairs) and define the kind of data it contains and any logic sequences that can manipulate it. The logic sequences are known as methods. A real instance of a class is called (no surprise here) an "object" or, in some environments, an "an instance of a class." The object or class instance is what you run in the computer. Its methods provide computer instructions and the class object characteristics provide relevant data.

The concept of a data class makes it possible to define subclasses of data objects that share some or all of the main class characteristics. Called inheritance, this property of OOP forces a more thorough data analysis, reduces development time, and ensures more accurate coding. Since a class defines only the data it needs to be concerned with, when an instance of that class (an object) is run, the code will not be able to accidentally access other program data. This characteristic of data hiding provides greater system security and avoids unintended data corruption. The definition of a class is reusable not only by the program for which it is initially created but also by other object-oriented programs (and, for this reason, can be more easily distributed for use in networks). The concept of data classes allows programmers to create new data types that are not defined in the language itself.

The structure of an Oracle database

Tables are the basic unit of data storage in a database. Tables hold all of user-accessible data. From the point of view of an ordinary user tables are the only objects he deals with. Each table is defined with a name and a set of named columns with specified width and data type. Once a table is created valid rows of data can be inserted into it. Rows can be queried, deleted, or updated. Tablespaces are the next bigger logical unit a database is divided into. Tablespaces are created by database administrators and group objects to simplify administrative operations.

The Oracle database has both a physical and a logical structure. The physical structure is determined by the operating system files and consists of data files, log files, and control files. The physical storage can be managed without affecting the logical structure of the database. The logical structure of the database is determined by one or more tablespaces which consist of tables, views, indexes, stored procedures, etc.

Structured Query Language (SQL)

SQL, an English like non-procedural language, is an international standard, hence it is the common language for all relational databases. The basic commands are easy to learn because they are in English not geek. SQL is used for all types of database activities. Programs written in SQL for other systems can often be moved to Oracle databases with very little modifications.

SQL is a standard interactive and programming language for getting information from and updating a database. Although SQL is both an ANSI and an ISO standard, many database products support SQL with proprietary extensions to the standard language. Queries take the form of a command language that lets you select, insert, update, find out the location of data, and so forth. There is also a programming interface.

Procedural Language PL/SQL

PL/SQL extends SQL. It allows you to logically group statements. PL/SQL procedures can be stored in centralized libraries for use in different applications. PL/SQL blocks may consist of any number of SQL statements combined with control statements like these: IF...THEN...ELSE, repetition statements like FOR...LOOP or WHILE...LOOP and unstructured commands like EXIT, GOTO.

ODBC Open Database Connectivity

ODBC, a standardized API, provides database access for client programs (for instance, Excel, Access). If an ODBC driver is available on the client computer, a so-called data source (DSN) has to be created and configured. A data source is a file in the client's file system as well as a logical name for the database the client will connect to.

Data modeling

Data modeling is the analysis of data objects that are used in a business or other context and the identification of the relationships among these data objects. Data modeling is a first step in designing an object-oriented program. As a result of data modeling, you can then define the classes that provide the templates for program objects. A simple approach to creating a data model that allows you to visualize the model is to draw a square (or any other symbol) to represent each individual data item that you know about (for example, a product or a product price) and then to express relationships between each of these data items with words such as *is part of* or is *used by* or *uses* and so forth. From such a total description, you can create a set of classes and subclasses that define all the general relationships. These then become the templates for objects that, when executed as a program, handle the variables of new transactions and other activities in a way that effectively represents the real world.

Meta, metadata, and metalanguage

Meta is a prefix that in most information technology usages means "an underlying definition or description." Thus, metadata is a definition or description of data and metalanguage is a definition or description of language. Meta derives from Greek, meaning "among, with, after, change." Whereas in some English words the prefix indicates "change," in others, including those related to data and information, the prefix carries the meaning of "more comprehensive or fundamental."

The Standard Generalized Markup Language (SGML) defines rules for how a document can be described in terms of its logical structure (headings, paragraphs or idea units, and so forth). SGML is often referred to as a metalanguage because it provides a "language for how to describe a language." A specific use of SGML is called a document type definition (DTD). A document type definition spells out exactly what the allowable language is. A DTD is thus a metalanguage for a certain type of document. In fact, the Hypertext Markup Language (HTML) is an example of a document type definition. HTML defines the set of HTML tags that any Web page can contain.

The Extensible Markup Language (XML), which is comparable to SGML and modeled on it, describes how to describe a collection of data. It's sometimes referred to as metadata. A specific XML definition, such as Microsoft's new Channel Definition Format (CDF), defines a set of tags for describing a web channel. XML could be considered the metadata for the more restrictive metadata of CDF (and other future data definitions based on XML). In SGML and XML "meta" means "underlying definition" or set of rules. One could describe any computer programming or user interface as a metalanguage for conversing with a computer. An English grammar and dictionary together describe the metalanguage for the English language.

What do we do with databases?
Databases are used to keep track of pretty much everything you can imagine. Mailing lists, books and CDs, insurance policies—everything that makes business run. The big thing we do with databases is to search them. In general, you search by specifying what you want in certain fields. If you're trying to sell Pearl Jam T-Shirts, you might search your mailing-list database to find all the people who are between the ages of 18 and 35, male, with an income of at least $12,000 a year because your market research shows that they'd be most likely to buy a T-shirt.

A database typically provides standard information pertaining to the items it describes. Each item has its own separate record made up of individual fields of information. For example, records of book s in an online library catalog provide the author(s), title, publisher, and subjects covered. A typical journal or magazine record will have fields for author, title of article, journal information (name, volume, issue, pages), and subject headings.

Full-text databases, such as Encyclopædia Britannica Online or the Boston Globe on CD-ROM, provide the complete text of articles, essays, etc. Bibliographic databases, such as Expanded Academic Index on Lexis/Nexis, provide citations to articles, etc. These records may also include a summary of the content, often called an abstract. Abstracts can be very helpful in determining whether an article will be of use to you in your research. Numeric databases, such as the 1998 Census Summary, provide information in a numerical or statistical format. Databases are all around us.

Using a database
Selecting the appropriate database or databases is often the biggest hurdle in beginning your marketing program and printing project. This is the responsibility of the marketing organization. They will find sources of information, either internally or externally, merge multiple databases to remove names common to both (called purging), or to add data about someone in one database to the record about that person in another database so that the new record will have more information to use in a variable data project.

Designing and building a database with Filemaker Pro
Decide what data you need or want. The first thing to decide is what data you want (or have available). Do you want to know the last three items purchased by someone? What someone's favorite color is? As a general rule, make fields for all the data you might ever eventually find useful. You don't have to use all of the data all of the time, but it's a lot easier to enter data all at once than to try and go back later and enter more data.

Decide how to break the data up into fields. A key thing to remember is that you can't use a part of a field. If you put my middle initial in the first name field, you cannot easily get rid of it. That means that it's usually a good idea to separate items into multiple fields if you can. Having a single "name" field makes it hard to search for someone's last name. Having a single "address" field makes it impossible to just get people in a certain city or state.

Open Filemaker Pro and give it a filename for your database. Unlike most applications, Filemaker Pro asks you for a file name immediately upon startup. It assumes that you will either open an existing database or begin a new one. Here is that dialog box:

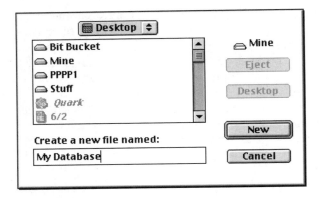

Create fields and decide what data type to make them. Each field in Filemaker Pro has a specific type. Besides affecting how things are sorted (numbers are sorted differently if their type is numeric or text), Filemaker has some nice facilities to make sure whoever is entering the data gets the right type in a field. For example, if a field is declared to only hold numbers, you couldn't enter your name into it by mistake without getting beeped at. Note *name* and *type* below:

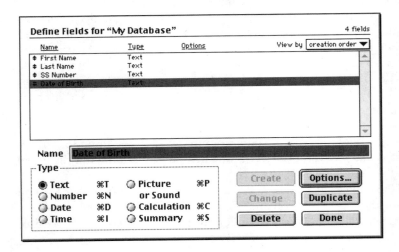

Add records to your database. Use Command-N or Edit:New Record to start putting information into your database. You can move from field to field with the tab key, or click the mouse in the field. Text is fully editable within each field. Fields are labelled as shown:

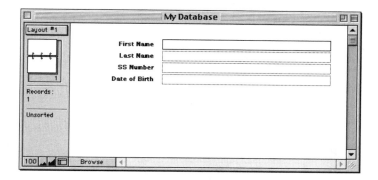

Filemaker automatically saves your data every time you get done entering or messing with a record, so there's no File:Save option.

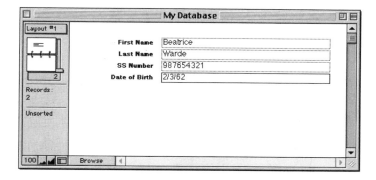

You can always add new fields to your database, so it can be configured to your current needs. Let's add a few more fields now:

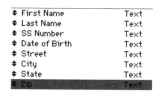

The Define function lets you add fields almost anytime. These new fields are then reflected in the input or Browse area where input takes place.

You can define the data in a field to be text or numeric. By defining numeric you can then perform mathematical operations, like adding the value of different fields and placing the result in a summary field. The summary can also be used to hold data for printing.

First Name	John
Last Name	Caslon
SS Number	123456789
Date of Birth	1/1/61
Street	
City	
State	
Zip	

The most important aspect of databases is the ability to re-configure the information and then output it in a standardized manner. The amount of data in a field can overflow the area defined on the screen.

Below, we have re-organized the data so that the fields that may be used for an address are ordered as such. Contrast with the one above.

First Name	First Name
Last Name	Last Name
Street	Street
City	City
State	State
Zip	Zip
SS Number	SS Number
Date of Birth	Date of Birth

The next step is to output the records for use by some other system. This is known as exporting records and we select the function from a pull-down menu under File, appropriately called File Menu.

Note that you can also import records. Most database programs can import the most common file formats. Since almost all databases output ASCII text and numbers, the format—that is, the way the fields and records are delineated—is important.

The most common formats are:
- Tab-separated text
- Comma-separated text
- SYLK, DBF, DIF, WKS, BASIC
- Merge or edition file

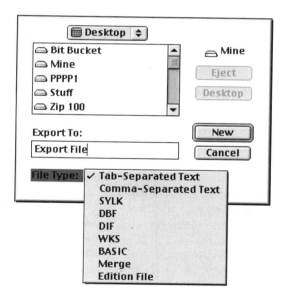

Once a file name and format are selected you can choose the fields you want to output. In many cases only a selected set of fields from each record will be used for the variable data mailing. This process is as simple as checking or unchecking the name of the field.

Specify field order for export

- ✓ First Name
- ✓ Last Name
- ✓ SS Number
- ✓ Date of Birth
- ✓ Street
- ✓ City
- ✓ State
- ✓ Zip

Summarize by...

● Don't format output
○ Format output using current layout

Cancel   OK

Here is what the ASCII file looks like:

John>Caslon>111 Main Street>Anyplace>NY>14623>123456789>1/1/61¶
Beatrice>Warde>222 Elm Grove>Anytown>MA>21616>987654321>2/3/62¶

There is usually a *Tab* (>) code between all fields and a *Return* (¶) code between records. This is the raw material for almost every variable data printing program.

You can open an ASCII file in virtually every kind of program on earth. In fact, many publishers take the data from databases into publishing layout programs when they compile directories, catalogs, and other data-intensive publications. However, ASCII has no format data so we could insert application specific tags in the database to define typographic style if the text in the field is not all to be in one style. Thus,

\iDavid\pand Frank
where \i means italic and \p means plain type.

would output David in italic and the rest of the text in plain type.

Keyword search strategies

A major advantage of databases is the ability to search and retrieve information. You can search within a specific field or through fields in a series of records

The following search example illustrates a typical strategy to follow when you search by keyword:

First, identify your search statement:

For example: What is the effect of television violence on children?

Second, state the terms that comprise your topic:

For example: television violence children

Third, think of different words or synonyms to express each word or term or concept:

For example: you might want your search to include the terms "tv" or "media" as well as "television."

Boolean search strategies (and, or, not)

Electronic databases often allow the user to employ Boolean search techniques to make a search broader or more focused. The three standard Boolean operators are AND, OR, NOT. By combining keywords with these operators, your search strategy will become more flexible.

Use AND when you want both terms to be present in the records you retrieve. This will narrow your search.

For example: violence AND television

Use OR to broaden your search. This strategy retrieves records with either of the terms.

For example: women OR females

Use NOT when you want to eliminate a particular term from your search results. For example: computer science NOT programming.

Be aware that when you use NOT you will eliminate records which contain both terms. Use NOT carefully, since there is the potential to inadvertently eliminate relevant records.

Subject and keyword searching--what's the difference?
When indexers look at a book or article to be entered into a database, they usually assign subject headings from a thesaurus or list of terms used specifically for that database. These "descriptors" or "subject headings" are then entered into the subject field for each record. When the researcher does a subject search, that field is where the computer looks for a match. This differs from a keyword or free-text search in which the computer looks for the keywords anywhere in the record—title, abstract, subject headings, etc. This is a much less "controlled" search than the subject search and will usually retrieve more records and less precise results.

Advanced searching techniques
Once you are familiar with a particular database, you can use more sophisticated searching strategies. Some of these include:

Field searching. Searching in a specific field, or a particular element of the record. Examples include searching for a particular author, a specific journal title, or a year(s) of publication.

Truncation. Truncation allows you search for the root of a word so the computer will pick up multiple endings. Since computers look for the word precisely the way you type it in, using truncation broadens your search. Most databases use either an asterisk (*) or a question mark (?) to indicate truncation.

Example:

psycholog* will retrieve

psychology psychological psychologically psychologist psychologists

Be careful not to truncate a word too much or you may retrieve unwanted matches. If you truncated the example above at *psych** you would also retrieve psychic, psyche, psychosis, etc.

Phrase searching or adjacency. Databases with phrase searching capability allow you to make your search strategy more precise. You can type in two or more words next to each other and the database will search for records that contain that phrase exactly as it is written rather than searching for each word separately.

For example, if you search the phrase *social work* in a database with phrase searching, your results would retrieve records relating to social work as opposed to items relating to the social aspects of work, a very different topic indeed. Not all databases allow phrase searching. Those that don't typically place an implied AND between the words. Some use a plus (+) sign instead of, or in addition to, the term AND.

Thus, the above example would retrieve records relating to both social work AND the social aspects of work.

Many databases use quotation marks (") around the phrase to restrict a search to only those hits that contain all the words defined, while others require a hyphen (-) between the words. Often you can even specify whether the words should be right next to one another or a particular number of words apart.

Example: Searching

"variable printing"

instead of

variable printing

would retrieve only records of the two words found, not every record with either word.

After the database, what?
Ultimately, you wind up with a database—either acquired as a single entity, or one created through the integration of multiple databases. The usual practice is to have the database output to a tab-delimited file, which includes the data you wish to use in the project. Tab-delimited ASCII is the most common format for use in personalized printing.

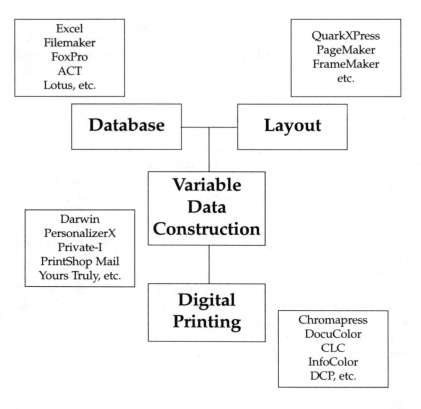

The database interfaces with the desktop layout program through the Variable Data Construction program. Many of these programs are covered in Chapter 6.

In some cases, the program itself performs all aspects of layout and construction. Bitstream PageFlex and Varis fall into this category.

You ultimately wind up with:

- a database output in ASCII form
- a layout program with the design of your page or pages
- a variable data construction program that maps the database fields to the layout
- a digital printer, either color or black or white

Glossary

Abstract Short description of the contents of an article or document.

Accession Number A unique identification number assigned to a record. Not the same as a library call number.

"And" Operator Connecting word requiring each search term to occur in every retrieved record, for example: adolescents and alcohol. "And" decreases the number of results.

ASCII American Standard Code for Information Interchange.

Bibliographic Database A database which indexes and contains references to original sources. It contains information about the records in it, rather than the original documents themselves.

Boolean Logic Use of operators "and," "or," and "not" to combine search terms.

Citation Short description of a record, typically including author, title, date, source, and accession number.

Controlled Vocabulary Standardized terms, often called descriptors, that are used to describe records in a database.

Database Collection of information stored in machine-readable form. Also called "file."

Descriptor A word or phrase precisely describing the subject content of a record and assigned by an indexer. Also called "subject heading."

Download Transfer of data from computer to a floppy disk or hard drive. Also called *save*.

Field Unit in a record representing a specific item of information, for example: author field, title field, abstract field.

Full-Text Database A database where individual records contain the complete text of articles, chapters, newspapers, etc. Sometimes includes graphs, photos, and other images.

Keyword Searching Use of any word to search a database, as opposed to descriptor searching, in which controlled vocabulary must be used.

Nesting The use of parentheses to override the default processing order of Boolean operators. For example: coloege students and (alcohol or beer, lots of beer, and pizza, and more beer).

Network Computers that are connected in order to share databases, software, printers, etc.

"Not" Operator Connecting word that eliminates records containing specific terms, for example: shakespeare not dissertation. Sometimes "and not."

"Or" Operator Connecting word requiring that at least one of the terms specified must appear in the same record, for example: teenagers or adolescents. "Or" increases the number of results.

Proximity Operator Connecting word requiring search terms be close to each other or in a specific order. For example: hillary *with* clinton retrieves: Hillary Clinton or Hillary Rodham Clinton.

Record Unique unit of information contained in a database representing one article, book, dissertation, etc.

Search Statement Instruction to the software to find records matching the term or combination of terms entered by the user. For example: teenage drinking and accidents and date is 1999.

Search Strategy Series of search statements organized to retrieve records that will answer the intellectual search request.

Selecting The ability to identify certain records for later printing, downloading, or emailing. Also called *marking, tagging, collecting*.

Set Group of records retrieved as a result of a search.

Standalone A computer workstation not attached to a network.

Stop Word Non-searchable common word which has no meaning to the computer. Usually prepositions and articles.

Thesaurus A list of standardized subject terms used in a database.

Truncation Symbol Punctuation marks, such as asterisks (*), that stand for any number of letters or characters. Also called "wildcard symbol." For example: teen* retrieves: teen, teens, teenager, etc.

4

Tips for
Dynamic Printing

The hottest driving force behind digital printing is dynamic printing or variable data printing (VDP). VDP software such as Yours Truly, Personalizer-X, Darwin Desktop, and PrintShop Mail lets you print something different on every sheet. Theoretically, this technology could someday mean that we'll get no more mass-market junk mail, and advertisers won't have to live with their chronic low response rates. How would you like to have 98% of your work thrown in the bin without being read? That's what advertisers live with, and they don't like it any more than we do.

Some VDP pioneers have already figured out how to print sheets that get several times better response than that. It requires much more than just buying a new press—it takes new production methods, new workflows, and new marketing thinking. As we all get better at VDP in the next 12-24 months, response rates will become easier to control. If you're considering getting into VDP, consider these tips from the pioneers:

1. Understand why a personalized page sells for more
It makes no sense to put a job on a variable-data press unless there's a payoff. Print providers must sell personalized pages for a higher price, because they cost more to produce. The technology is more expensive, the workflow is more complicated, the consumables are

more expensive, and operators are more scarce. To succeed, you need to know how to maximize the payoff—how to use the new technology to generate economic value. What makes a personalized sheet sell for more? For one thing, personalized ad mailers produce more responses, more sales, fewer pieces thrown unopened into the trash. In short, they produce dramatically better results for the advertiser.

2. Learn to maximize the "VDP value added"

Okay, okay, we hear the hoots: only some personalized mailers produce better results. Some campaigns have been flops. Why? Because you can't just switch to the new technology and become an instant advertising genius—you need to understand what makes a mailer "tick" so you can use the new tools to good purpose. For one example, put a different product picture prominently on the mailer—a picture chosen because of something specific that you know about the individual. If you do it right, the picture will earn the customer's attention—and that's a proven principle of successful direct mail.

Of course, to show something you know the customer will like, you have to know something genuinely significant about each person in the database. The photos can also be more subliminal. You could select images of a young couple for a mailing about starting a family or a great-looking older couple for promotions about retirement plans. Images are important, so pick them carefully.

Moral: successful VDP campaigns require good marketing people and a good marketing database.

3. Use your data to "make it easy to say *yes*"

Whether it's through TV, print or radio, a key principle of direct marketing is "make it easy to say Yes." One way marketers do this is by offering an 800 number, so it's easy for you to pick up the phone and place an order.

Another way is by accepting credit cards: it's more convenient to buy using a credit card number. A great way to "make it easy" with VDP is to use your computer to fill in the customer's order form. Pre-print the data (name, address, etc) in the "Yes I'll buy" section. That way, the recipient is that much closer to filling in the order blank because you made it easy for them.

4. "You may already be a winner:" personalization for dummies
The classic sweepstakes mailer "Dave, you may already be a winner" no longer produces dramatically better results. (It produces marginally better results. Not dramatically better.) Why? Because consumers have already gotten numbed to seeing their name inkjetted onto an envelope or letter. Let's face it, the novelty has worn off.

We have now seen our names on promotions, on pages in our magazines, and on all manner of materials. Now it is no longer just your name—it is how you use the name.

The first job that an ad must accomplish is get your attention at least for an instant, so the mailer doesn't go straight into recycling. You have to excite the reader's brain for a moment. But we no longer get excited by seeing our own name—it's not new. Plus, some advertisers have put everyone's names on worthless offers, not on personalized offers. *Dear Frank, you may be a loser.*

Result: we've all learned that seeing our name doesn't mean anything special.

5. But there's still reason to start with the "for dummies"version
For one thing, it's much quicker to get started if all you're doing is imprinting the name. Okay, we said this was passé. Well, not passé, but rather old hat. Do it new hat.

There's not much planning to do with "name merge" in marketing or in production: almost any campaign can have simple personalization added to it. For another thing, a "for dummies" job lets everyone "walk before they run" in the new workflow. Database people can learn what's involved in feeding data to production.

So think of innovative ways to get someone's name into the promotion. Production people can practice receiving simple data from a database. And everyone can learn the importance of clean data, because they'll have plenty of chance to see how inconsistent their data is! It's much better to go through that with a simple job than a complex one. And while all this is going on, the marketing people can start thinking about varying the content in some meaningful way, in future campaigns. To do that, they'll …

6. Start with the mailing list

Look at your data before you design the offer. The best campaigns start when a marketer looks first at an existing database and asks "What can I offer this individual that they're likely to want?" That's new: it's the opposite of looking first at the product and then asking "How can I find buyers?"

Far better is to look through your databases in the first place, and ask "Is there anything can I offer this customer?" If a given database has nothing unique and significant about each individual, don't bother trying to use it for VDP—except "VDP for dummies"!

Look beyond the mailing information for the real value of a database.

7. Personalize the outside, not just the inside

Most folded mailers get discarded without ever being opened. What a shame it would be if you designed a clever, truly personalized offer, and hid it inside something that got ditched! So if your offer is folded, be sure the outside shows something personalized that's truly eye-catching. The good news is that if you do get them to open it, you've got their attention longer: the moment a reader takes action, even just opening the folded piece, you've accomplished an "involvement trap" and their attention span goes up.

The involvement trap is a key marketing approach. Get the recipient to take an action. Then they may take another action. Get the picture?

8. Watch out for bindery spoilage

It's not your father's printing industry where you can just overprint to cover the waste. Waste in the bindery means someone won't get that great offer. Have a plan and a workflow for re-dos. One VDP printing firm prints every VDP run twice. 100% waste they say, but it eliminates re-dos, which is a costly problem.

9. Pre-print the static parts of the page, if you can

The majority of the printing cost in VDP is in the "consumables:" the ink or toner, the belts, the plates, whatever components a particular printer or press uses. To minimize your cost, minimize how much you print on the variable-data press. Print all the static (non-variable) information on a conventional press, then feed those sheets through the variable-data press. Watch out for data jealousy.

10. Clean up the data
VDP is the first technology to combine two adages. From the computer industry: "garbage in, garbage out." From the printing industry: "Doctors get to bury their mistakes, but a printer's mistake is seen by the world." Imagine the fun when erratic data enters VDP production: you get a vast supply of incorrect press sheets, produced with total automation.

Just what we needed: fully automated "garbage out." At a higher cost per page, no less! When you first start working with a given database, expect to spend some time discovering whether it's clean or not, and plan on delays to have someone go back and fix it. Otherwise you'll find yourself immersed in a third classic adage: "Failure to plan on your part does not constitute an emergency on our part!"

Variable data printing is the hottest technology in the printing industry. . . if you do it right.

Generalized workflow
The key to effective personalized printing is in the workflow, the manner in which information flows from database to layout to print. Here are the major steps to keep in mind as we now start to get down to the nitty gritty.

1. Collect data from one or several databases and organize into one.
2. Define the project in terms of marketing goals and results.
3. Design the material and plan for personalization levels.
4. Clean up and organize the data for consistency and correctness.
5. Organize data into identifiable units and standardized coding.
6. Link variable data to the layout and prepare file for for output.
7. Organize the combined file into a PostScript data stream.
8. Screen preview or run several samples; correct if necessary.
9. Run the job through the Raster Image Processor and digital printer.
10. Process printed sheets through bindery/finishing operations.
11. Doublecheck all output for correctness; postal processing.
12. Convert for other applications; save for future use.

Here is a simple chart on the next page to help organize your thinking about variable data printing workflow.

Variable Data Generalized Workflow

Data Acquisition/Analysis	1. Collect your data from one or several databases and organize into one.
Marketing Concept	2. Define the project in terms of marketing goals and results.
Creative Concept/Production	3. Design the material and plan for personalization levels.
Data Finalization	4. Clean up and organize the data for consistency and correctness.
Data Stream	5. Organize the data into identifiable units and standardized coding.
Data Construction & Linking	6. Link variable data to the layout and prepare file for for output.
Print Stream	7. Organize the combined file into a PostScript data stream.
Preview/Preprint/Proof/Correct	8. Screen preview or run several samples; correct if necessary.
Print Production	9. Run the job through the Raster Image Processor and the digital printer.
Post Print Processing	10. Process printed sheets through bindery and finishing operations.
Verify/Audit	11. Doublecheck all output for correctness; postal processing.
Conversion/Archive	12. Convert for other applications; save for future use.

5

Applying
Dynamic Printing

With all of this technology, a major application of variable printing is, essentially, fancy junk mail that in lesser forms has existed for decades, but some companies, publishers, ad agencies, and commercial printers have found creative uses for variable printing by personalizing catalogs, brochures, phone cards, iron-on T-shirt transfers, refrigerator magnets, packaging, financial portfolios for "high net worth" clients, newsletters, postcards, wine and beer bottle labels, vinyl pressure-sensitive labels, and many other types of printed materials—they even print the icing on cakes.

Others have found success by using variable printing strictly as a piece of a marketing program and focus not on the process itself but rather its position and value relative to database marketing.

Junk mail fun facts
- Almost 4 million tons of junk mail are sent each year in the United States.
- 60% of that goes straight from the mailbox to the trash bin, unopened, and not recycled.
- Each American receives an average of 1,169 pieces of junk mail every year.
- Americans received 15 billion catalogs, made with 2.5 million tons of paper from 42.5 million trees, in 1996.

- Producers of generic junk mail are happy to get a 2 percent response rate.
- $320 million is spent hauling junk mail to landfills and incinerators, generating airborne pollutants and consuming fuel in the process.
- Paper represents 40 percent of the solid waste generated in the U.S.
- The Fresh Kills landfill on New York's Staten Island is visible from space.

How to succeed in database marketing

Peter Takacs of Prevail Associates, Santa Rosa, California, has a lot to say about variable printing. Takacs feels that some users are pushing variable printing in the wrong direction; that it should be sold as a database marketing system and not sold as print; that the products being marketed must be high-margin; that a marketing program must have continuity; that it must produce measurable results; and finally, "we can lead a marketer to our suggested goal, but they know their product and customer base best."

Takacs says, "To sell it [variable printing] into marketing, sales people must talk and think like marketers." According to Takacs, print salespeople must do the following to be successful with variable printing:

- Direct mail is testable, predictable. With testing and tracking on a small scale, you can effectively predict results from a large-scale campaign.
- Salespeople must understand database marketing and sell variable printing as an enabler to successful database marketing, not just another type of printing.
- Salespeople must go to decision-makers, not traditional print buyers, who haven't had a historical reason to be concerned with database marketing.
- Salespeople must clearly show clients that the "pathway" to program success must include database marketing, and by extension, variable printing.
- Salespeople must be aggressive and should bring a marketing expert with them to client meetings.

The problems with variable printing as a means of database marketing, says Takacs, are several. It is difficult to sell to a client simply as personalized printing; the salesperson must help the client use variable printing as a tool for building a marketing program. There is usually no single decision-maker who approves expensive marketing programs and the salesperson must appeal to the job sensibilities of each person in the decision-making sequence: putting a financial spin on a presentation to the client's CFO, or a sales-building presentation to the VP of sales.

Satisfying customer needs in the Netherlands
Royal KPN N.V., the company which owns the Dutch phone and postal services, wanted to create a service which lets consumers request information about products and services and receive a customized catalog in the mail within 48 hours.

Customers access the service via telephone, Web, or teletext service and request information on a range of products and services, including travel, home furnishings, computers, electronics, cars, and financial packages. Once the request is made, a four-color, personalized catalog is delivered to their door within 48 hours. A customer can receive additional information, including expert advice, manufacturers' specifications, advertisements, comparative test reports, and local dealer or supplier addresses for requested products, for the price of a phone call, around $1.50.

Toets 9220 ("Dial 9220") allows KPN to gather consumer data while meeting the consumer's need for personalized information. This led to an alliance with Moore Corporation's Interactive Solutions Marketing division. The Moore-devised printing system is based on its Intelligent Color Imaging technology which allows production of short-run, full-color, variable-page catalogs while providing management of KPN's customer database.

For example, if a customer requests information on home electronics, Moore's technology selects all the products and services that fit the customer's electronic profile. Then this variable data is sent to a Xeikon digital color press and the customized catalog pages are printed, folded, perfect bound, and trimmed. The finished catalog is then delivered to the Dutch Post for overnight or same-day mailing. Moore's digital print technology allows the entire process to be completed within 48 hours. More than 3,000 36-page booklets are produced each week.

Toets 9220 has attracted participation from premium advertisers including Mercedes-Benz, Citröen, Phillips, and Whirlpool. Participants are selected on the basis of market share with featured products and services determined by customer demand. Advertising revenue is used to subsidize catalog production, distribution and awareness campaigns.

Consumer response is strong. The Toets 9220 campaign has so far reached 18 percent of the Dutch consumer market and has elicited a 5 percent response rate. Of those who respond, 45 percent purchase a product or service within two months while virtually all (91 percent) refer to the booklet when making a purchasing decision.

> *"The issue isn't how to do variable-data printing—any fool can do that and lose his shirt. The questions are: how to make money and how to be productive with it."*
> — *David deBronkart*

Moore Corporation

Moore Corporation operates its Interactive Marketing Solutions division at its Research Center on Grand Island, NY. Jeff Gebhart is the Manager of Application Marketing Development at the facility who helped get the Toets campaign off the ground, and is working with a British company on a similar program. This division of Moore has printed a number of variable programs, including Subaru's, and is possibly the largest company in the business now. Moore operates eleven Xeikon DCP/32 presses at facilities in New York, the Netherlands, and the United Kingdom.

Gebhart showed several promising applications of variable printing, including printing of transaction statements intended for high-end credit card users that include small four-color ads for items related to the cardholder's recent purchases; full-color investment statements for high net worth individuals, and other examples of merging transaction printing, which has traditionally been black-and-white with perhaps a spot color and of low resolution, with four-color, high-resolution digital printing.

Moore is also developing a Web-based document fulfillment system called Message Master, which is intended for the internal use of large corporations with far-flung offices and divisions. Message Master incorporates the United States Postal Service's CASS system of address verification and rejects any non-compliant addresses, as do all of Moore's mailing applications. CASS (Coding Accuracy Support System) improves the accuracy of carrier route, five-digit Zip, Zip+4, and delivery point codes that appear on mailpieces.

Users of Message Master connect to a Moore-designed web site and from there they can specify documents to be ordered, printed, and mailed, with a full preview of the document and of all recipients on the Web page display. This system is still under development but Gebhart says that Message Master is now ready. It is a promising new technology that lets anyone become a direct marketer of sorts without having to learn all the tools typically associated with the production process.

Moore also offers a high-end transaction printing system called MIPS, which uses webfed ion deposition print engines combined with selectively-engaged flexographic print units to produce multiple-color products, though currently process color printing is not supported. The system is driven by Moore's proprietary XLC front-end system, which collects all necessary information from databases and merges it with static data on-the-fly, with no caching or buffering of rasterized pages. The same system is used to drive Moore's Xeikon digital color presses through a customized interface to the digital press, though the Xeikon RIPs are used to print repetitive, short-run color jobs.

Gebhart states that the XLC system is fast enough to drive multiple digital presses at their full-rated print speed, even while the system is processing incoming information. He says that this capability is what allowed Moore to snare clients of other providers of variable printing who could not provide finished jobs on time because they used RIPs which took up to eight hours of processing time before the job could be sent to the press engine.

Output speed will be a major contributing factor to a company's competitiveness in the near future. The XLC system is currently a closed, proprietary system running on the NeXT operating system but Moore is developing an open system that operates with Adobe Acrobat Exchange (PDF) and QuarkXPress (via XTensions), which should be available shortly.

Whirlpool Corporation

Brett Knobloch, Manager of Interactive Consumer Marketing at Whirlpool Corporation in Benton Harbor, Michigan, is currently piloting a program that makes effective use of variable printing. Whirlpool is the largest home appliance company in the world and manufactures appliances under its name and others.

Knobloch is creating a marketing program that takes advantage of what he calls "life events," such as purchasing a new home, remodeling an existing one, or replacing a set of elderly appliances. People in these situations have the time to research and compare appliances, unlike someone whose dishwasher has just exploded and needs a replacement right away. Whirlpool is targeting event decisions with print media ads which include a toll-free telephone number to call for more information.

All calls are answered in Whirlpool's call center. When a customer calls about appliances, the phone operator helps the customer narrow down a selection based on needs, then uses a proprietary Web interface to build a custom appliance catalog for that customer. If a consumer just wants general appliance information, a conventionally printed product catalog is sent.

The data entered by the phone operator is collected and send electronically to ColorStream Technologies in Chicago, a digital print and fulfillment service, and is merged with a predefined layout produced by Whirlpool's corporate design firm. Images selected from a database of digitaized photographs taken by Whirlpool's internal photographers are merged with the layout and variable text, and printed on one of ColorStream's two digital color presses. After finishing, the catalog is mailed to the customer. This process is performed six days a week.

Knobloch's objectives are to deliver a catalog of the same quality as the conventional offset-printed catalog in the same timely fashion; to reduce cost of conventional printing and inventory due to frequent product changes, and to create better one-to-one communication with Whirlpool customers. In addition to the personalized catalog, customers will receive additional messages via e-mail that thanks them for calling, confirms the catalog shipment, and keeps the customer aware of the brand.

ColorStream receives data files daily from Whirlpool and and uses a third-party application to connect the Whirlpool database to ColorStream's processors. Using Barco's PageStreamer software on a Xeikon press, and Bitstream's PageFlex software to drive an IBM InfoColor press, ColorStream uses the disk cache available on both of these systems to store pre-rasterized images and page layouts as much as possible, to reduce processing time and press idleness. Tim Graves, a production manager at ColorStream, maintains that for most jobs, the two RIPs are able to drive the presses while processing other jobs.

Graves states that customer awareness of variable printing is growing rapidly and predicts that 1999 will be the year in which variable printing finally "arrives," if processing power increases and software tools for these applications become more readily available.

Build your own Buick
Thebault DI, a division of L.P. Thebault Cos, of Parsippany, New Jersey, developed a four-part "interactive" newsletter program for the Buick division of General Motors. Thebault DI is a full-service advertising and marketing printer with six- and eight-color sheetfed presses, two Heidelberg GTO-DI direct-to-plate-on-press imaging offset presses for short-run process color, full- and half-size offset web presses, and four Agfa Chromapress digital color presses, which, according to Jac Bloomberg, Vice President and General Manager of Thebault DI, are used strictly for printing personalized direct marketing documents.

Bloomberg feels that digital presses are too expensive and slow to use for short-run static printing and uses the GTO-DI presses for such work—adding value with personalization is the only way to profitably sell digital color printing. Bloomberg also stated that "most people who get into digital printing fail to market it properly."

For the Buick program, Thebault DI used a database generated by EDS, GM's database service provider, that was delivered ready to run with a few minor modifications such as converting all-uppercase words to upper- and lowercase. No further data manipulation was required and the database was ready to feed into the Agfa Personalizer-X application, used with QuarkXPress to generate variable documents.

The first-phase newsletter contained minimal levels of personalization. These were sent to current Buick owners whose cars were from two to four years old, and to selected non-Buick owners based on demographics of age and income: a 35-year old man with an income of $40,000 per year might receive a newsletter centered on the Buick Regal, while a 60-year old woman with an income of $100,000 might get a newsletter describing a top-of-the-line Buick Riviera. A prepaid reply card was bound into the newsletter, which included questions about the type of car they might be interested in, the color they might like, and available options.

The second-phase newsletter was based upon the response, or lack thereof, from the targeted customer. If there was no response, the newsletter reflected that; if there was a response, Thebault DI took the opportunity for further newsletter personalization, and a second run of newsletters was mailed out along with another reply card where the customer could specify the exact model, color, and options of the Buick automobile that they were interested in.

The third-phase newsletter, based on data from returned cards of the second phase, showed the exact model and color specified and had a banner headline of the customer's surname, the model, and the color chosen, e.g. "The Smith's Jade-Green Regal." Additional information such as options and a suggested retail price of the car was also printed on the piece.

The fourth-phase newsletter was sent only to those who actually purchased a new Buick. This phase was delivered by two different pieces: one thanking the customer for the purchase and offering a number of coupons that could be used at local establishments, and another that contained a detailed post-sale questionnaire.

This all sounds like a lot of work, but Bloomberg estimates that the entire program netted about a 25 percent response rate and more importantly, was the means by which Buick sold 7,000 new cars with a $21 million return on the investment made in the program. Approximately two million total pieces were mailed. It is unclear, however, whether those sales were a direct result of the program, or whether they were also a result of cross-selling from other media such as TV and newspaper ads.

Lufthansa Airlines

Few products have a shorter shelf-life than airplane seats. Communicating to consumers and travel agents with relevant localized and time-critical information is an essential element to keeping seats filled. But delivering that information is harder than mollifying a bumped passenger.

"Information in the airline industry pours in faster than anyone can absorb and disseminate it," says a spokesman for Lufthansa's Quick Response Program (QRP) promotion campaign, "and that includes such mundane information as changing price information, new-flight announcements, special offers, and everything else that drives this business."

Intensifying the problem, coupled with the crush of data, was the need for the German airline to create a greater presence in its ten U.S. gateway cities. Attracting business travelers at these locations is key to filling seats on the highly contested North Atlantic routes, as well as increasing membership in its Miles & More frequent-flyer loyalty program.

Solution: Create a turnkey marketing program for Lufthansa's promotion coordinators in each of the ten cities that enables cost-effective four-color art execution and material production within 72 hours. The heart of the program is the QRP Workbook, a three-ring binder that each promotion coordinator receives containing organized images of customizable templates of letters, self-mailers, deluxe invitations, postcards, banners, counter cards, and a deep library of digitized photographs and images.

Each on-site promotion coordinator determines which database to draw from and indicates their graphic, template, and media selections on an order form and writes the copy and headlines for variable boxes. The form is then faxed to Chicago-based Flair Communications, the promotion agency coordinating the campaign, and the Mac-platform Quark templates are modified to each coordinator's specifications. The digital image, once approved by the client, is transmitted or overnighted to a digital printer that merges the database file and prints by Zip-sort sequence on a Xeikon digital printer. Time from order-entry to in-the-mail: 72 hours.

"Lufthansa's bookings and profitability on average for the ten offices was up 44 percent," according to the spokesman, "which are results we thought would take more than two years. The database, on average, increased 16 percent. But another boost to the airline is that the QRP has provided a means for each of the ten gateway cities staff to interact one-on-one with air travelers and travel agents," he adds. "The Quick Response Program consistently delivers customized sales material within 72 hours with cost efficiencies while maintaining Lufthansa's worldwide quality standards and corporate graphic imagery. Yet the system is flexible and lets coordinators be creative as well as effective."

Variable printing for the apparel industry
Typical clothing manufacturers turn over 60 percent of their product line per year. Oswego Print of Portland, Oregon, receives apparel tag orders electronically through a Web site, prints the tags, and ships them to an offshore clothing plant, and also prints customized catalogs for apparel manufacturers that are tailored for a particular store.

Ric Kimbell, founder and chairman of the Oswego group, a marketing services firm that serves the apparel and entertainment industries, spoke at the Seybold San Francisco conference in September, 1998, on the issue of database printing:

"First of all, we ask what makes a good variable data printing client? . . . a good variable data client needs to have a large number of products. Someone like Jantzen for example has 35,000 product SKUs [Stock Keeping Unit]. The second thing is they have very short life cycles. This product changes 60 percent annually. So, you can see they begin to have a problem. The third thing is they have very short development cycles for getting their products to market. This also makes for an ideal client. And, the fourth thing is they have a highly segmented markets. They sell to all strata of dealers from a single mom and pop shop all the way through to J. C. Penney and Sears.

"At Oswego, we define variable data as data that changes over time. . . . We do very little one-to-one marketing, but we have an extraordinary base of ever-changing content for our clients. The shorter the time frame, the more variable the data. Variable data is not just direct marketing. Variable data does not change in every pass of the press necessarily. It is information that requires database management of some kind. What makes variable data printing valuable? First, the managing of information for a customer is very valuable to that customer. Almost all of your customers have no idea how to manage visual information. So becoming a visual information manager, we've heard the term media asset management, but somehow managing that data for your clients make you valuable. The ability to focus selling materials to specific customers is valuable. For example, Columbia Sportswear will want to do a catalog specific to J.C. Penney. They'll only want 600 of those particular brochures that have data for each store, actually.

"Because of short life cycles, literally by the time a catalog is developed, it's obsolete. So all these things become very important to a client and that's why you can charge much more for variable data printing . . . You're offering three or four value added services beyond the aspect of actually printing. Printing is only the result of being involved in these other aspects of their business.

"So, how do you attract a variable data client? Well, first of all, you need to specialize in vertical markets. We've chosen three. I've mentioned them to you. But you could look at virtually any market that has a lot of products in it. The financial markets, the automotive markets, the appliance markets, all have companies with hundreds and thousands of product SKUs that need to be put into printed marketing materials.

"Second, become an immediate expert. At our company we hired people in the apparel industry that had at least 3–5 years experience that understood the sales and marketing problems with the apparel industry, and the same with the consumer electronics market.

"Third, you analyze their business. With Jantzen we sat down and for three months we asked what their problems in getting information out were. They found they could design, build offshore, and deliver a swimsuit faster than they could get either a brochure or a hang tag label to go on that swimsuit. So, that was very important to them that they shorten that critical time area to get it to market.

"Fourth, the answer's always a workflow solution and not printing. You do not want to be a printer. Printers work on very low margins. What you want to be is someone who integrates themselves very far down into the workstream. At Jantzen for example, we start in the planning production department and award it through them all the way through to a final garment tag. So we're involved in every portion of their business."

Making menus
Darden Restaurant Corporation, which operates 1,200 Red Lobster and Olive Garden restaurants in North America, was printing menus on an offset press with numerous plate changes required for regionalized versions of menus. Significant time was spent in producing films, proofs, plates, and in press makeready. Jobs required time to dry before they could be printed on the reverse side. The company was falling behind in the ability to quickly produce menus and the numerous other printed pieces used in many restaurants such as the stand-ups on tables, special menus for liquor and desserts, and promotional materials.

To keep up with the demands of store managers, Darden's in-house creative and printing group acquired a Xerox DocuColor 40 and a Xerox Majestik color copier, each driven by a Fiery RIP that processed jobs created on a number of Macintosh computers. The time to produce a job went from five hours with offset to just an hour with the new digital color printers, and the cost to produce the run plummeted from $2,500 to $500.

The food service industry requires fast response times to accommodate regional tastes and price sensitivity. Darden now produces menus that can be quickly customized for each restaurant location, a major concern when over a thousand restaurant managers all demand some sort of customization. The completed materials are shipped to each location within a day of printing. The increased capacity has also let to the printing of many of the company's marketing materials, internal communications, business cards, newsletters, point-of-purchase displays and regional management reports.

Customized shopping lists
Many stores now collect customer purchase information at the time of check-out with a "Shopper's Club" card or some other similarly-named program that provides discounts on selected items and allows check-writing privileges. Customers swipe a card in a reader at the check-out counter to obtain the discounts, and the customer's

entire shopping list is recorded. It would be very easy for a super-market to create a personalized incentive mailer to customers based upon their buying habits; for example, if the customer regularly buys No-Stinkum kitty litter, then the store might include a coupon for Poops-B-Gone (honest) litter as an incentive to try a different brand.

PODi's Rab Govil avers that several grocery chains have already begun to plan such database marketing programs, but at the same time, customer goodwill might be at risk at stores that require them to sign up for a card to obtain a discount.

> *"Actually, I would stand in line at the checkout counter hearing those cheerful clerks address the previous customers and just dread the moment when they would stumble over my Finnish name, as they inevitably would. 'Hello, Mr Smith!' 'Hello, Mr Michaels!' 'Hello? er . . .'*
>
> *"I feel that mandated friendliness is more of a turn-off than a feature, and I strongly dislike the Big Brother-like aspect of having a complete stranger know my name before I introduce myself. I would try to stay away from that store in the future."* —Anthony Majanlahti

It's all in the details

One of the most successful personalization campaigns involves a bridal registry. Some department stores were discarding the collected data after the wedding, but one held on to it. The registry had the name and style of particular dishware, the name and address of the married couple, the name and address of the gift givers, plus the piece that was given. Thus, the database could be organized to tell what pieces the couple did *not* have.

With variable data software, promotions were developed to the married couple with discounts on the pieces that were missing from their collection. 10,000 mailers went out with a response rate of 8%. This represented a close rate of 100% since only buyers responded—all 800 of them. Each purchased an average of $252 in product and the program netted over $200,000.

This is a perfect example of how database information and variable data printing can work together for successful direct marketing.

Not convinced

Dolly Jackson, Director of Development at Whitworth College in Spokane, Washington, gave variable printing a try but has since reverted to her previous fund-raising methods because she didn't see a change in response. Ms. Jackson states: "We had a huge turnover on our staff and didn't have the technical support or the machinery to effectively personalize/merge our fall appeal. Using variable data allowed us to get our pieces personalized on a non-standard mailer. It was more than what a traditional mailing house could do for us.

"I don't think the response rate was affected because so many who mail are able to personalize pieces these days. I remember when I first received *Games* magazine and there was a page on the inside of the magazine that had *my* name and address on it (in some advertisement)—it was impressive! Now, I get Publisher's Clearing House with my name and personal information peppered throughout. It has lost its uniqueness.

"One thing that my contact at [Ms. Jackson's printer] told me recently is that some clients who have used variable printing to an extreme have turned off some of those to whom they mail. The recipients get concerned that a mass mailer has so much personal information about them—it feels like an invasion of privacy. Before, vendors may have *had* lots of information about people on the mailing list. Now, the recipients *know* how much information vendors have, and *knowing* makes them nervous."

Caveats

Ms. Jackson's concerns about privacy are current events in the database marketing industry. So far, there have been no market studies about the adverse effects of personalization whether in direct mail or in person at the supermarket. Marketers should proceed carefully as consumer concerns about privacy have become serious issues, which could be a reason why pull marketing is so successful: consumers in pull situations willingly volunteer information about themselves in order to get something; there's nobody collecting personal information about them without their knowledge.

It's possible that the revelation of the extent of involuntarily-collected information a database contains about a person could create an angry anti-consumer instead of a potential customer.

Quick facts

Here are some interesting facts about direct mail:

The average person is bombarded by 3,000 marketing messages per day, a six-fold increase over 20 years ago.

One percent of all names and addresses in a database are obsoleted every month.

Third-class mail has increased thirteen times faster than the growth in population.

45 percent of the average direct mail campaign is postage.

After three mailings to the same list, a promotion loses its power.

The average run for a variable data job is:

1–1000	55%
1001–5000	20%
5001–10000	10%
100001–20000	5%
Over 20,000	5%

The most common formats are:

Sheet, un-trimmed, un-folded	20%
(includes labels, certificates, letters, some post cards)	
Sheet, un-trimmed, folded	10%
Sheet, trimmed and folded	20%
Sheet, cut out multiples	30%
Sheets, collated, stapled, bound	10%
Other formats	10%
(includes perfing, diecutting, embossing, laminating,	

Variable data programs are categorized into four levels:

1. Mail merge

    Like Microsoft Word, they take data from a list and merge names and addresses, in many cases, with templates or pre-pared pages. Mail merge has been around for long time and it is very much a form of personalized printing—but on a very basic level

2. Standalone application

    These are variable data front ends that are not tied to any particular application. PrintShop Mail, Xeikon Private-I, and EFI FreeForm are examples. Some provide added flexibility by allowing personalized printing on virtually any RIP.

3. QuarkXTensions

    These programs are XTensions to QuarkXPress, which is one of the most popular programs for page and document lay-out. Programs include Agfa Personalizer-X, Scitex Darwin and FocusGold, among others. Adobe's new layout pro-gram, InDesign, may be a factor at some time.

4. Dedicated high-end systems

    These are industrial-strength systems, from Barco, Bitstream, and Varis, which are capable of extensive personalization, but also integrate asset and content management, job track-ing, and system control.

6

Variable Data
Printing Programs

In addition to the database and the variable data library—the collection of images and/or text files to be inserted—the other necessary component for variable-data imaging is a software program that integrates textual and graphic variable data from a library into a page layout, sometimes based upon a set of data-handling definitions or rules. These rules can be as simple as a static list of page elements or as complex as a set of conditional logic statements, e.g. "if gender = female, use picture X; if not, use picture Y".

Most desktop variable printing applications work within Quark-XPress as a Quark XTension. A copy of QuarkXPress and a Power Macintosh or Windows-based computer system will also be a required component of the variable printing workflow. Most variable printing applications operate on the Macintosh, though upcoming variable printing systems such as Bitstream PageFlex require Windows NT client and server systems.

A QuarkXPress XTension is often only part of the complete package. Usually, a specialized RIP (Raster Image Processor) is sold with a digital press that is designed specifically to support the unique and demanding process of variable imaging.

Data in a database must be exported to a plain text, tab-delimited file from the client's database. The client supplies this file, any images, and the final page layout to the shop that will print the job. The plain text file is imported into the particular program used to generate the personalized pages. Some of these programs offer data manipulation rules—a rule is a directive to the program and takes the form of 'if <condition X> exists, then do <procedure Y>', or, more simply, "if gender = male, then set salutation to 'Mr.'"

A problem occurs in the production phase: who is responsible for creating these rules? At what point in the process is responsibility for accuracy handed off from the client to the printer? Rules cannot be specified in the data file; the programs are expensive and usually protected with a hardware key, so it is impractical for the client to perform this step. This leaves an operator at the print shop responsible for correctly following the client's written instructions for rules-based processing, unless the client does it in the print shop, and it leaves the client responsible for writing up exact instructions for the print run. Both methods are impractical.

This is a relatively new business, so new ways of conducting it will need to develop so that data accuracy is not left in the hands of the wrong person. The currently available programs for producing VDP are not designed for use in commercial printing; they are targeted at in-house printing operations of a large organization, which might maintain a digital color press as a part of their reprographics area.

The upshot is this: with few exceptions, a customer cannot walk into a commercial print shop, which does not know the customer's marketing needs, hand over a disk containing the database, page layout, and variable images, and expect to pick up a print job a few days later. The production process requires the intervention of the person most familiar with the data, the marketing program, and the desired result. A press operator cannot know these things, but a smart shop with an employee who is familiar with these issues can do well with commercial variable printing.

Challenges and barriers created by variable printing
A significant barrier to profitable variable production is the fact that a variable print run is composed of unique pages. A static digital print run is RIP-once, print many, analogous to a conventional press,

where each sheet is exactly the same as all the others. Variable printing produces pages that can vary in content from very little to completely different. In a PostScript workflow that is not optimized for variable printing, this means a complete rasterization of each page before it can be sent to the imaging engine. In the case of established imaging technologies, such as an imagesetter, a platesetter, a color proofer, or a prosaic office laser printer, driving the engine at its full rated speed is not really the prime concern—accurate output is.

What is a RIP?

A raster image processor (RIP) is a system that converts PostScript-language graphics files into rasterized images (bitmaps) that are then sent to the marking engine, which can be as simple as a laser printer or as complex as a digital press or platesetting device. Every PostScript device includes a RIP, from the simple ones present in most laser printers to the standalone, high-performance RIPs with gigabytes of disk storage and several hundred megabytes of random-access memory typically used in the printing industry.

Nearly all RIPs used with current digital presses incorporate proprietary extensions to the PostScript language that pre-process static images (the ones common to all pages of a variable print run) and merge these with variable data at print time, which really speeds up the process. This method of forms caching is the primary reason why variable printing has been possible at all, and the various applications that generate variable pages are typically very tightly coupled to one or more particular, optimized RIPs. A generic PostScript RIP usually cannot efficiently process variable information unless an application is optimized for that RIP. A plain RIP, such as that used with a film imagesetter, will rasterize every page as if it were a unique document. This could take forever on a long print run.

Proprietary extensions to PostScript allow pre-rasterization of static and variable images on a job's pages which are stored on the RIP's internal disk or in a page buffer; the objects are merged at print time along with any text, which RIPs quickly, preventing the enormous overhead of rasterizing all page data for each VDP page. Some of these programs can operate with any printer or digital press, but the result will always be a standard, unoptimized, and above all slow composite PostScript print job where each page is processed as if it were a separate document.

Each vendor implements these extensions differently. The PostScript Level 2 Red Book includes definitions for "forms caching," or the storage of static pre-interpreted, non-rasterized image data, but some hardware vendors have chosen to implement their own PostScript extensions with non-rasterized or rasterized static data. These proprietary methods for caching typically perform better than the standard PostScript caching system, at the expense of compatibility.

In variable printing production, driving the target print engine at its full speed is critical to not only productivity, but to the actual process itself, particularly for digital web presses such as the Xeikon or other high-speed digital color printers. A Xeikon web cannot be stopped and started without a tremendous waste of paper because a stoppage dissipates the electrical charge required for the toner application process. Restarting the web requires feeding about 20 feet of paper through the press to re-charge the web. So keep it fed with data.

The sheetfed Indigo E-Print engine is slower than Xeikon engines, but in the case of complex variable printing this could be an asset; if the press is made to wait for the RIP to finish processing, it simply sits and waits, then feeds a sheet into the engine when the job has finished processing. The Indigo UltraStream increases output speed.

RIPs designed for the first generation of digital color presses, which are still the predominant type of system in use today, cannot drive the press at full speed when processing variable pages. Consider that a letter-sized page (8.5x11-inch) rasterized as a process-color print job at 600 printer spots per inch will occupy 67 MB per separation, and there are four separations per page. This is an enormous amount of information to store and process, and most RIPs can't process data fast enough to feed a digital color press at its full speed. If the RIP cannot process the job quickly enough and then compress the resulting data, the print engine could keep the web moving until the data is transferred from the RIP, leaving large blank areas on the web.

For example, complex jobs might require hours of RIP processing before they can be printed, and in the meantime the press is sitting there unused. A dictum in conventional pressrooms is "keep those cylinders turning!" since idle presses aren't generating any revenue. The same is true for digital presses. Some vendors try to alleviate this by filling up a page buffer with rasterized pages, but these can be depleted fairly quickly and require that the press be stopped until the RIP can fill the buffer back up again.

Most vendors of digital presses and RIPs offer a variable printing application specific to that RIP and/or print engine. Typically, these applications are written by the RIP vendor, such as Scitex or Agfa, or by an outside software developer like Atlas Software BV, who wrote the Private-I software for Xeikon that's based on Atlas's PrintShop Mail program. Atlas also provides PrintShop Mail to Splash Technologies.

Software / hardware pairings

Darwin	Xerox DocuColor (Scitex RIP)
Personalizer-X	Agfa Chromapress
Private-I	Xeikon (Barco, Xeikon RIPs)
VIP Designer	Xeikon (Barco RIP)
VarisScript	Xeikon (Varis RIP)
Yours Truly	Indigo (Harlequin RIP)
FreeForm	EFI RIPs
PageFlex	IBM InfoPrint (IBM RIP)
Focus Gold	any, forms-caching optional
PrintShop Mail	any, forms-caching supported
DataMerge	any, forms-caching optional

Darwin could be used on other RIPs than Scitex because it optionally generates PostScript code, but all the benefits of forms-caching are lost if it is not used with a Scitex RIP. Focus Gold, PrintShop Mail and DataMerge are sold as general-purpose applications—they are device-independent and can operate in any PostScript environment from an Apple Color Laserwriter to any digital press with a PostScript front end. These applications can also be purchased with optional drivers for specific RIPs to implement PostScript Level 2 forms-caching.

Most variable printing applications simply truncate text to fit the specified area if the copy is too long to fit a static text container. While this is not a problem with a carefully-designed layout and properly formatted data, it does introduce a limitation into a workflow. For example, a variable text container in a page layout for a surname may not be long enough to accommodate all surnames in the database if this eventuality is not accounted for in the design process.

All programs offer a preview function for the review of inserted material but this can become impractical for runs much over a few hundred, so variable text containers need to be made as large as possible without compromising the design. Some variable printing systems such as Barco's PageStream and BitStream's PageFlex can take basic text insertion to the next level: resizing text, resizing text containers, adjusting hyphenation and justification, and performing other methods of copyfitting texts of varying lengths into a specified text area on a variable page. Scitex Darwin can substitute an alternative layout if a given condition, such as a long surname or page title, causes reflow or awkward line endings, is encountered at print time.

Foreign languages can present a problem if the language uses a non-Roman alphabet, such as Russian, Arabic, or Japanese. Mixing these writing systems with the Roman alphabet may be possible but in all cases localized versions of the database, page layout, and variable-data applications must be purchased and installed, along with any system-level support, such as Apple's various Language Kits. Further problems arise if non-Roman text is exported to ASCII; such character strings typically uses a two-byte code for each character so the receiving application must not only be able to decode this text, it must use the same character mapping as the originating application, for which there is no current standard.

For example, Russian text exported from a Russian Windows version of Filemaker Pro will not be transportable to a Macintosh running a Russian version of QuarkXPress. The workaround for this example would be to move the Filemaker Pro database to a Macintosh running a Russian version of Filemaker Pro, then exporting the data as a Macintosh ASCII file which can then be imported into a Russian version of QuarkXPress.

Applications like Word, Excel, Filemaker Pro, QuarkXPress, and Pagemaker can make the character encoding conversion internally when the native files for these applications are moved between platforms and only then exported for use in other applications. Roman languages that require diacritical marks, such as å, ë, í, ô, ñ, æ, and others can present a problem because these diacritical marks are outside of the 7-bit ASCII range, which is the common denominator between the database and the variable-data application. Diacritical marks use 8-bit ASCII codes, and there is currently no standard for transliteration of so-called "high-bit" ASCII between the various computer platforms. Transliteration problems will arise when the data is exported from another platform. The proposed Unicode character mapping standard will eliminate this problem, but unfortunately Unicode is not yet well-supported. The workaround described above works well in these cases, and language-specific versions of applications are not required for most Roman-alphabet diacritical marks except for those used in Vietnamese, which requires specialized fonts.

When using foreign-language text in an English-language version of QuarkXPress, the text will not be hyphenated properly. This is a big problem if the automatic hyphenation feature in QuarkXPress is turned on, as it will try to hyphenate foreign words based upon hyphenation rules for English, which can cause illogical word breaks that might not be noticed if the operator only reads English. The multi-lingual version of QuarkXPress, Passport, includes hyphenation dictionaries for many European languages, as does Adobe's new InDesign program, which can be mixed in a single document.

The lack of reliable auditing features can be a drawback to variable printing, especially of sensitive or confidential material. Auditing functions ensure that every page sent to the press is theoretically printed—it passed through the imaging stage. Most desktop variable printing applications and digital color presses cannot perform auditing functions during a press run because there is no interface to the post-press process. Most digital print jobs need to be trimmed, or require further finishing operations like folding and binding, and some might require specialized finishing operations like die-cutting, perforating, embossing/debossing, foil-stamping, or gluing.

There is always a spoilage factor in these finishing operations, and current CIP3 integration that is available with large conventional presses and bindery equipment does not exist on digital presses. Trying to determine which 25 of a 10,000 piece run got mangled in the folder would be a nearly impossible task. High-speed black-and-white systems that are used to print utility bills or bank statements, for example, typically print optical marks on the edge of the paper and use an Optical Mark Reader (OMR) to verify that each piece is accounted for at each step in the production process. If a piece is missing, it is identified and the operator is alerted so the missing piece can be rerun and sent out. Typically, pieces ruined in finishing have to be culled and returned to the press operator to be reprinted.

What is CIP3?

CIP3 (Cooperation for Integration of Prepress, Press, and Postpress) is a system designed to integrate communication between prepress, press, and post-press processes. It allows for the specification of a job's production instructions, and more importantly it contains instructions about how each device in the process should be configured. These configuration instructions can include:

- *ink key settings on a sheetfed or web offset press*
- *other press setup instructions*
- *folding instructions for a folding machine*
- *binding instructions for a perfect binding machine*
- *cutting instructions for a cutter or three-knife trimmer*
- *other instructions for equipment that supports CIP3 and is able to communicate with other equipment in the process.*

Variable printing systems need CIP3 integration and none currently support the technology. It is the means by which an efficient auditing and verification system can be designed for a variable printing workflow.

CIP3 controls and feedback systems are an important feature that should become standard on all future digital presses as speed and capacity increase to the point where automated finishing will be a requirement. At present, only Agfa offers an auditing feature with the Chromapress and IntelliStream RIP, and this is limited to verifying press output. There is no provision in any digital press for integration with automated finishing operations, and since Xeikon-based presses rarely jam or misfeed, this is a feature of questionable benefit.

Many variable printing applications support the common barcode schemes such as ISBN, UPC, and EAN. To produce U.S. Postal Service PostNet barcodes, additional software must be purchased and integrated with the user database. A PostNet code for each record can be generated and stored as a separate field in the database, and then can be tagged with a PostNet barcode font when imported into a variable printing application or a QuarkXPress page. Barcodes can also be used in quality assurance as a means of auditing variable print jobs after finishing; this will require a barcode scanner and a link to the original database to verify that each requested piece has been printed and is ready to mail or ship.

Finding qualified operators may be the most insurmountable barrier to starting a variable printing operation. Some of the applications can require a person who is both a designer and a database expert if data is delivered raw and requires extensive manipulation before it can be incorporated into a variable layout. There are differing viewpoints on the involvement of the designer or press operator with the data handling aspects of a print run. Some maintain that the responsibility for managing the database belongs in the MIS department. For efficient workflow, data should be delivered "ready to roll" without the need for a designer or press operator to become involved with data handling, as they have things to do that they already know how to do.

With this in mind, several of the variable printing applications offer only minimal data-handling features, since the workflow assumes that the database is delivered to production in its final form. Others maintain that the ability to modify and "massage" the data after it is delivered is an important feature, and some applications offer extensive data handling functions on a par with some dedicated database management systems, and they are quite difficult to learn.

> *"Rarely, if ever, will you find an individual with the right and left brain functions required for database manipulation and creative document design."*
> —*Marc Orchant, Market Development Manager, Digital Printing Systems, Agfa Division, Bayer AG.*

Accountability issues: at what point in the process does accountability start or stop? Should further processing of data be necessary after it is delivered to production? Should graphic designers of variable layouts be expected to purchase and learn the data handling functions of these programs and apply them according to client instructions? Should a digital press operator's job description also include "database administration"? In nearly all cases, the answer to these questions should be "no," but in real-world operations this is probably not possible. The responsibility of database management should stay with the originator of the data as much as is practical.

There are no current workflow standards for the production of variable print jobs, nor are there coherent management, marketing, and sales strategies for printers offering variable services. Printers lack the data management techniques that can add tremendous value to a variable print sale. They tend not to market themselves well, and especially with variable or short-run digital printing.

Print sales people still do not initiate variable sales calls with the right people in an organization. Variable print orders are much more likely to come from marketing managers than from traditional print buyers, who really have not had a historical need to understand the requirements of database marketing and variable printing. We think that graphic services will integrate database functionality over time.

Overview of variable-data applications

Nearly all variable-data production tools can produce the following degrees of variability:

- *Personalization*—adding a name to boilerplate text: the old "Dear Joe Blow" salutation in much "personalized" junk mail. Such a level of personalization is dated, unimpressive, and likely to end up in the trash even if read. On average 60 percent of such pieces are not read, according to the Direct Marketing Association. Poor construction of personalized text leads to poor value perception of the material to the reader. Much of this personalization is overdone and in a manner that can be a bit insulting to the reader. It is not necessary to repeat the customer's name in every sentence.
- Versioning—producing multiple versions of a base publication, each defined by a chosen parameter such as geographic location, income, education level, etc. This level of variation ensures that the piece is targeted more closely to a recipient's demographic than would a generic (national) version of the same publication. Versioning can be extended to substitution of sections, advertising, or pages selected from a list according to a set of rules.
- *Customization*—producing highly individualized documents, each varying substantially from the other, as in the case of a completely customized direct-mail catalog targeted at one specific customer's buying habits, prior ordering history, and a host of other demographic vari-

ables of interest to the producer. This is the peak level of variability—each recipient gets a different document.

These distinctions in variability can be further broken down, from the simplest to the most complex, in terms of the degree of variation in the final pieces:

- addressed to "resident," with identical contents
- addressed to "resident" and sorted by geographical parameters, with contents chosen by selective bindery (the "Valu-Pak" coupon mailings are a good example)
- name and address on piece, sorted by regional parameters (country, state/province, city, postal code). This can also include selective bindery, such as that used by many national magazines like *TV Guide* and *Time*
- address merge—name and address on mailing and enclosures
- mail merge—name, address, and salutation
- document assembly—merge prewritten paragraphs
- data merge—name, address, salutation, and name or other variable information within text
- database merge—a link to all fields in a database
- hybrid documents—a combination of variable and static pages
- database and image merge—links to text in a database and images named within that database
- rule-based database and image merge—conditional placement of most text and/or images based upon a set of rules specified by the producer
- completely unique document—every image pixel and text character differs from recipient to recipient

There are several criteria for variable-data production tools which apply to any workflow and equipment installation.

Building pages
For defining variable content within a layout page, those applications which insert variable text and images into predefined content containers or insertion points can be classified as fixed-layout applications. These have no ability to adjust containers or content for fit. Most variable printing applications fall under this classification and are capable of producing a database and image merge.

Those with the ability to redefine data containers and/or content, primarily to accommodate text of varying length, can be considered as dynamic-layout applications and are capable of producing completely unique documents. The only programs that do this are Barco's VIPLine and Bitstream's Pageflex, but it is expected that this rather important feature will soon become standard in all variable printing applications. Most current programs cannot perform dynamic layout, but some can replace any page of a document with another page according to specified rules.

DataMerge includes an XTension called Group Picture that allows grouped items on a QuarkXPress page to be saved to disk. These can then be referenced as variable images and used as page replacements where needed. Darwin and Focus Gold can select any number of different layouts within a QuarkXPress document according to rules-based selectors.

All software packages intended to produce variable content support at least the following functions:

1. Insertion of variable text from a database into a defined text container. Typically, this text copy is a field from a database record. Some support rules-based insertion of text from a file, such as "insert cats.txt if pet = 'cat'," or insertion of a certain word, such as "insert 'Mr.' before Name if gender = 'male'." They usually support hyphenation and justification, and text reflow.

2. Insertion of images into a defined image container. Variable images can be inserted two ways: defined as a field in the database that contains the filename of the image to be inserted, or they can be referenced in a library of images and defined with a rule within the application, such as "insert petey.tif if pet = 'parakeet'." Some applications allow scaling and rotation of images within a specified picture or text box in QuarkXPress, although this is a practice to be discouraged without the proper RIP or program support.

Here's the first side of the 5.5x8.5-inch postcard designed for The Old Time Company:

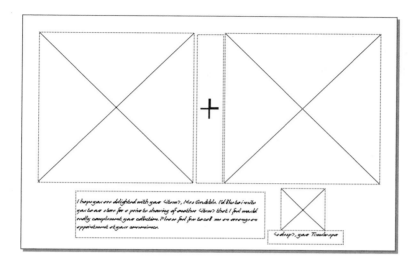

It might not look like there's much on the page, but all of the static elements are present and placeholders for variable text information have been identified by the designer with angle brackets < >.

The reverse side of the card looks like this:

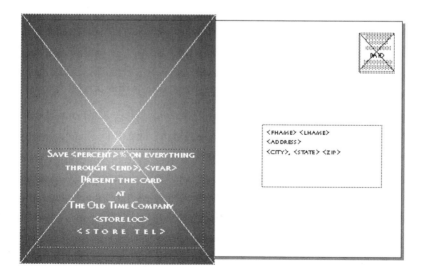

Here, additional placeholders are present, showing that variable text can consist of far more than just a name and address. A laser comp and a digital color proof of the document should be made for client approval. It's probably a good idea to proof all variable images and to run the entire job through a preflighting application like Markzware Flight Check or Extensis Preflight Pro to check for potential problems before building the variable-data job.

The database should be prepared by a database specialist as follows:
- remove old, invalid data
- remove duplicate records
- check spelling, especially of words to be used in the variable content
- make titles and honoraria consistent
- sort as required, such as on Zip+4 Zipcode for a postal discount
- define fields to be exported
- define field *order* for export, such as «firstname» «lastname» «address» and so on, if the fields aren't already sorted as needed. Field order is irrelevant in most cases once they are defined during the construction phase, but many database professionals prefer to have more order to their data
- add names of image files to an image filename field in each record, if the variable printing application requires this
- create conditionals and filters for any required variables, such as salutation, demographic information, and other data created from the results of a data manipulation, and store the results in appropriate fields
- export the database as an ASCII tab-delimited file or as a DBF file. Provide production with a printed list of all field names.

Consider dynamic content generation, where content is derived as a function of the database record data, such as bar charts and pie charts. This may happen during data mining or on-the-fly.

Software approaches to variable-data production
We'll use our marketing promotion for The Old Time Company to profile several variable printing applications.

The goal

The Old Time Company wants a set of color postcards mailed out to previous customers. The customer's last purchase was noted and a similar item, based on the customer's collecting preference, also noted, is chosen and shown alongside the item the customer bought previously. The new item is chosen to resemble the purchased item, for example, if the customer bought a small vintage alarm clock, another vintage alarm clock is chosen. A short paragraph of obligatory marketing-ese is below the images of the items, which requires variable input of the purchased item, a salutation based upon gender, the customer's surname, and a repeat of the item type. The text reads:

> *I hope you are delighted with your vintage <item>, <sal> <Lname>. I'd like to invite you to our store for a private showing of another <item> that I feel would really complement your collection. Please feel free to call me and arrange an appointment at your convenience.*

Our designer enclosed the variable data in angle brackets to easily distinguish it from static text. Next to this text is the name and a photo of the salesperson who assisted the customer the last time they made a purchase at a particular store. Here's a sample of the front of the card, as delivered by our designer:

I hope you are delighted with your vintage <item>, <sal> <Lname>. I'd like to invite you to our store for a private showing of another <item> that I feel would really complement your collection. Please feel free to call me and arrange an appointment at your convenience.

<salesp>, your Timekeeper

The recipient instantly recognizes the item he or she already owns, on the left, and probably recognizes the sales representative. The image on the right shows the item chosen by the sales rep as possibly being of interest to the customer based on sales history and the sales rep's knowledge of the customer's preferences.

On the back of the card, the customer's local store and store phone number are given, and the customer's mailing address is printed on the right side.

The Old Time Company wants to offer different discounts to different customers, based on past business, and also wants varying lengths of discount eligibility, and this information is included in the database.

Here's the back of the card:

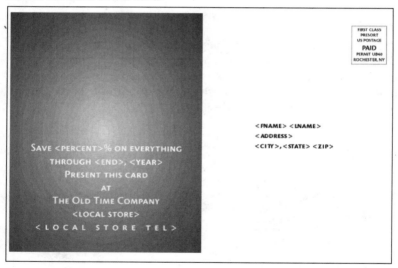

The designer has indicated where the variable information is to appear, just like on the front of the piece. There are no variable images on the back, just a static vignette created in QuarkXPress as a blend of two process colors.

The goal is to see how each application handles this task, and to what degree each can customize the cards based on the database and instructions provided by The Old Time Company.

Scitex Darwin

This Macintosh-only application consists of two parts: Darwin Co-Pilot, a Quark XTension, and Darwin Pilot, a separate application used to control QuarkXPress and within which the operator defines rules for placement of text and graphic variables. Darwin is tightly coupled to the Scitex SX3000 RIP, which is sold as an option with the Xerox DocuColor 40, 70, and 100 digital presses.

Darwin allows the creation of very specific rule sets. In addition to the expected rule sets for variable text and images in otherwise static pages, alternate pages can be specified for substitution depending on the rule defined for that page or pages. For example, if it is known that some recipients of a catalog are married with children, then Quark pages X, Y, and Z that contain child-specific items will be placed on pages 10–12 of the catalog. If it is known that other recipients are single, married without children, same-sex or opposite-sex unmarried couples, retired couples, widowed or divorced singles, then other, more appropriate pages can be substituted.

Pages carrying items like child car seats, minivans, educational software, and such probably aren't of much interest to a young single person, so there's no reason to offer them if other items that the recipient is more likely to be interested in, such as sporty cars, computer games, or fashionable clothing, can take up the same space. In addition, multiple-language documents can be made, with a page rule to substitute a page in one language for another, depending on a rule trigger.

Darwin offers some basic data-handling features, such as conditionals ("if <condition X exits> then do this") and other exceptions, and it supports all of the text and image features of QuarkXPress, such as text on curves, scaling of images, clipping paths, kerning, and runarounds, but only on the DocuColor 40 at present.

Due to limitations in the "PES" interface between the RIP and the press engine, variable data printing on the Xeikon-based DocuColor 70 and 100 is subject to some fairly strict rules. All Xeikon-based presses offer varying levels of bit-depth per device pixel from one to four. Scitex specifies variable text and image coverage per page as follows: bit depth 1, 100 percent; bit depth 2, 50 percent; bit depth 3, 33 percent; bit depth 4, 25 percent.

There are also limitations on how closely variable elements can be spaced on a page. Scitex defines a page grid that must be used according to the chosen bit depth. At bit depth 1, the grid is spaced at 0.24″; at bit depth 2, it is 0.12″; at bit depth 3, it is 0.08″; at bit depth 4, it is 0.06″. Presumably, these limitations also apply to the Splash and Fiery RIPs sold by Xerox with the DocuColor 70 and 100, since Xerox is the only reseller of the Xeikon presses that relies on the PES interface; all of the others bypass it. Xerox offers its VIPP workflow as an alternative (see page 244), and is currently developing a direct interface between the RIP and the press engine.

Darwin at work

Darwin works with QuarkXPress versions 3.32 and 4.0, and it is strongly recommended to update any version of 4.0 to the latest available from Quark's Web site www.quark.com, which at the time of this writing is 4.04.

The Darwin Pilot offers a minimal interface to all of its functions. Commands are chosen from the control panel; there are no relevant commands in the drop-down menus at the top of the screen.

The Darwin Pilot Control Panel.

The Scitex Launchpad in QuarkXPress displays an icon for Darwin, which is dimmed out if the Darwin Pilot is not running. Any other Scitex XTensions also appear in the Scitex Launchpad. Clicking the Darwin icon displays the Darwin Co-Pilot palette.

Darwin ON   Darwin OFF

The Darwin Pilot Control Palette

Once all of the needed files are gathered, a Darwin job is prepared by first defining the job and a profile in Darwin Pilot. A profile defines the fields in the database to be used, and is usually created from the exported ASCII database file which should have as the first record all of the field names of the database. A new job and profile are created when the user clicks the "New" button in the Darwin Pilot palette.

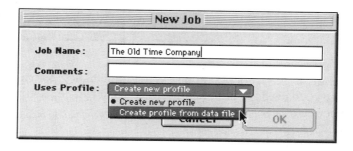

The profile creation step asks for the data file, which is the same one that contains the actual data. A profile could be created manually if the field name information is omitted from the first record of the file.

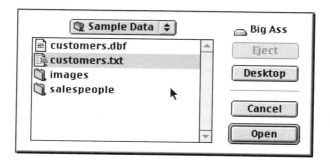

Once selected, the profile window shows all of the fields in the data-base. New fields can be added at this stage if necessary, in case the database was missing a field.

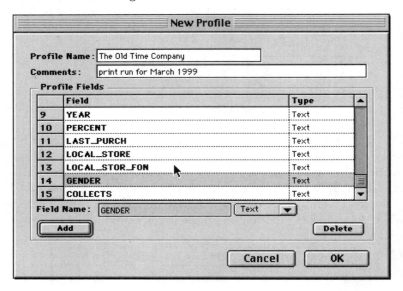

A field can also be redefined in the New Profile dialog, for example if the Zip code needs to be sorted numerically, it can be redefined as an integer field here.

Once the profile is created and saved, the next step is to import the database file. Clicking the Data button on the Darwin palette opens the Import dialog, which preselects the same data file used to define the profile. Here the fields to be imported can be selected, although in most cases all of the fields will be imported.

As we noted in the database section, data in fields can be defined as text, or numeric, or as other types of information. This helps when formatting output.

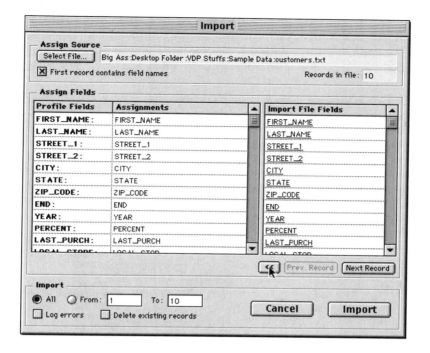

The mouse pointer is shown over the "Auto Assign" button, which automatically selects all fields in the database. Specific records can be imported, but at this point in the operation, all of the data to be processed should have been defined and identified in advance. Creating additional work for the operator leads to errors and lots of finger-pointing.

Clicking the Import button does as advertised, and it may take a few minutes for the process to finish.

Imported data can be edited, but this is something that should only be done upon request. The operator has better things to do than to correct spelling or address errors. This is why the database must be fully vetted, audited, and cleansed before being handed off for a press run.

Now Darwin has the data needed for the press run. The next step is to define the location of any variable images and text, and to place them in the Darwin Library, which acts as a central repository for all of the job's variable data. Darwin recognizes bitmapped images in TIFF or EPS format, vector artwork in EPS format, plain ASCII text files, and QuarkXPress files as variable items. We'll see how a Quark page can be used as a variable item a bit later.

The variable data library is defined with the Library button in the Darwin control panel. This is a nicely-designed routine; all that's needed is for the operator to click and drag job elements from the job folder into the open Library dialog window.

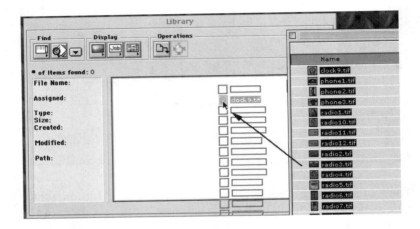

Darwin creates thumbnails of each item and can show them as a list, or as thumbnails. The thumbnail view is very handy when creating rules that select specific images because the desired image can simply be dragged to the rule that operates on it from the Library dialog.

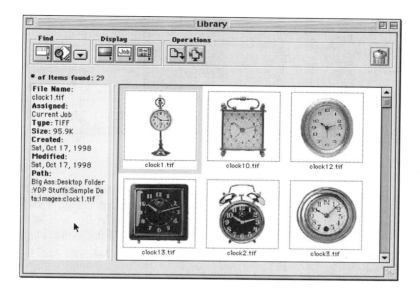

Text files are added to the library in the same manner. A small snippet of the first sentence or two of the file is shown as a reference when in the thumbnail view which makes it easy to identify multiple files. This is useful if entire text blocks are designated as variable, meaning that the content of each designated box is replaced with the specified text file. This can also be used to great advantage in multi-lingual projects.

A completely different QuarkXPress page can be specified with a rule. Here's an example of a different page being used if the COUNTRY field meets a certain test, in this case, Finland. This substituted page is defined in the Darwin layout and is simply another page in the variable QuarkXPress document, altered to accommodate different languages, different text breaks, or any other exception to the standard document pages. Substituted pages need to have the same variable text fields and picture boxes as the main pages.

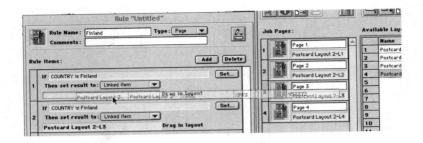

Creating the variable page in Darwin

To define the variable content, the desired layout (specified in the "Pages" setup) is selected from the Darwin control panel, which opens it up in QuarkXPress. A list of available fields, rules, and other items defined in Darwin Pilot appears in the Co-Pilot palette. Here, the first variable, a database field, is inserted where indicated by the designer.

It will be necessary to delete the placeholders once finished. Database fields and rule results can be placed as variable text. Fields and rules are simply dragged to the desired position on the page.

Once placed, the variable text field is shown enclosed in guillemets (French quotes). Here, all of the variable fields in the text box have been placed:

I hope you are delighted with your vintage ≪LAST_PURCH≫, ≪saluta-tion≫ ≪LAST_NAME≫. I'd like to invite you to our store for a private showing of another ≪LAST_PURCH≫ that I feel would really comple-ment your collection. Please feel free to call me and arrange an appointment at your convenience.

Variable images are placed similarly; an image rule can be dragged to the target picture box. A placeholder image is used in the box.

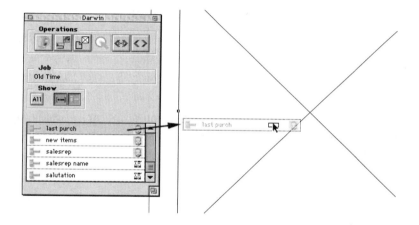

Once placed, the placeholder can be centered within the box with Command+Shift+M.

It looks like a gray blur but it does show position (see next page):

After placing all of the variables, an on-screen proof can be made to make sure that each finished piece contains the correct information. The front of the card looks okay here:

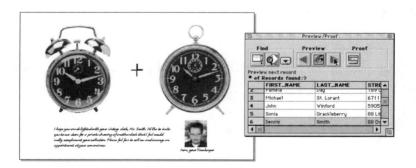

The back of the piece looks as expected, and the address and telephone number of the store match the region of residence.

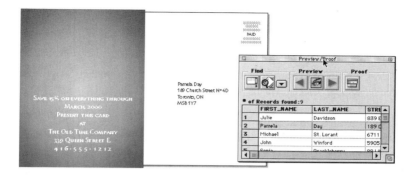

After proofing, the VPS job can be sent to the Scitex SX3000 RIP, which is sold as an option with the Xerox DocuColor 40, 70, and 100 digital presses. Darwin supports other output devices but only performs PostScript forms caching when used with the Scitex RIP, a significant factor in production speed. Darwin renders each variable document separately before it is sent to the RIP, so pre-processing can be quite slow.

Summary
Darwin offers quite a number of powerful features that can be learned easily; makes heavy use of drag-and-drop, a very intuitive approach as compared to specifying items in menus or dialog boxes; supports all of the enhanced text handling features of QuarkXPress 4.x, such as text on a curve, and seems very well-integrated with the QuarkXPress application.

Pro: easy to learn; excellent rules-based system for defining variable-data; allows entire pages to be substituted; excellent documentation and tutorials.

Con: Requires a hardware key ("dongle"), only operates with QuarkXPress, expensive ($995 for one user, $3,995 for four users); some hardware limitations on the DocuColor 70 and 100 preclude advanced text features of QuarkXPress 4.x.

Agfa Personalizer X 2.0

This is an XTension for QuarkXPress 3.3 and 4.x. Personalizer-X does not offer any rules-based processing like Darwin, but does allow selection of specific records for printing by specifying a search term or filter which operates on a specified field, such as "select only those records where 'Occupation' = 'dentist'."

Images require the addition of an image filename field in each database record and a variable image file name entered into this field.

The rules-based method of generating the salutation based on the contents of the gender field used in the Darwin example won't work with Personalizer X. Another field for salutation would have to be added for this job to work in Personalizer X. This is a factor when defining the database prior to export. Users of Personalizer X need to be specific about the need for preprocessing of a database before it is delivered to production.

Personalizer X allows variable text and image boxes to overlap, unlike Darwin, and it also supports linked variable text boxes, which allows reflow of variable text to other pages or other text boxes. Agfa bypasses the PES interface on the Chromapress (Xeikon) and there are none of the limitations present in the Xerox DocuColor with regard to variable coverage or advanced text layouts.

Setting up the variable run with Personalizer X is simpler than with Darwin. It also offers offset records and clustered records. Offset records let you specify a numerical offset, in the number of records, for each variable box on the page. Clustered records determine which records are placed on each variable page.

Both offer step-and-repeat functionality, either by clustering a group of records in a precise location on a larger sheet, or by offsetting them so that after bindery the final product is properly collated.

The basic setup information is entered in the Data File Settings from the Personalizer-X menu. The desired settings, any filtering criteria, the location of the variable images folder are entered here.

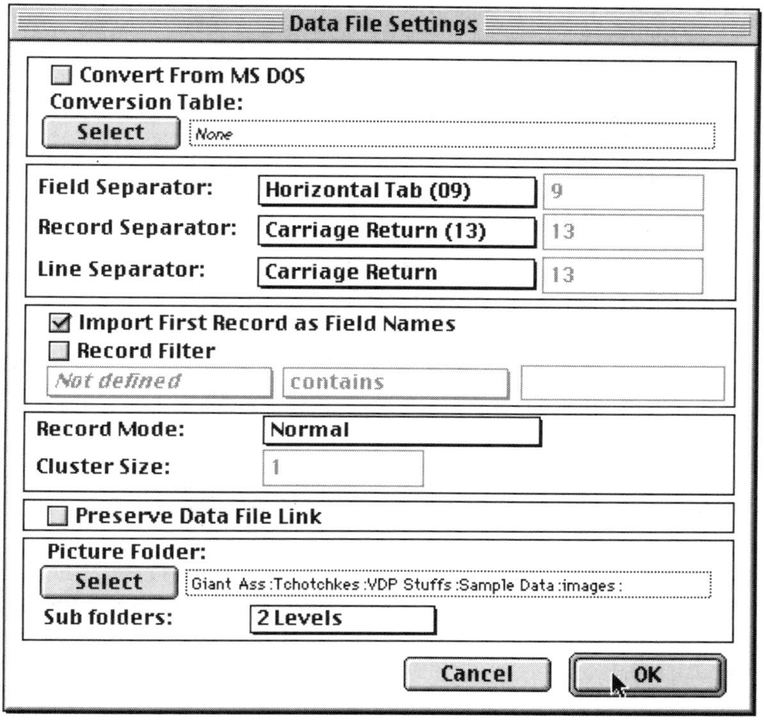

Data File Settings		

☐ **Convert From MS DOS**
Conversion Table:
[**Select**] *None*

Field Separator:	Horizontal Tab (09)	9
Record Separator:	Carriage Return (13)	13
Line Separator:	Carriage Return	13

☑ **Import First Record as Field Names**
☐ **Record Filter**
[*Not defined*] [contains] [ ]

| **Record Mode:** | Normal |
| **Cluster Size:** | 1 |

☐ **Preserve Data File Link**

Picture Folder:
[**Select**] Giant Ass :Tchotchkes :VDP Stuffs :Sample Data :images :
Sub folders: [2 Levels]

[Cancel] [▶ OK]

Now the database file is defined by choosing Select Data File from the Personalizer X menu. Choosing Data File Link further refines the database information.

Note that you can define separators for fields, records, or lines.

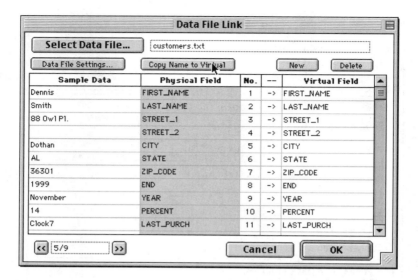

Field names need to be copied to "virtual," a not-very-clear step. Fields can be added or deleted here, but data cannot be modified in Agfa's Personalizer X. Any changes must be made in the original database file.

The process of defining variable text and image boxes is straightforward as it is all driven by field names in the imported database. The user selects a text box and names each one on the page from the Personalizer X menu:

After this step, the database field is applied to the contents of the text box by choosing Variable Text Field... from the menu. Multiple fields can be assigned within each box. Each instance of a text field prompts this dialog box:

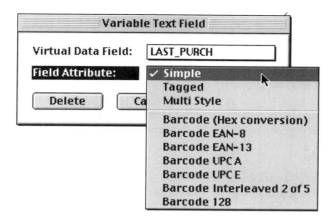

A field name is chosen from the pop-up menu. Various types of barcodes can be specified here, along with text styles such as bold or italic, and whether any QuarkXPress tags found should be applied.

An example of QuarkXPress's formatting tags:

Tag Filter Version:

<v1.70><e0>

Style sheet definition:

*@body=[S"","body"]<*L*h"Standard"*kn0*kt0*ra0*rb0*d0*p(0, 9,0,14,0,7.2,*

*g,"U.S. English")*t(0,0,"2 "):*
Ps100t0h100z10k0b0c"Black"f"
Palatino-Roman">

Styled Text:

@body:<$>QuarkXPress tags are a powerful means of styling text as it is imported into a layout.

If imported, this snippet of text would appear already styled and the "Body" style sheet would be added to the list of available styles.

QuarkXPress tags are a powerful means of styling text as it is imported into the layout program. A database application can be programmed to insert these ASCII tags (which are similar in concept to HTML markup tags) into the field contents of a database, saving a lot of production time. It also assures that the client's style choices are maintained in production.

The Agfa manual is unclear about the application of barcodes, but apparently the selected field must contain the ASCII barcode data with a checksum byte, and unspecified barcode fonts must be installed, though most any commercial PostScript Type 1 barcode font should work.

Once a field is chosen, the live data for the current record is displayed in the text box. As expected, all of Quark's typographical features can be applied to variable text.

Designating a variable image works similarly: a QuarkXPress picture box is selected and the user chooses Variable Picture Box from the Personalizer X menu.

Here it's easy to see that variable picture filenames must be supplied as fields in the database. Since we did not include these fields, we'd have to go back, add a field to each record for each variable picture, and enter the picture's filename into the field.

Once the variable picture box is defined, the actual image is displayed in the box. Opening the Data Browser allows one to preview each variable page.

Having the ability to proof pages is very important in finding problems before they are printed. You can step through the proofs and see if long names or other data did not fit properly, for instance.

I hope you are delighted with your vintage clock, m Smith. I'd like to invite
you to our store for a private showing of another clock that I feel would
really complement your collection. Please feel free to call me and arrange an
appointment at your convenience.

Your Timekeeper

This job was not prepared correctly for Personalizer-X. Without the data-handling rules present in other applications, the salutation generation fails, as does the selection of the right-hand image, and the name and picture of the sales representative. These could be accommodated by creating new fields at the expense of additional time spent preparing the database.

Personalizer X offers a step-and-repeat function similar to that already offered in QuarkXPress, but it preserves the variable information in each element. This is useful for small items such as business cards or ID badges that can be ganged-up on a large press sheet.

Generating the final output is a multi-step process. First, the job is exported, which creates one or more variable data files with links to each image. Then the job is saved as a PostScript file using the usual print-to-file routine in the chosen printer driver. Then all of the files are imported into the Agfa ChromaPost software on the Chroma-press RIP for output. Because it requires the ChromaPost software, Personalizer X can only be used with Agfa digital presses.

Summary
A great program for workflows where the data arrives perfectly-defined without requiring any manipulation, which is as it should be. Possibly the easiest of all programs profiled to use.

Pro: Supports barcode generation, offers several field layout options, an advanced step-and-repeat function, linked variable text boxes, very tightly integrated with Agfa's Chromapress. *Con:* Tight integration with Chromapress precludes use on any other system, requires a hardware key, no conditional rules, definition of variable fields and images can be tedious and time-consuming, expensive ($995).

Focus Gold by Vision's Edge

This is by all appearances an industrial-strength suite of Quark-XPress XTensions. Focus Gold offers strong conditional rules-based exceptions and text-handling, a system of alternate field content replacements, and the ability to substitute different page layouts based on a set of "keys," or custom rules, that trigger the desired layout when a specified condition is met during processing of the database file. This functionality comes at the cost of usability; this set of XTensions has a learning curve far higher than any of the other profiled applications, probably because it does so much.

The set of programs that comprise Focus Gold were originally developed by Vision's Edge as a custom application for *Reader's Digest* magazine. According to Julie Roberts, Vision's Edge Product Manager, future revisions of the programs will include new dialogs, menus, and other changes to make the product's features more accessible. A less-comprehensive version, Focus Bronze, is expected to be released in 1999 with a much more simplified user interface.

Focus Gold requires significant preparatory work before anything can be printed. The user must define all of the fields manually as these cannot be abstracted from the database file (the next release will do this). The following parameters need to be defined after creating the field structure:

- alternates—substitutions that can be made for specific or blank field contents; default content can be inserted into the layout if the database field is empty or contains a specific word.
- keys—where the conditional rules are stored. Different layouts can be swapped in according to the results of a conditional rule contained in a key.
- sets—a collection of elements that share the same keys
- labels— (optional) these are user-defined names for displayed fields; an alternative to the cryptic default names

that display codes for the set, key, and data file of a variable image or text element.

The number of images, text boxes, and other variable elements in a set must be defined when the set is created by the user. This is rather exacting, although these values can be altered later.

Focus Gold offers optional plug-in device drivers that support advanced variable printing functions available in some RIPs and printers. Focus Gold supports a huge number of variables per job, far more than any RIP could ever hope to churn through, but it's a nice feature for very specific types of work: up to 2,000 text variables per document, a nested system of sets with up to 16 sets and 16 variable images or lines, and over 1,600 possible layouts. If this type of capacity is required, then Focus Gold is the only application available on the desktop that can handle such a job.

One feature is the Variable Parameter File (VPF). This is a small file prepared by the manager of the variable print run that's designed to be handed off to a designer along with a small set of sample data; the supposition here is that the designer doesn't need to see the actual data in order to create a layout that is compliant with the actual data, which could be useful in highly confidential documents. Live data is only used once the job is handed off for production. The designer will still need to have Focus Gold installed in order to use this file when building the layout. This VPF would ideally be generated by someone with an intimate knowledge of the database and of the project goals. However, a designer can just ignore the VPF and use placeholders in the layout like the ones used in The Old Time Company card layout, in which case the variable fields would need to be created by the project manager.

Creating a VPF is not a simple task, and it is the first thing that must be done when starting a new job with Focus Gold. We'll use our Old Time Company project once more:

First, the QuarkXPress layout provided by the designer is opened. To help get the field names into the VPF, a text box can be drawn on the pasteboard and the ASCII database file imported into it. The first line of text should contain the field names. This way the field names will be visible while setting up the VPF.

Choosing Utility->Focus VPF Editor->New... presents this blank VPF dialog:

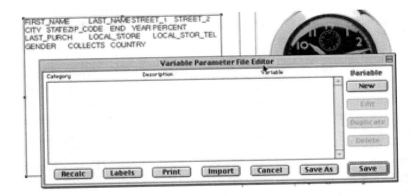

Clicking New defines the first field and displays the Variable Editor dialog. Note that entries cannot be pasted in from outside of the Variable Editor; items can only be copied and pasted within the dialog, which is a bit of an annoyance. Editing a variable field presents this cluttered dialog:

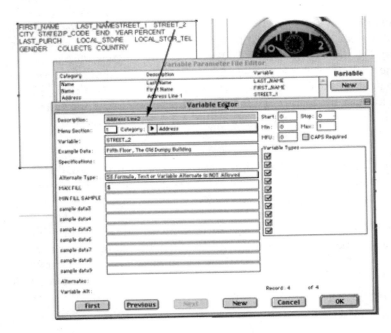

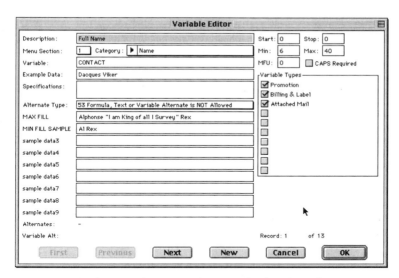

Here, sample data can be entered to test for line length.

A variable parameter file must be specified before any layouts are defined. This is done in the Focus Designer Preferences from Quark's Edit->Preferences menu.

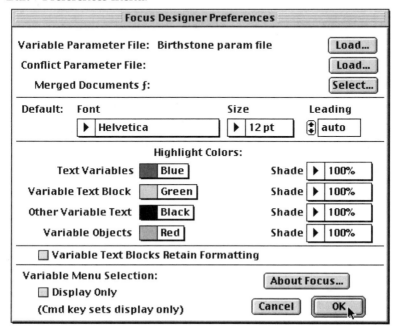

Inserting variable fields into a QuarkXPress document is fairly straightforward: a variable field is defined at the cursor location with the pop-up menu in the Focus Designer palette:

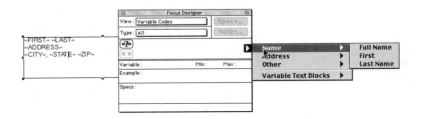

Variable fields appear within guillemets. Focus can show the specified sample data from View->MAX/MIN FILL SAMPLE DATA in the Focus designer palette so the operator has a good idea of whether the text box is sized appropriately:

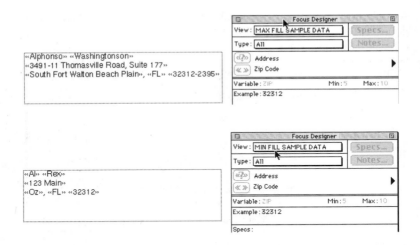

The next step is the definition of variable sets and keys. A variable set is a set of variable text blocks, text boxes, graphics and/or lines in a QuarkXPress document that are all triggered by the same formula and have the same keys.

The balance of the images and examples are pulled from the Focus Gold tutorial that is included with the product. It is a similar idea to our Old Time Company mailer—a postcard mailed to a list of customers—and suffices to show the rest of the program's capabilities.

Defining Sets.

Keys correspond to responses that may be generated from the variable set's assigned formula. Each key triggers a full set of variable text blocks, text boxes, lines and graphics.

For example, if key data in the merge file indicated Alaska, variable text about Alaska could be inserted into the document, variable lines can be drawn to point to Alaskan cities on maps, or graphics depicting Alaskan scenes can be automatically imported into the Quark-XPress document.

Setting up Keys

After setting up keys, variable text blocks must be defined. This is can get a little annoying but we got through it. Variable text content is stored in special text boxes on the document's pasteboard and is inserted into live text boxes on the document page according to the results of a key trigger.

This is text that can vary, but it is not contained in the database. Text blocks used in this manner are created as part of a set. Focus Gold also uses variable text boxes, though how these differ from variable text blocks is not clear. Links are then created to text boxes on the live page that correspond to the contents of the variable text blocks.

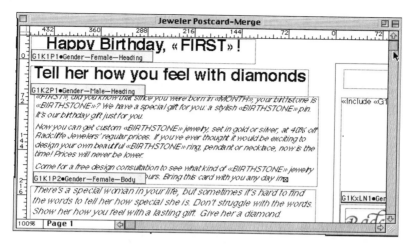

Variable text blocks on the pasteboard.

After having tried a few pages, this approach may not be as annoying as we first thought. It does provide another level of variability.

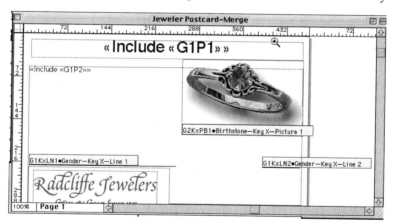

Live text boxes on the document page with links assigned to a specific variable text block on the pasteboard..

Variable images are assigned by creating a key for each instance of a variable image. For example, each of the Birthstone keys has a specific image of a piece of jewelry tagged to it that uses that month's birthstone.

Rules for keys are created in the Formula window. Here a simple test is performed to determine the birthstone image used in the piece based upon the recipient's month of birth.

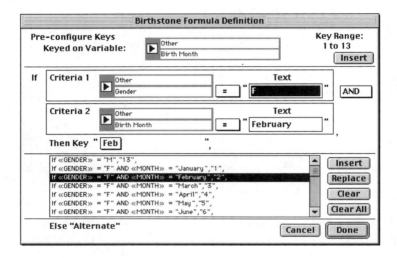

These formulas can contain numerous levels but are limited to Boolean operators such as AND, OR, AND NOT, and such.

Once all of these procedures are finished, the job can be merged with the live data. The merge process starts with defining a database file to use for the merge and specifying a filename prefix for all of the files that will be generated.

The Merge Dialog, set up to save to disk

Focus Gold does not merge variable data with the template on-the-fly, but rather creates individual QuarkXPress documents for each database record from the template document, which can be saved to disk or printed as they are created. Large jobs with thousands of records create the possibility of thousands of QuarkXPress files being generated. This could be an inefficient method of merging variable data for very large jobs. Each file is sent to the printer or press as it is created, then the next record is created and printed, and so on.

The print process is mostly hands-off, but there's no means of controlling static image caching, and there's no support for image replacement at the RIP. This can result in very slow processing times as the RIP must generate each page as if it were a unique document.

Vision's Edge offers optional modules for certain digital presses but these were not included with our evaluation software. These files can be saved to disk as separate QuarkXPress files, but they are not saved when generated while printing.

Summary
The software is a little intimidating but it is a very powerful variable data program.

Pro: Advanced data manipulation tools, more or less unlimited number of variable items per document. RIP independence is an especially nice feature.

Con: High learning curve, jargon-laden user interface, documentation could be a little better, software generates a QuarkXPress file for each record in a database. Vision's Edge is addressing some of these problems in the next revision of the software, which is being released as we go to press.

A new version of the Focus Gold program adds a floating Set Assistant palette which makes accessing the powerful variable layout capabilities of Focus Gold more intuitive for designers. It also includes the ability to turn on and off both variable and static layers in a variable document, serialization of variable documents, automated data importing, and PostScript forms-based output for quicker printing of variable data printing documents.

Users can place text variables within the copy of documents to personalize the message as well as creating sets of page elements that can vary in content and location depending on the information stored about a recipient in the users' database.

Documents can even contain variable bar codes in a variety of popular formats. Focus Gold merges the data into that QuarkXPress document, personalizing it to target its intended recipient.

Focus Gold allows users to build personalized documents with the precision they have come to expect from the QuarkXPress interface. Both text and page elements may be customized throughout the document to create fully-variable documents. Once the document's design is complete, the merging of data is done in preparation for high-speed personalized press runs. Through a system of plug-in output filters, Focus Gold can support a variety of output devices. All data is stored in tab delimited or fixed record length text files which can be output from any database, allowing access to data stored on any type of database.

Focus Gold carries a manufacturer's suggested retail price of $3,895 and a demonstration version is available for download from the Vision's Edge Web site at www.visionsedge.com.

Meadows Information Systems (MIS) DataMerge Pro

DataMerge Pro is a suite of QuarkXPress Xtensions that provide variable output. The software sells for $1,495, although a "light" version is available for $595 which does not include the custom printer and press forms-caching driver mechanism present in the more expensive version. DataMerge Pro also includes MIS's Group Picture XTensions, which lets the user save a set of grouped elements on a Quark page as a file that can be opened and placed within QuarkXPress and can also be used as a variable element.

This is another method of swapping entire pages into a variable document, similar to what Darwin does with its Page rules, although unlike Darwin these pages cannot contain variable content. A QuarkXPress for Windows version of DataMerge Pro is expected in 1999. As we went to press, DataMerge was acquired by Banta Corporation, a printing company with technology in all areas of printing, with an emphasis on direct marketing.

Meadows has developed a version of DataMerge that natively supports Xerox's VIPP, an extended PostScript toolkit that sits on the RIP and uses in-RIP composition, a technique that sends the static elements to the RIP for storage, then sends the variable data as a set of PostScript code macros. More information on VIPP is presented at the end of this chapter. Meadows has also been contracted to supply DataMerge Pro with the new Hewlett-Packard Color LaserJet 8500, a relatively fast desktop "digital press."

The software is similar in some respects to Agfa's Personalizer X. The user must define all variable fields manually, and variable images must be defined as a field in a database that contains the image's file name. MIS (now Banta) states that the next revision of the software will automatically generate variable fields from field names present in the database.

To create the Old Time Company mailing with DataMerge, the "DDF" (database definition file) is created first. This is where the field names are entered by the user.

Choosing DataMerge->Setup->Database Definitions defines the DDF. Here's where DataMerge can store up to 200 different DDFs, each pertaining to a specific job. Click "New" to name the DDF, then click "Edit."

This displays the Edit Database Definition dialog. Here's where the source database type can be set: whether it uses tabs or another character as a field delimiter, and from what type of computer the database came from.

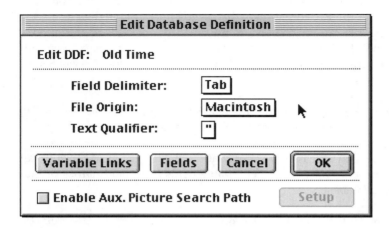

Clicking "Fields" shows the Field Names dialog. All text and picture fields must be typed in the order that they appear in the database. After each field is entered, click the up-arrow button to advance to the next field entry. When finished, click the giant "Create Variable Links from Field Names" button.

This is a somewhat tedious and error-prone method of defining variable text and image fields.

The resulting variable links are pointers to a specific field in the database. The variable link's name is used to assign text or images in the document, not the actual field names. Clicking the Variable Links button produces the Variable Links dialog:

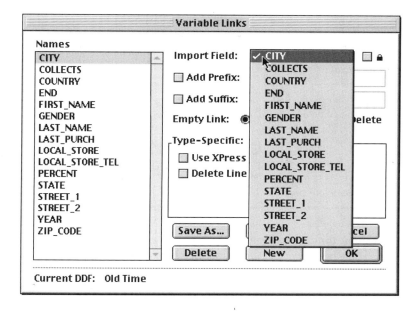

The links appear alphabetically and not in the order of the database fields. Links must be defined as text or picture links from the "Type-Specific" pop-up menu.

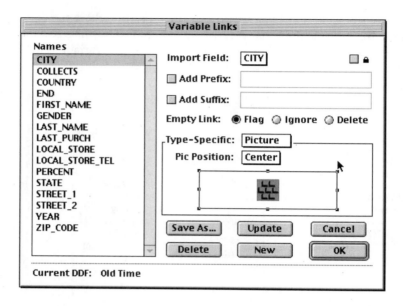

Picture handling is specified with the "pic position" pop-up menu. Images can be placed within a picture box as top-left aligned, centered, or centered and scaled to fit the box. Images should always be saved at the desired final size as resizing them in QuarkXPress can result in slow processing and undesirable image quality.

Links can be reassigned to different fields, prefixes and suffixes can be added (such as appending ".eps" to the end of an image file name in the field or "Hello, <fname>" to a text field), and text stored in a database can be formatted with QuarkXPress formatting tags. Selecting the "Use XPress Tags Filter" box will use QuarkXPress formatting tags to style the inserted text.

The "Delete line if completely empty" option is useful for fields that typically may be blank, such as the second line of an address. The Empty Link handling options allow an error flag to be inserted to catch the operator's attention, it can be ignored, or if the "Delete" option is chosen, the picture boxes will be deleted if there is no referencing image file name in the database; text links will be removed. In order for a blank text line to be removed, both "Delete line if completely empty" and "Delete" in the Empty Link handling area must be chosen.

Here, we've specified what to do when the STREET_2 field is empty.

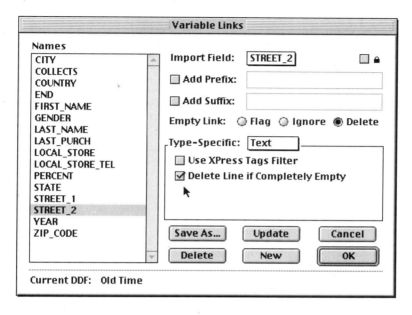

Each time a change is made to a variable link, the "update" button needs to be clicked to finalize the change.

To start the variable layout process, the DataMerge Palette needs to be visible. Specific word(s) in the layout can be selected as variable fields by choosing the appropriate variable link from the DataMerge palette and clicking the "Assign" button.

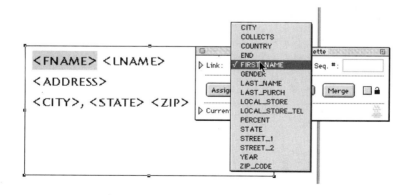

DataMerge places green underscores below variable text links, instead of using guillemets like many other programs.

There's no real advantage to either method, although programs that use guillemets might have trouble with French and Russian documents that use the guillemets for quotation marks.

Variable images are marked similarly; the picture box that will contain the variable image must be selected, then linked to the image filename field from the Link pop-up menu. In the case of the Old Time Company, we had to add this field, and three more: one for the salutation, one for the sales representative's name, and one for the sales representative's photo.

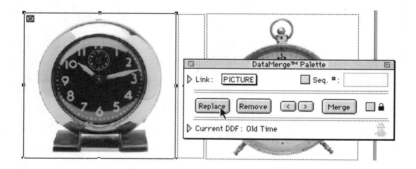

A small green box appears in the upper-left of the picture box to identify it as a variable image.

To proof the job, the user chooses Merge from the DataMerge palette, which is shown on the next page:

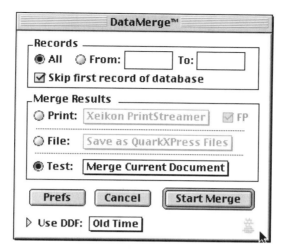

The "Test" option gives an on-screen preview of the merge results. The database file is only used at merge time, and a prompt will appear asking for the database file:

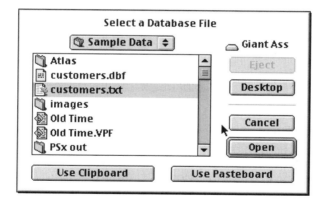

The database is merged with the document and the results can be proofed on-screen:

JULIE DAVIDSON
839 EIGHTH AVE.
FOSTER CITY, CA 94401

DataMerge supports forms-caching on specific RIPs through the FormPrint option. MIS supplies several RIP-specific printer "modules" for Splash, Fiery, and EDOX equipment, and other modules can be purchased for use with the Xeikon DCP and VIPP-driven Xerox products. To use this feature, choose "Merge" from the DataMerge palette and then select "Print" in the "Merge Results" area. Here, a Xeikon DCP digital press is specified. Clicking the "Start Merge" button shows the machine-specific options available. Here, the static data (the form) is sent to the RIP first, then the variable data is sent to the RIP after the form has been imaged and cached.

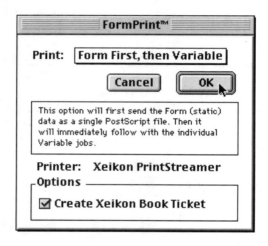

Multiple forms can be stored on a RIP's hard disk after they have been imaged, and can be referenced by a number from 1 to 99 in the Laserwriter page setup dialog's "Printer-Specific Features." Users need to remember the form number, because it'd be easy to specify the wrong one or overwrite another by mistake.

Summary

Meadows Information Systems has devised a simple means of producing variable-data output. The product can drive any PostScript printer but has the option of printer-specific modules that enable forms-caching on supported RIPs. Drivers for Xerox's VIPP PostScript database printing system are also available. A good solution for high-volume work that does not require any data manipulation at the production stage.

Pro: Simple, works as expected, good documentation and tutorials, supports multiple RIPs from different vendors, supports Quark tags embedded in database fields, no hardware copy protection, Windows version under development.

Con: database field names must be manually entered (to be remedied in an upcoming release), no means of performing conditional logic on database contents, pictures must be tagged as variable with a database field containing the image's file name, a little expensive ($1,495 for the standard version, $595 for "light" version without forms-caching).

Atlas Software BV Printshop Mail/Xeikon Private-I

Atlas Software of the Netherlands sells PrintShop Mail and is the OEM of Xeikon's Private-I software and also supplies the program to Splash; all operate identically. However, Xeikon's version specifically supports only the Barco PageStreamer RIP (sold along with the digital press) and the Xeikon VDS system, whereas PrintShop Mail specifically supports EFI FreeForm, Splash VI and DiamondMerge, and Scitex VPS RIPs.

Private-I by itself cannot print anything; users must purchase Private-I Print to output variable jobs to the Barco or Xeikon front ends—this is probably because Private-I can be downloaded for free from www.xeikon.be, which lets prospective buyers try the program out before buying. Private-I Print requires a hardware key. Both use the PostScript Level 2 forms-caching feature that allows the RIP to drive the print engine at its fastest-possible speed. PrintShop Mail can print to any PostScript Level 2 device without additional software. We will use the Private-I version of the software to produce the Old Time Company mailing.

Private-I is a standalone VDP application that imports standard EPS pages from QuarkXPress, PageMaker, FreeHand, or any application that can generate an EPS page. This gives the software a bit more flexibility than others since it gives the user a choice of which application to use for creation of the layout. All the other programs require QuarkXPress. An imported EPS layout is used as the basis for the variable print run and must remain static. Variable text and picture boxes are placed over this static background.

Immediate disadvantages to this approach should be apparent: any change to the static images requires that they be opened, edited, then exported as EPS files again, and variable text reflow may impinge upon static artwork. Both programs default to a DBF file format for database imports. A custom import can be specified to import delimited ASCII text files, but if the originating database application can export a DBF file, it should be used instead.

All picture and text boxes that are intended to contain variable information must be deleted from the original layout. In this case, everything except the postal indicia, the vignette, and the large "+" symbol is variable text or image. Each page in a document must be exported as an EPS file from QuarkXPress (or from any application that can export EPS files). Once exported, the pages are placed into Private-I as static background images.

In the Private-I application, choosing File->New creates a new variable document.

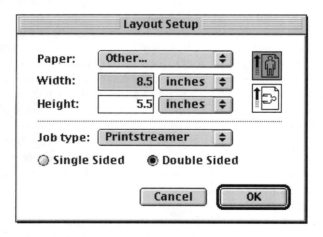

A blank page results, with options to select the front or back side (if duplex is chosen). EPS backgrounds are placed on each page through the File menu, much as in any desktop layout program.

Here, the back of the document has the back side of the Old Time Company mailer placed as a static background. Note that bleeds are not maintained when a Quark page with bleeds is exported as EPS.

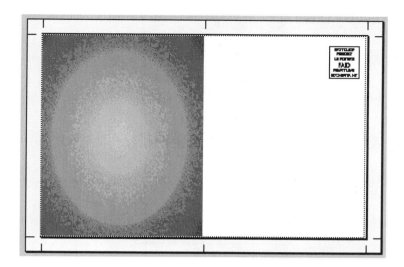

Already we're in trouble because we used QuarkXPress 3.3 for this job; a Quark XTension called PS Utilities is required that will allow a bleed to be preserved when exported to EPS. QuarkXPress 4.0 supports EPS bleeds.

A printing bleed amount can be specified in Private-I by choosing Layout->Impositioning:

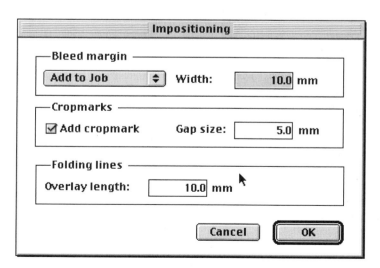

With the PS Utilities XTension loaded in QuarkXPress 3.3, a bleed can be specified for the EPS file:

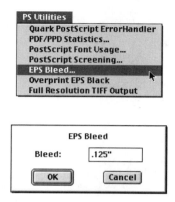

The new EPS file reflects the addition of the bleed amount.

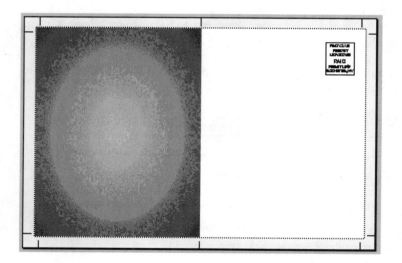

Transferring bleed information to EPS files is critical if they are to be used with Private-I. Many page layout and illustration programs require user-specified bleed information when creating EPS files.

The next step is adding the variable elements to the layout. Private-I treats static imported EPS art as the document master, and sends this master as the cached form when printing the job. Variable information is treated as a separate object layer above the background, and is sent as variable data to the RIP when printing, where the variables and processed static backgrounds are combined.

Text variables are created by drawing a text box to contain them, just like in QuarkXPress. In order to match the exact placement of each element to the designer's layout in QuarkXPress, it's necessary to write down each element's X and Y coordinates, along with the width and height of each element. This is a serious hit to productivity and requires a lot of time to duplicate a designer's layout in Private-I. We expect this to be improved.

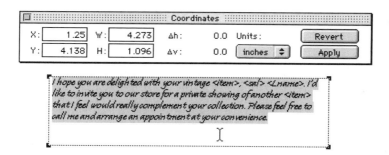

Even with exact text box coordinates and size, text flow will not be accurate as Private-I has no provisions for tracking and kerning. If tracking and/or kerning is applied to text in an original QuarkXPress document, lines may break in different places if the text is copied and pasted into Private-I, even with the same typeface and point size specified. Text pasted from QuarkXPress reverts to 12-point Geneva, so an additional step must be taken to apply the correct typeface and point size to the pasted text.

Original Text Box in QuarkXPress.

I hope you are delighted with your vintage <item>, <sal> <Lname>. I'd like to invite you to our store for a private showing of another <item> that I feel would really complement your collection. Please feel free to call me and arrange an appointment at your convenience.

The same Text Box replicated in Private-I.
Notice the different line breaks.

Assigning text variables is a bit awkward. The user must type variable names and enclose these with guillemets, which are typed by pressing Option + \ (opening guillemet) and Shift + Option + \ (closing guillemet). As variable names are defined, they are added to the floating list of variables:

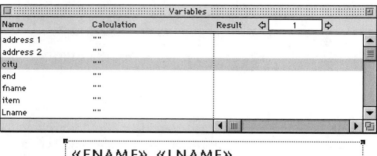

Variable picture boxes are drawn the same way: the box coordinates and size must be copied exactly from the original QuarkXPress document. The program's Step and Repeat command, unexpectedly hidden in the File menu, is not used to repeat page elements; it is used to define a step and repeat for the job on the Xeikon digital press.

Picture handling in Private-I is unforgiving: all images must be saved as EPS files, regardless of whether they are vector or raster images. TIFF images must be opened in Photoshop and saved as "Photoshop EPS" files—DCS EPS files are not supported. Variable images must be located in the same folder as the database file and the Private-I file.

Private-I ignores many Macintosh conventions: you cannot copy and paste elements within the program, although you can paste text into a Private-I text box from another program. When moving an object to another location, nearly all layout programs will move the object in a straight line if the shift key is held during the move.

Private-I does not allow this. There's also no easy way to scroll through a document without using the scroll bars; many layout and illustration programs will pan and scroll if the user holds down the option or spacebar key.

To assign the database's fields to the variables just defined in the Private-I document, the database must be specified by choosing Database->Open. Private-I opens the database and presents all of the field names along with the contents of the first record in a Fields palette.

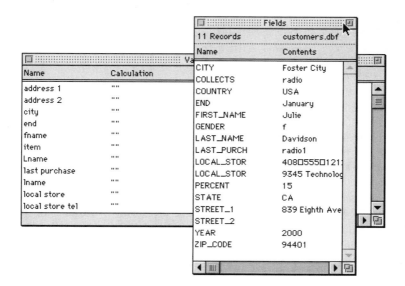

You will notice that the long fields LOCAL_STORE and LOCAL_STORE_TEL have been truncated. To fix this limitation in the native DBF file format that Private-I uses, we went back into FileMaker Pro, shortened these field names, then re-export the database to a new DBF file which we opened in Private-I:

local store	STORE	STATE	CA
local store tel	STORE_TEL	STORE	9345 Technolo
new item	" "	STORE_TEL	4080555012１
percent	PERCENT	STREET_1	839 Eighth Ave

Assigning a field to a variable is a simple matter of dragging the field to the variable desired. It's a little confusing, though, because fields are listed in the order as they appear in the database, but variables are listed alphabetically. Drag a field name over the corresponding variable name, and the field name will appear under the "Calculation" column of the variable palette:

Lname	LAST_NAME	LAST_NAME	Davidson
last purchase	LAST_PURCH	LAST_PURCH	radio1
lname	LAST_NAME	PERCENT	15
local store	STORE	STATE	CA
local store tel	" "	STORE	9345 Technolo
new item	" "	STORE_TEL	4080555012１
percent	PERCENT	STREET_1	839 Eighth Ave
sal	" "	STREET_2	
salesrep	" "	YEAR	2000

The "Calculation" column is a hint of some of the things that Private-I can do with imported data; in fact, Private-I possesses the most complete set of data manipulation tools of all the programs profiled.

To create the salutation, a calculation must be performed on the GENDER field. Double-clicking the "sal" (salutation) variable in the variable data palette produces the calculation dialog. Here, the salutation is determined by creating a conditional statement with Private-I's IF operator:

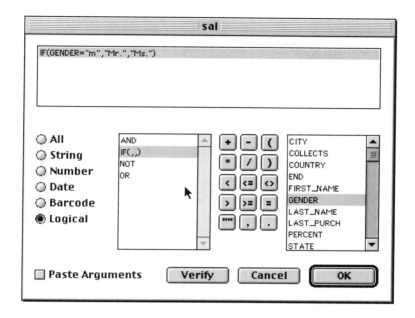

Operators in Private-I use a sort of shorthand for their calculations. In this case, the IF operator takes the contents of the GENDER field as its first input value, and uses the second input value, "Mr." as the text to be returned if GENDER = "m"; otherwise, "Ms." is returned to the variable and then to the variable document during processing.

We'll use Private-I's conditionals to define the contents of the picture boxes and of any other undefined text variables.

To define the sales representative, we'll select Lev as the US representative, and Antoine as the international representative. The results go into the document under the sales rep's photo. Results of Private-I calculations are always shown in the variables palette.

Using a calculation to determine the image to be placed alongside the customer's last purchase can be done, but it requires a series of nested IF conditionals; a single IF conditional is shown here:

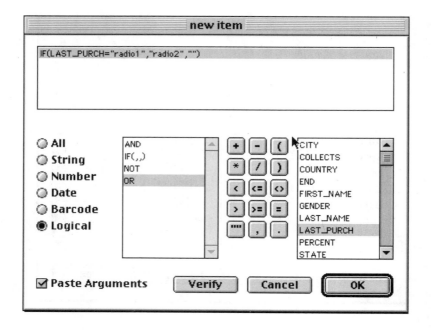

This calculation takes the value of the LAST_PURCH field and simply substitutes another image in place of the image specified in the LAST_PURCH field.

With Private-I's string-handling features, a calculation can be designed that would return the numeric values at the end of an image filename (for instance, it would return a "9" if the LAST_PURCH field contained "radio9") and replace the number at the end of the filename with a new one within a specified range.

Image substitution based on database data is a key attribute of variable data printing.

A sample card is shown on the opposite page:

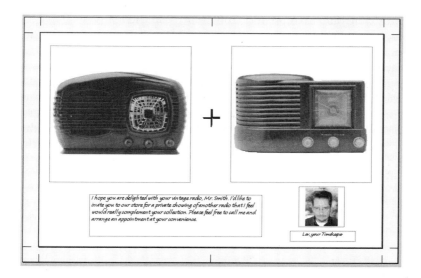

Private-I allows the placement of fold lines and crop marks, and lets users specify the number of step and repeats on the press sheet, and document printing order.

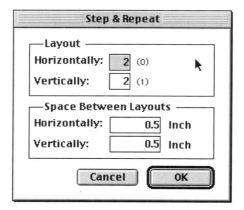

Summary

Private-I/PrintShop Mail presents a unique approach to the production of variable documents, and it is a good choice for applications requiring rigorous database manipulations in the production stage.

Pro: Strong data manipulation tools, fairly easy to learn, available for Macintosh, Windows 95, and Windows NT. *Con:* Static elements cannot be edited within the program, program interface is at odds with Macintosh conventions, only works with EPS files, limited typesetting controls, cannot reference variable images outside of the database folder, dimensions and coordinates of variable elements from designer-supplied Quark or PageMaker pages must be noted and applied to variable elements created in Private-I, line breaks may differ from those in the original page layout, calculations can be lengthy and difficult to interpret, requires a hardware key for printing to Xeikon presses, expensive for unlimited use.

PrintShop Mail and Private-I Print are sold according to how many "prints" the user wants to buy: 25,000 prints, $395; 200,000 prints, $1,395; unlimited prints, $3,995.

Digital Works' Digital VIP
Digital VIP is completely different from any other variable printing application or system. It is a Web-based client-server application and only requires a Java-capable Web browser and a reasonably fast Internet connection for operation on the client's computer.

> **What is Java?** *Java is a programming language invented by Sun Microsystems that is designed to be independent of any particular operating system or computer type. The actual Java code that a programmer writes is compiled to "pseudocode," an interim code state that maintains operating system and platform independence, unlike, for example, a C++ program that is compiled to operating system and platform-dependent machine code. To execute Java pseudocode, an interpreter must be written for each operating system and computer platform. The interpreter is compiled machine code, and it exists to translate Java pseudocode into executable machine code for a particular operating system or hardware platform, such as Windows NT running on DEC Alpha hardware, or Linux running on PowerPC hardware.*
>
> *The model for Java is descended from the unglamorous UCSD p-System invented in the late 1970s at the University of California at San Diego.*
>
> *Java is currently available for Windows 95, 98, and*

NT; MacOS 7, 8, and 8.5; Linux, SunOS, and other implementations of Unix.

Digital VIP started as an in-house program for Minneapolis-based Digital Marketing, Inc. With some heavy programming efforts, the product was commercially launched by Digital Works of Florida. It is sold as a complete package to any print shop that wants to get into variable printing but might lack the personnel and expertise to work with some of the programs already reviewed.

For $25,000, a print shop with a digital press obtains a Web site operated by Digital Marketing, Inc., extensive sales and operator training, and two days of customer sales calls with a Digital Works sales expert. When a customer builds a variable job with Digital VIP, the results are converted to a PostScript file which is then sent to the subscribing print shop through a fast Internet connection. This file can then be fed to the RIP driving the digital press. Each record processed by Digital VIP and sent to the shop is charged 3.5¢, and a monthly bill is mailed to the print shop for these charges.

Currently, Digital VIP only operates with Xerox DocuTech black-and-white digital presses. Printing black on preprinted four-color document shells is the most common use, though entirely variable designs can be used as well. Digital Works anticipates full support of digital color presses by 2000.

Customers who use the system upload their own fonts, ASCII databases, images, and EPS page layouts that are stored on the server. Any page layout that can be saved as EPS can be used with Digital VIP. Images can be TIFF or EPS. Once the customer database is loaded on the server, additional records can be added online without having to send a revised database to the server. The server offers the ability to select certain records of the database with simple filters, such as "select all records where 'city' = 'Fargo'." Complex data manipulation is not available, so the database should be provided with all required information.

Typefaces are PostScript Type 1 only; TrueType is not supported. Digital Works owns the Adobe Type Library, so customers do not need to include font files with the job unless the fonts are not Adobe's, in which case they must be included with the job.

If the customer doesn't use the services of a graphic designer, there are several "canned" templates and typefaces available for use.

This is a very flexible and above all simple means of getting a variable printing job from the customer to the printer. The customer need not purchase or learn any new software, and all of the components of the job are stored on a fault-tolerant server that the customer connects to remotely. If a customer's computer crashes or is for some reason disconnected from the server, the session will resume at the point where the interruption occurred.

For printers, the only thing coming to them will be an error-free PostScript file that requires a minimum of intervention other than loading preprinted shells into a DocuTech.

A Digital VIP job starts with the customer sending all required files to the print shop's Digital VIP Eeb server, either electronically or on disk. Once all the files are loaded, the user starts up a Web browser, enters a username and password, and can begin building a variable print job interactively.

All screen images used here are of the pre-release version of VIP. Our Old Time Company project was not submitted to Digital Works and the data used in the examples was supplied as is. This image shows the initial home page of a hypothetical print shop's VIP server.

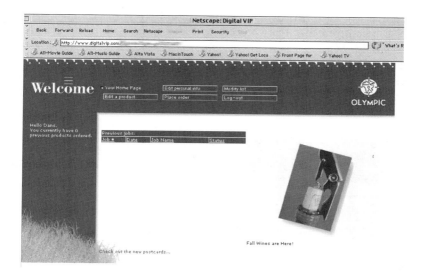

The first step is to select the list to be used for the particular job. The entire list is presented, and the user can accept it as is or create a filter for record selection. Here, filters to select all addresses with a specified city name in them has been applied and the search results have been saved.

The second step is to select and edit a "product," which is the desired page layout such as a postcard or a four-page newsletter that can be printed on a tabloid-sized sheet. If the job uses preprinted color shells, the product file is the same file used to generate the films or plates of the shell.

Here, a postcard layout has been specified to create a mailer for a local restaurant that has variable text and black-and-white images. Text assignment is based on variable selection fields. It is shown as a template for variable printing. Each of the small check-boxes to the left of the template is a step in the process that must be completed before the finished layout can be accepted. In these steps, the user specifies particular elements of the job.

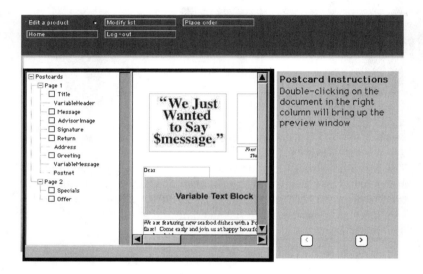

To set text or images for the variable fields, the customer clicks on each item with a checkbox next to it. Here, the message that is to go below a photo of a restaurant manager can be specified as selection fields in the database.

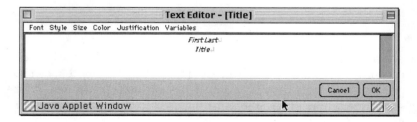

A manager photo is chosen from three provided images.

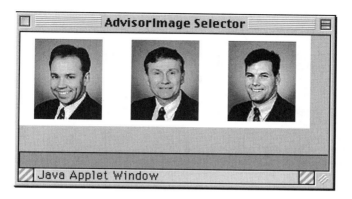

The text of a message is specified next. This can be easily modified and as the window shows, typefaces, font size, style, justification, and other typographical specs can be assigned. The "Variables" menu will insert any available variables into the text, which is otherwise static.

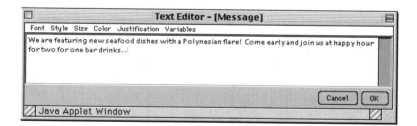

As each step is completed, a tick mark is shown in the checkbox, signaling that the step was completed. The next page is similarly set up to the customer's satisfaction.

Now a preview of the card, showing all of the static elements, can be seen by double-clicking the current page in the column at the left of the template. Here's the front of the card:

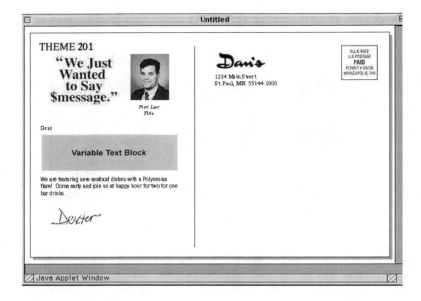

The back of the card contains a facsimile of the color images that have already been printed on an offset press.

The customer saves this new layout. All of the pieces are in place, so the next step is to place an order with the print shop, using the selected list and template. After clicking the "Place Order" button on the main page, the customer selects the desired product:

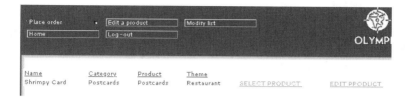

Then the "Chaska" list is selected, and the layout and list are displayed in a preview window. The customer can proof each piece on screen by clicking any of the variable records in the list.

To soft-proof the cards on screen, the customer double-clicks the page number of the template.

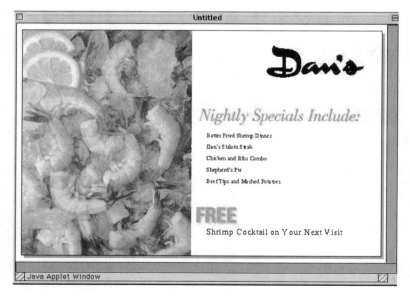

To place the order, the customer completes a form with final instructions regarding paper stock, shipping, and overages:

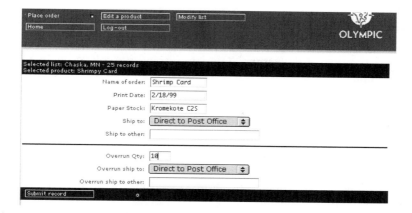

After confirmation, the server then processes each variable piece and builds a print-ready file for the entire job, along with an electronic job ticket, electronic purchase order, and detailed instructions. A checklist consisting of variables for each piece is included so the printer can verify that each item was printed successfully. The printer is billed 3.5¢ for each piece, which can be added to the markup on the per-piece rate charged to the customer.

Summary
Digital VIP is, so far, the simplest and most accessible variable printing application available. Customers will find it easy to create their own variable products without having to buy, install, and, above all, learn any new applications. They can use Windows, Macintosh or Unix platforms. Professional graphic designers can create any type of artwork for the system and export it to EPS for use as a template or for the basis of offset printed four-color shells.

Pro: No software requirements other than a Java-capable Web browser, low learning curve, secure password protection, server data redundancy allows resumption of a session after a connection loss or client system crash, no special press operator training. *Con:* Limited typographical controls, no control over kerning, tracking, H&Js, and other advanced typographical features, currently only supports black-and-white printing, additional expense for preprinted color shells may dissuade some customers, support for static image caching for the upcoming color version of the system is unknown.

Other variable solutions not profiled

Xerox VIPP

Xerox has turned its former XGF data format into a RIP-level variable-data system called VIPP (Variable Information PostScript Printware), a set of PostScript macros that operate with most RIPs used with Xerox DocuColor presses and black-and-white high-speed printers. This method essentially creates an ASCII workflow from client to RIP, resulting in much faster sending and processing times. This lets the print engine run at full speed, because the graphic-intensive portions of a job are processed beforehand and the variable portions of the job are small, quickly processed PostScript macros. The RIP picks up the rasterized images and merges them with the variable data. This differs greatly from all of the QuarkXPress-based applications and is not constrained by the fact that QuarkXPress was never intended to be used for variable printing, even with add-on XTensions. It is a simple, elegant solution that promises greatly increased throughput for a digital press.

In the VIPP workflow, graphic elements can be created in any application that exports PostScript; the PostScript files are sent to the RIP, rasterized, and saved. Then the Database Master (DBM) is created, which defines specifics such as page size, typefaces, colors, and the location of static elements, which are already rasterized, and of variable elements. The DBM is a PostScript file that can be generated by an application or by a skilled programmer. Currently, Meadows' DataMerge offers this capability in conjunction with QuarkXPress.

The ASCII database must be converted to a PostScript database file (DBF)—essentially, an ASCII file with PostScript headers and a specified field delimiter. The VIPP data file format follows this model:

```
%!PS-Adobe-2.0
%%Creator: Program X [can be any value]
%%Title: [filename].DBF
%%Orientation: Portrait/Landscape
(|) SETDBSEP [defines the field delimiter]
500 SETBUFSIZE
XGF ([filename.DBM]) SETJDT [specifies the job master]
FIELD1|FIELD2| . . . |FIELDn [fieldname declarations]
Ms.|Veronica|Mushpie|25 Berkeley Road|Rochester|
NY|14607|716-555-1212| . . . |FIELDn [variable data]. . .
%%EOF
```

This format would not be too hard to create from a tab-delimited ASCII database; most word processing programs can be set up to perform this task with macros. DataMerge creates the DBF file automatically, and a competent MIS analyst could certainly create a program that generates a PostScript DBF-formatted file from a corporate database.

VIPP offers the ability to generate charts and other business graphics from PostScript instructions in the DBM file. A macro that draws a 3D pie chart using values found in the DBF file looks like this:

```
1178 592 MOVETO [sets the starting position]
/Minion-Regular 10 SETFONT [specifies font and size]
[()VALUE1()VALUE2(). . . VALUEn] [variables in DBF]
50 [/SpotSize 0 /SpotOffset -9.75 /3D true /SliceBurst
/LabelDashColor White /ColorTable [XLGREEN LRED LGREEN
RED]] DRAWPIE [defines chart type and colors used]
```

These charts are generated as the job is processed. The algorithm that creates a pie chart, among others, takes as input, values present in the DBF file and quickly generates a chart. Other chart types can be created by a programmer.

Once all the files are stored on the RIP, the job can be printed. One can see from these examples that a fast RIP can chew through such simple PostScript code very quickly. A minor drawback to VIPP is the PostScript coding requirement for the DBM file—there's currently only one application that can create this for the user (DataMerge) and any charts present in the layout must be coded by a programmer. Until other applications support VIPP, the user must be comfortable with understanding and writing PostScript code.

> *"I'm so tired of telemarketers calling for and getting mail addressed to David Brandy, Brady, Browly, Broudie, Browdie, Browdy, Broody, Browley, Brooley, Brumly, Brownie, Groudy, Grody (to the max!), Grouty, and worse. If you want to sell me something, you should at least try to spell my name right."*
> *— David "rhymes with Bowie" Broudy, commiserating with Mr Majanlahti on their mutually unpronounceable surnames.*

EFI's Fiery FreeForm

Fiery FreeForm is a server-based approach that works through a PostScript printer driver. According to EFI, this allows the use of any application to create both a static background and variable information. For example, a designer can create a static layout in FreeHand and send it to the RIP as a static form by specifying that it is a "master" page in the application's Print options.

A marketing manager can then create a layout in nearly any application, as long as the variable data correctly overlays the static form, then can open the application's Print dialog and specify the desired master page, then sends the variable data stream. The Fiery RIP will treat the job as a forms-cached process.

As with Private-I and PrintShop Mail, static and variable text cannot be commingled. Creating a layout to exactly match the master page can be difficult especially in database and word processing applications that lack precision image and text controls found in page layout software.

However, the ability to print the overlying variable data from a sophisticated database management application like Filemaker Pro adds quite a bit of flexibility to the variable elements that can be printed, since FileMaker supports numerous types of graphics and can create charts based upon database fields.

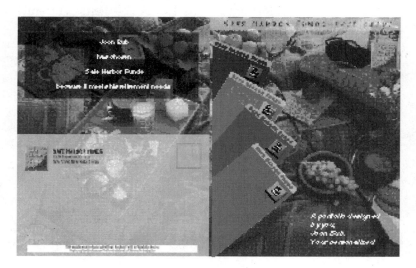

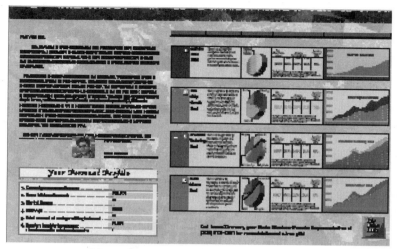

Master Page overlaid with FileMaker Pro data.

The example files from EFI show a complex FileMaker database with variable charts and objects that are overlaid on a QuarkXPress master page (as shown above) and the results are quite impressive.

To summarize the three steps used by Fiery FreeForm:

Master data
Fixed images common to every page. Only needs to process once, saving time.

Variable Data
Text, graphics or images that change per page. Master Data (background) has already been processed.

Final Document
Variable data overlays the master data image.

On the next page is the master page that has all the static images.

Master Page layout from QuarkXPress.

Indigo Yours Truly

Yours Truly is a multi-application system developed solely for use with the Indigo family of digital presses, including the sheetfed E-Print, TurboStream, and UltraStream, the webfed Omnius packaging press, and the sheetfed Omnius Card Press which is designed for printing plastic or paper cards such as phone cards and sports cards.

Yours Truly requires QuarkXPress and a Macintosh computer. It is included with all Indigo presses along with page imposition, variable card layout, and high-fidelity six-color process printing tools.

The system uses a number of intermediate job file formats collectively referred to as ILYT. It allows minor changes to be made on the Indigo RIP without recreating the entire PostScript file from a Macintosh. After the page template and variable data fields are defined, Yours Truly creates these ILYT files:

- the Job file—contains the page geometry, the number of color separations (up to six), number of copies, and page placement and assignment information.
- the Page file—defines the location and dimensions of each page on a press sheet, and contains the characteristics of each variable data "channel" on that page. A Page file is created for each separate page of a job.
- the PR variable data file—specifies all of the variable elements to be printed with a job, linked to personalization channels in the Page file.
- the Element file—contains all of the variable elements to be printed with a specific page. One Element file is created for each page.

Variable pages must be imposed on the client machine using the Yours Truly-Layout application in QuarkXPress. Variable containers on a page are defined with a "personalization box" drawn in Quark-XPress, and further modified with choices from the Yours Truly modification menus that are added to the QuarkXPress Item->Modify menu, which allow adjustment of the variable container's origin, size, color separations, and content type (text or image). From this modification menu, a new QuarkXPress page is created that is exactly the size of the specified variable container.

Variable data files in Yours Truly are either QuarkXPress pages or plain PostScript files. If a QuarkXPress page is specified, it must be populated with variable data for each variable page in the entire job. For example, for each finished printed item in the job, there must be a corresponding QuarkXPress page containing all of the variable images and text for that job. These pages can all be in the same QuarkXpress file. This is a labor-intensive process, so Indigo provides Yours Truly-Link, which serves as a pipeline between a database and a variable page layout in QuarkXPress.

Yours Truly can use live Filemaker Pro databases or plain ASCII tab-delimited database files. Yours Truly-Link helps automate the production of the QuarkXPress variable page file described above by inserting the required text and images into the variable page file. This program requires that all images are identified by name in a database field. There is no means of creating conditional rules.

The Yours Truly-Card utility adds the ability to step-and-repeat multiple static background images onto a single press sheet, and variable data is applied afterwards using the methods available in the Yours Truly-Link program.

The Indigo Yours Truly suite of utilities represents a rather different approach to building variable documents, but in the end it seems no more difficult than the other applications. It does force the user to work within an imposition rather than reader spreads, but an experienced operator should find this to be an asset rather than a liability.

Bitstream PageFlex

PageFlex is a client/server application that runs under Windows NT only. It consists of three components: Producer, Server, and Designer. Producer collects and manages all files used in a variable print job, and is used to define the variable content of a job template. The PageFlex Server is the actual production component—it uses input from PageFlex Producer to populate variable templates, created in PageFlex Designer, with data based on rules applied to customer profiles. Page layouts are fully dynamic, making PageFlex one of the few solutions with this ability, and content containers can grow or shrink to accommodate the requirements of the data being merged into the document template. The Server creates a PostScript stream, merges high-resolution pre-rasterized images using an OPI process, and sends the job to a digital press.

PageFlex Designer is the tool used to build a PageFlex document template. It uses PDF files generated from documents created in QuarkXPress, Pagemaker, Ventura , or any other application that can generate a PDF file. PageFlex Designer is the only current application that effectively uses the PDF file format to any extent for variable printing. This PDF file can be used as the foundation of a PageFlex template, where the user defines the containers for text and images to be used in the layout. PageFlex templates are comprised of static data and variable containers, which can be modified with "springs" and "struts," Bitstream-ese for mechanisms in the template that can expand, contract, or reposition a container based on layout rules defined within the template.

Bitstream PageFlex jobs can be saved as XML, HTML, and PDF files instead of being printed. PageFlex's internal format is based on the

XML markup language, which makes for relatively easy information interchange with other XML applications, and the product is compatible with ODBC-compliant databases such as Oracle and Microsoft's SQL Server.

Currently, the IBM InfoColor 70 and 100 are the only presses that use the PageFlex architecture; Bitstream is planning to open the product to other vendors' press engines.

Barco Graphics VIP Designer
Barco offer several products that complement the FastRIP/X RIP and the PrintStreamer page buffer sold with Xeikon digital presses. As with the Bitstream products, Barco's VIPline offers dynamic page layout with text reflow, field containers in any shape, overlapping fields, dynamic page composition directed by the position and size of page objects, and offers variable objects within other variable objects directed by conditional rules.

The system can accommodate page templates created in any desktop package as long as they can be saved as PostScript files, and includes a QuarkXPress XTension that helps ease the process of creating a template. The template and variable elements are rendered into Barco's proprietary VIPScript which is interpreted by the VIPBinder software, which generates the actual variable content. Master and variable elements are rasterized on the FastRIP/X and stored on the PrintStreamer page buffer. From there, these elements are combined into a variable page and sent to the Xeikon press.

The FastRIP/X is based on a Compaq/DEC Alpha AXP computer system, a 64-bit RISC (Reduced Instruction Set Computer) system.

> *What is RISC?* A computer processing unit that is designed with as few instructions as possible in order to streamline the system's throughput is known as a RISC (Reduced Instruction Set Computer) processor, such as the DEC Alpha and Motorola/IBM PowerPC (used in Power Macintosh systems) processors, or "chips." A processor that uses a large number of instructions, such as the Intel Pentium, are referred to as CISC (Complex Instruction Set Computer) and requires more system overhead, is less efficient in operation, and requires that

the system be operated at a higher speed in order to achieve the performance level of a RISC processor.

The Barco RIP offers two screening methods—traditional or *AM* (Amplitude Modulated) screening, and *FM* (Frequency Modulated) screening. Barco calls the AM screening system "Classic Screening" and named the FM screening system "Monet Screening." (We anxiously await the release of Wassily Kandinsky, Joan Miró, Georgia O'Keeffe, and Edward Hopper Screening.)

> **What's the difference between AM and FM Screening?** *The two methods differ in the placement of halftone dots. AM screening varies the size of the halftone dots to produce gradations; FM screening varies the number of dots in a given area to produce gradations. Advantages to FM screening include the lessening of the "dottiness" sometimes present in AM screening, the elimination of screen angles, which are required in AM screening, finer detail in continuous-tone image reproductions, better rendering of light or pastel colors, more tolerance for press misregistration (within reason), and the technique is effective with lower image resolutions unlike AM screening. Disadvantages are increased dot gain in some cases, darkening of midtone and shadow areas in other cases, increased difficulty in off-press proofing, and a grainy appearance in areas of flat tints and in the highlight areas of image reproductions. Both methods can be combined to produce hybrid screening, although the Barco system does not support this.*

Barco is the only vendor that offers the option of FM screening for digital presses. Careful testing and image evaluation should be performed to determine the optimum image preparation process for FM screening. An image preparation method for AM screening can't be used to produce images for FM screening without this testing and evaluation, as the images will appear decidedly different if FM screening is used without proper preparation for it.

The big advantage to Barco's "Monet" FM screening with a digital press, specifically the Xeikon press, is that printer spots can be imaged at 1 bit per spot while achieving a similar level of image reproduction quality that is obtained when running the Xeikon press at 2, 3, or 4 bits per printer spot. This lets the RIP drive the press at a faster rate since less data is required to be sent to the press from the RIP when using 1 bit per printer spot.

The Barco RIP also offers an automatic process for eliminating banding in vignettes and gradients. The RIP recognizes vignettes present in incoming PostScript data and converts them to continuous-tone images, then adds a bit of "noise" to the image to remove the appearance of vignette banding without reducing the image quality. This is a common prepress technique used in Photoshop blends and gradients to help eliminate banding.

The FastRIP/X also uses a dual-channel interface—it can accept PostScript data streams, and it also accepts Barco's proprietary imaging format, which includes the VIP products and is the format sent to the RIP from the VIPBinder system. The RIP also performs trapping internally, a nice feature but something not terribly critical in many digital printing systems.

VIPBinder is a server-based application that pulls together all of the pieces of a variable job, using data and rules specified in the VIPScript file. Completed jobs can be stored on the server and regenerated with a new or changed database as needed.

The PageStreamer was originally intended to serve as a collation buffer, allowing jobs to be printed in sequential page order no matter how many copies were required. IBM's Collator product for the InfoColor press operates on the same principle: an enormous bank of hard disk drives is used to store pages that have been rasterized, up to 2,000 (separated) color pages. Barco uses the PrintStreamer buffer to store variable pages as well as collated sets of pages. However, complex or large jobs can empty the PageStreamer before new data is ready to be sent to the buffer, which means the press will be idle until another set of pages has been RIPped and sent to the buffer.

The PageStreamer also offers imposition of rasterized pages, which is a very important feature. Rasterized pages, including variable pages, can be imposed on the PrintStreamer without the worry of breaking variable data links because the pages and variable elements are already rasterized and merged at print time. Pages and elements are compressed using a *lossless* image compression algorithm when they are received from the RIP, and decompressed on-the-fly when they are sent to the press.

> *What's lossless compression? There are two types of compression used with bitmapped images, whether they are images scanned from a photograph or rasterized pages from a RIP. Lossless compression, typically based on the LZW (the initials of the developers: Lempel-Ziv and Welch) compression scheme, is a means of compressing an image without throwing away any information; when the image is decompressed, it is exactly the same as it was before compression.*
>
> *"Lossy" compression, typified by the common JPEG format, discards data in order to achieve greater magnitudes of compression than is possible with LZW or other lossless compression methods. Images that are compressed with JPEG encoding can be subject to defects known as compression artifacts, which are areas in the image that had data discarded, and the decompression method has tried to interpolate the missing data by examining adjacent areas and attempting to recreate the missing data.*
>
> *For this reason, the JPEG format is mostly unsuitable for use in high-quality image reproduction, although at lower compression levels the method usually does not discard enough data to make a noticeable difference in the image quality. But when a lower compression level is used, the image isn't compressed much more than it would be using LZW compression, so there's no real impetus behind using JPEG for the graphic arts. It remains a suitable compression scheme for on-screen graphics such as those used on Web pages, but used carelessly it can destroy an image's reproducibility in print.*

The VIP Designer application is a QuarkXPress XTension that implements Barco's VIPScript environment into XPress and simplifies the production of variable print jobs. VIP Designer offers basic features, supporting text on curves, text within any text box shape defined in QuarkXPress, placement of variable images, a Filemaker Pro interface, record filtering, and automatic splitting of a large database into a number of smaller jobs, which is sensible considering the limitations of the PageStreamer (which are applicable to every other front-end system used to drive Xeikon press engines). It also supports Apple Events, which allows integration with other Apple Events-aware programs such as charting or database applications. VIP Designer does not offer rules-based conditional printing.

Barco's VIPline is a high-end page layout system for generating variable data pages. It offers most of the features of VIP Designer except for the Apple-specific ones, since it runs under Windows NT. VIPline takes PostScript files as input from any PostScript-based page layout or illustration applications. VIPline supports dynamic page layout, as does the Bitstream PageFlex system, which allows variable elements such as text and image boxes to expand or contract as needed, or based upon a set of rules constructed by the user. VIPline offers rule-based creation of dynamic layouts that can vary according to the contents of a database record, giving it a significant edge over most QuarkXPress-based variable printing systems.

Both VIPline and VIP Designer generate VIPScript files, an ASCII data stream that represents the variable content, similar in concept to the Xerox VIPP system, except that VIPScript is a proprietary system whereas VIPP is a PostScript-based system. VIPScript creates a VVD (VIP Variable Data) file that contains all variable text extracted from a database, the names of any image files to be used, and the master or static page upon which the layout is based.

The VIPline system is a graphical VIPScript editing system that takes PostScript as the basis for input and generates VIPScript from this information. VIPScript is sent to the VIPBinder server, where VIPScript files and PostScript pages and page elements are pre-processed before being sent to the RIP. Since VIPScript is an open specification and is ASCII-based, it should be possible for any developer to create extensions to QuarkXPress, Adobe InDesign, and other page layout and illustration applications that can generate VIPScript files for the Barco system.

Varis Corp. VariScript

Varis Corp. recently announced a cooperative effort with Xeikon to produce what may be the most advanced variable printing system yet. The system incorporates a Xeikon DCP/32 or DCP/50 digital press with a Varis digital front end, replacing the Barco or Xeikon RIP usually sold with Xeikon presses. The Varis system, which is called VariScript, has been used with great success in the transaction printing market, which uses high-speed, low-resolution black-and-white printers to generate bills, statements, and and other utility-level documents, supporting full variability at speeds of up to 1,000 pages per minute.

The VariScript RIP can use data from any application and can be configured to pull database records, text, and images from any computer on its network—it can also connect to ODBC-compliant databases like Oracle and SQL systems. It uses no spooler and is fast enough to drive a digital press at its top-rated speed while processing a variable job. Some RIPs cannot print while processing variable jobs, leaving the press idle. The system is composed of the High-volume Page Output (HPO) controller, a RIP based on three fast RISC processors that incorporates custom hardware rather than software to perform specific functions much more rapidly than a software-based system can, and it includes dedicated hardware for halftone screening and color management.

The VariScript software runs directly on the HPO. The HPO can process files pulled over a local- or wide-area network from Macintosh, Windows, Unix, and other operating systems and does not depend on a specific application such as QuarkXPress, and it supports the use of two-byte fonts like those used in Japanese and Russian. Any application that can write a PostScript file can be used with VariScript. It is database-driven, meaning that the data is processed against a set of rules which define one or more layouts.

These rules are simple text-based conditionals. The page layouts are user-designed PostScript or PDF pages with "prototypes" (placeholders) in position for variable text and images. VariScript gathers all pages and graphic elements, disassembles them into PostScript graphic states, then reads the database and rules, applies the rules to the objects, selects the objects to be printed and sends the composed page to the digital press.

The HPO has the computing power to "RIP on-the-fly," or generate pages while others are being printed, by generating bands of raster data and sending each band to the press immediately after processing. No spooling system or disk cache is required, and last-minute changes can be made without re-processing an entire job.

The VariScript software that resides on the HPO performs file pre-flighting of incoming jobs and can operate in simulation mode for proofing purposes. VariScript can also be run on a Sun computer for proofing or for work that doesn't require the processing speed of the HPO. VariScript generates a job ticket for each run that contains complete job instructions up through binding and finishing. It can generate many types of barcodes without the use of special PostScript barcode fonts. The VariScript workflow starts with the creation of a page template using any page layout or illustration software that can export a PostScript file. Variable data is identified several ways—as a database field, a text field, or an image field.

Database fields have direct links to specific fields in a database and are enclosed in «guillemets»; text fields are not linked to database fields, but any text string specified in the job ticket can be substituted according to any rules attached to that field. Image fields accept TIFF files based on rules, the contents of a particular database field, or images can be stored directly in an image database and be swapped into the page template directly. There can be many page templates used in a particular job, and different templates can be substituted to match a specific rule, for example "use template XYZ.ps if field 'pet' = 'cat'."

A VariScript electronic job ticket contains all of the conditional rules used in a job and provides the location of all components used in the job, such as the network addresses of servers that hold the images and the databases, and holds information about a specific print engine, its resolution, web width, color, and duplexing capabilities. All variable data fields used in the job are identified with their location and links to any databases. The job ticket can also contain instructions pertaining to copy fitting, such as adjusting font size to fit a field container.

Once the job ticket arrives at the HPO, the system identifies all components needed to produce the job and starts to pull files from the servers specified in the job ticket. Using other special instructions in the job ticket, the HPO assembles pages, renders them into bitmaps, and sends these to the print engine.

VariScript offers the most complete audit and verification features currently available on digital color presses—its system scans printed pieces as they are printed with a barcode reader or a CCD camera. Verification can be accomplished by page scanning or by reading barcodes within the document or printed on a trim area. It incorporates connectivity to post-press equipment such as folders and binding machinery, and monitors each piece through the entire production process. A report is generated that can be sent to any system on the network which contains the status of a current job; any spoiled jobs can be rescheduled and reprinted.

VariScript supports the RS-485 industrial local network interface which can be used to connect a variety of finishing equipment and roll-handling systems from Pitney Bowes, C. P. Bourg, Böwe-Systec, Stralfors, and others. The HPO can also drive a Zebra label printer through an RS-232 serial port for automatic application of box labels.

The Varis/Xeikon partnership bodes well for the variable printing industry and promises to provide the fastest, most accurate variable printing system available, but the system's very high cost, just under $700,000 including a 20-inch-wide Xeikon DCP50/D press, might be a bit of a sticking point to all but the most performance-driven users. The base price of the same press, with the Barco PrintStreamer RIP, sells for $560,000. As of this writing, the system is not available, so it remains to be seen if the promise of the VariScript system will work as well for high-resolution color variable printing as it currently does for low-resolution black-and-white transaction printing.

According to Forrest Gauthier, President of Varis Corporation, VariScript was developed with process color support from the beginning, and the system will require only minor improvements for use with Xeikon engines. Gauthier expects the Xeikon/VariScript system will be available by the second quarter of 1999. The system can drive the press at full speed while processing jobs, and it may well provide a better return on investment than most other RIP/Xeikon combos, which except for Xerox's VIPP, cannot usually RIP and print at the same time.

PDF and variable printing
With the current high level of buzz about PDF in the printing industry, it might be a bit of a surprise to learn that, as far as variable print-

ing is concerned, PDF is still a relatively unimportant player. There is no mechanism in the PDF file specification that supports the population of a template with variable data. This may be remedied in the upcoming release of Adobe Acrobat 4.0, which will be the debut of the next generation of the PDF specification (currently 1.2, soon to be 1.3), but details about any new features in the specification are sketchy and unreliable.

Adobe's new Extreme architecture promises greatly enhanced support for variable printing with PDF, and Adobe's replacement for PageMaker, code-named "K2," now called InDesign, uses PDF as its native file format. InDesign promises a level of extensibility past what is already available with QuarkXPress and XTensions or plugins, since the entire application is based upon modules. Features are added to InDesign by simply plugging in a plug-in. A variable printing module for InDesign will certainly be at the top of most current vendors' lists of applications to support.

The only use for PDF in variable printing currently is as a basis for a template, as used in Bitstream's PageFlex, or as a master form with EFI's FreeForm, where a PDF page can be sent to a RIP as a static master page over which variable data can be overlaid. Of course, a PDF file can also be exported to an EPS file, which can be used in just about any application. The potential for PDF to impact variable printing in a big way is there; Acrobat Exchange already supports variable text fields in electronic forms, which can be exported out to a data file, but it isn't capable of accepting variable images or swapping in variable text from a file.

Future support for variable printing of text and images with Acrobat Exchange is anticipated but not promised. However, PDF forms are still a great way to collect information, whether used on a Web site or as an electronic form that can be downloaded or delivered on a CD-ROM, and they're a lot more tidy than a form-based HTML page.

What's ahead?
Look for incremental improvements in press speeds and much greater improvements in processing speed over the short term. New technologies on the horizon like the joint-venture NexPress with a possible toner-based digital color system, and Scitex's Digital Printing subsidiary with its work on a high-speed, fully variable

color inkjet web "press." Both hint at possibly revolutionary techniques for putting variable images on paper or other substrates.

Kodak's former Diconix subsidiary actually had a working variable inkjet web press in operation in the early 1980s, but that product never emerged commercially. Diconix was sold to Scitex in 1993, and apparently the old Diconix prototype was kept around long enough for Scitex's engineers to use it for the basis of a modern version that prints in CMYK and also images both sides of the web.

Expect this unit, and the highly-secret NexPress (even here in Rochester, the US-based home of NexPress LLC, information about the system is impossible to obtain) and other startling new digital printing technologies to debut at the Drupa 2000 exhibition in Dusseldorf, Germany in May, 2000.

Innovations like MAN-Roland's DICO re-imageable gravure and lithographic presses could lead to, with sufficient computing horsepower and stable, quickly rewritable image carriers, the ultimate digital color press: a full-size variable-image web offset or gravure press putting genuine ink on paper (instead of toner) at potentially current web press speeds. Think personalized newspapers, magazines, books, and more for the same or slightly higher price as the mass-printed counterpart. This is, of course, a long way off, but current research is leading in that direction. Advances in finishing, auditing, and closed-loop monitoring systems must keep pace with press developments and in some cases must eclipse it in order to ensure that the right custom newspaper, for example, actually gets delivered to the right person.

Variable printing is a relatively new business and is currently the "value-added" champion of the entire printing industry. To be profitable, one must adjust to this new business as a marketing expert in addition to being a printing expert. Additional personnel with competencies in marketing, database management, and network skills will be required to operate a variable printing business, and in order to provide the most value-added services, additional equipment may be required such as finishing, packaging and mailing machinery along with the required labor. Look for variable printing applications to become less tied to QuarkXPress and more portable between the client and the output provider. Currently, it would be very difficult for the average end-user to walk into a commercial printer and hand over a disk with a layout, a database, and not much else. Significant preparation of these materials by specialized personnel will be required for some time until these applications are able to produce a press-ready data stream at the client's end of the process.

Internet-based technologies like Digital VIP and Moore's Message Master eliminate the requirement that the end-user purchase expensive, specialized software, at the expense of lower design standards. The ideal variable printing application will let the end user generate the entire job, merging all of the elements into a metafile that can be processed efficiently on most any type of variable printing system.

Standards must emerge that define intermediate metafile formats, efficient variable page element caching, RIP-on-the-fly systems, auditing and verification controls, and post-press finishing interfaces before variable printing can become just another service offered by nearly any printer. At the same time, the amount of value added will decline as the technology becomes more commonplace and less of a speciality. Providers of variable printing need to account for this eventuality in their long-range business plans.

What to look for in a variable printing application

Selecting a method for producing variable printing can be a difficult decision. Each one profiled here has strengths and weaknesses. Space considerations prevent the coverage of other variable printing applications; a summary of features and abilities of most currently available variable printing application can be found at the end of this chapter.

Much of the decision can be based on the type of organization that plans to use variable printing: a large organization with an in-house reprographics department might purchase or lease a digital color press for short-run and variable printing, which can be produced with easy access to corporate databases, directed by the project manager. All of the variable printing applications would be well suited to this type of operation. On the other hand, a commercial print shop would have little need for the data manipulation features in some of the applications, and depending on the type of equipment, could operate profitably with a relatively modest application like Personalizer X, as an example.

Print shops that employ a variable printing specialist can offer value-added services to customers who do not want to be bothered with setting up a variable print job, who send in only a layout, a set of rules if any, and an ASCII database. Shops that offer this level of service will have a definite competitive edge, but finding the right person to perform this task could require significant effort.

The following points are pertinent to the selection of a variable printing application:

- Ease of use—in many cases, the person generating the variable print job is probably not an experienced prepress technician but rather a marketing manager or a graphic designer. Users will balk at learning yet another application especially if it requires extensive and tedious study
- Training requirements—does the software vendor offer training, in the form of a live instructor or possibly a CD-ROM simulation? Most applications come with comprehensive documentation, but that may not be enough.
- Integration with current workflow—does the application require other software to do its work? Does it run under more than one operating system? Most of the current ones require QuarkXPress, and only run on a Macintosh computer. While most print shops use Macintosh computers, many corporations do not.
- Data manipulation abilities—Many users won't require this, but others will. It depends on the usefulness of the supplied database; an organization with a competent database administrator can generate a database with all of the required information and fields that won't require any further manipulation.
- Compatibility with any RIP-specific features—it makes sense to purchase the application offered by the vendor of a digital color press, or to purchase a third-party application that specifically supports the variable features of a particular RIP. A generic application won't be able to access the efficient forms-caching features present in all RIPs that drive digital presses.

The table on page 264 is a simple summary of some of the variable data construction programs.

It covers:

Supported applications and graphic formats
Most often QuarkXPress, but the variable data program may use a graphic format for more flexibility.

Variable text commingled with static text
This approach is a lot more flexible than the variable overlay approach.

Database connectivity
ASCII, DBF, or ODBC are three primary approaches.

Rules-based conditional statements
A key feature.

Record selection via filter
The ability to define which records are placed at which point in the document.

Barcode generation
The ability to automatically generate a barcode—you still require a barcode font in most cases.

Supports pre-processing of static elements, forms caching
This includes interpreting or rasterizing certain elements to reduce RIP processing.

Automatic copyfilling, dynamic containers
This allows the program to make text fit in a text box as required by the layout.

Supports any PostScript device
That is, the program is not linked to a specific RIP.

Output format
Usually PostScript, but there may be proprietary approaches.

Supports QuarkXPress 4
Not all QuarkXPress 4 features are supported by all programs.

Variable-Data Production Tools for Digital Color Presses

Company	Scitex	Agfa	Xeikon/Atlas	Indigo	Meadows Info	Vision's Edge	Varis	Xerox	Digital Works	EFI	Bitstream	Barco
Product	Darwin	Personalizer-X	Private-I, PrintShop Mail	Yours Truly	DataMerge Pro	Focus Gold	VariScript	VIPP	DigitalVIP	FreeForm	PageFlex	VIP
Supported Applications or Graphic Formats	QuarkXPress	QuarkXPress	Any EPS	QuarkXPress	QuarkXPress	QuarkXPress	Any EPS	Any	Web Browser with Java	Any	Any, also has Quark xtn	Any, also has Quark xtn
Platform	Macintosh	Macintosh	Macintosh Windows	Macintosh Windows	Macintosh Windows**	Macintosh	Any	Any	Any	Macintosh Windows	Any	Any
Variable Text commingled with Static Text	Yes	Yes	No	No	Yes	Yes	Yes	Yes	Yes	No	Yes	Yes
Database Connectivity	ASCII	ASCII	DBF	ASCII, FileMaker	ASCII	ASCII	ASCII, ODBC	User-defined PostScript db	ASCII	n/a	ASCII, ODBC	ASCII, ODBC
Rules-based conditional statements	Yes	No	Yes	Yes	No	Yes	Yes	No	No	No	Yes	Yes
Record selection via Filter	Yes	Yes	Yes	Yes	No	Yes	Yes	No	Yes	No	Yes	Yes
Supported Presses or RIPs	Xerox DocuColor 40, 70, 100	Agfa ChromaPress	PageStreamer, Splash,	Indigo E-Print, TurboStream, Omnius	Splash, EFI, Xerox VIPP,** HP 8500	Any, optional modules available	Xeikon DCP	DocuColor, DocuTech, other Xerox	not specific to any RIP	EFI	IBM InfoColor	Barco FastRIP/X
Page Substitution	Yes	No	No	No	Yes	Yes	Yes	No	No	No	Yes	Yes
Barcode Generation	No	Yes	Yes	No	Yes	Yes	Yes	No	No	No	Yes	Yes
Automatic Copyfitting, Dynamic containers	No	No	No	No	No	No	Yes	No	No	No	Yes	Yes
Supports pre-processing of static elements, forms caching	Yes, with Scitex RIP	Yes	Only on supported RIPs	Yes	Only on supported RIPs	Only on supported RIPs	Yes	Yes	No	EFI only	Yes	Yes
Supports any PostScript device	Yes	No	Yes	No	Yes	Yes	n/a	n/a	Yes	No	No	No
Graphic Input Formats	TIFF, EPS, QXP	TIFF, EPS	EPS	TIFF, EPS	TIFF, EPS QXP	TIFF, EPS	TIFF, EPS	TIFF, EPS	TIFF, EPS	n/a	TIFF, EPS PDF	TIFF, EPS
Output Format	PostScript, Scitex VPS	PostScript	PostScript	PostScript	PostScript	PostScript	n/a	n/a	PostScript	PostScript	XML, HTML, PostScript, PDF	VIPScript
Supports QuarkXPress 4	Yes*	Yes	Yes	Yes	No**	No**	n/a	n/a	n/a	Yes	Yes	Yes

* Text on curves only supported on DocuColor 40.   ** In development   n/a — not applicable

7

Variable Printing
Design Considerations

Graphic designers were the first group to widely adopt electronic layout systems, but many have been self-taught and unfortunately a number of them do not have production knowledge. There are an infinite number of ways to prepare document layouts for press, and an infinite number of ways of making a layout unprintable without applying a lot of time and expense. Issues peculiar to digital printing and especially variable printing are new and many designers have not had experience with the limitations of these systems. As with conventional printing, the first, critical step in starting a new job is talking with the printer who will be producing the job to determine what, if any, limitations exist with a particular digital press.

Some variable printing systems can use a PostScript file as the basis for a page template. This allows a designer to use the tools with which he or she is most comfortable: Corel Draw, Ventura Publisher, Adobe Illustrator, InDesign, and PageMaker, MacroMedia FreeHand (this *InterCapping* trend has got to stop!) and others can all be used if the system only requires a PostScript file to start the process. Other systems that rely upon a QuarkXPress XTension (Darwin, Personalizer-X, Focus Gold, DataMerge) restrict the designer to using QuarkXPress on a Macintosh computer. While this isn't such a bad thing, as many designers already use this platform and software, it does impose creative and performance limitations. A designer must always start a variable job with a given system's requirements well in mind.

Here are some potential pitfalls in the creation of designs for digital color and variable printing, some of which may cause a customer to reject the job:

- The resolution of supplied images is too low, resulting in "pixelated" output.
- The paper stock chosen for the job performs poorly on a digital press. Papers for digital printing must be able to withstand the high temperatures used in the fusing process; papers that don't meet the press manufacturer's specifications can crack, bubble, resist toner deposition, or resist toner fusing, where the fused toner flakes off the sheet.
- Large areas of solid color or screened tints can exhibit variation in toner coverage, and screened tints may show blotchy areas even in small areas.
- A bleed is specified but doesn't appear because the press's image area wasn't taken into account.
- A product can't be trimmed, folded or bound because the page layout was incorrect, or a bound product was not created with sufficient gutter area to accommodate the binding.
- Vignettes, blends and gradients exhibit significant "banding," or noticeable stripes in the vignette.
- Variable text is cut off because the text container is too small to accommodate the longest word in a field.
- Too much variable information on a page causes press or RIP errors, or results in missing elements from the page.

There are, of course, many more things that can go wrong with any print job whether it is printed digitally or conventionally, without even going into the subjective area of what constitutes "good" design.

Variable data coverage

As we mentioned in Chapter 6, some combinations of RIP and press engine can impose certain limitations on the percentage of a page that can contain variable information, or limitations on certain typographic and special effects. Specifically, the Xerox DocuColor 70 and 100 cannot print more than 25% variable coverage at their maximum quality setting—all Xeikon presses can print color images at varying "bit depth" settings; the maximum quality and slowest processing speed is 4 bits of data per printer dot, while one bit of data per printer dot increases the variable coverage to 100%. Other bit-depth settings have corresponding effects on print quality and speed.

The Xerox presses have such limitations because they use the relatively slow Xeikon "PES" interface, so if a job is to be run on a DocuColor 70 or 100, this must be taken into account. The DocuColor 40 does not have this limitation, and neither do any of the digital color presses from Agfa, IBM, and of course Xeikon. Indigo presses use a completely different technology and aren't limited by the RIP-press interface. Always be sure to check on press limitations before getting so deep into a project that reworking it becomes impossible.

> *"Why is there never enough time and money to do it right*
> *but always enough time and money to do it over?"*
> —*Werner Rebsamen, RIT*

Substrate issues

A designer who is in charge of paper selection must follow up on a paper choice and find out if the paper has been approved for use in a digital press. The paper or press representative should be able to confirm a paper's printability in a digital press. This also applies to any other substrate such as Teslin, Tyvek, synthetic papers, carton stock, and to any flexible substrates like poly films.

Papers come in a bewildering variety of finishes. Common copier paper is a good example of an uncoated paper—the smoothness of an uncoated sheet is achieved with massive, steam-heated steel "calendering" rollers in the papermaking process. Coated papers have a coating made of various compounds such as kaolin, a type of clay. Coatings can be glossy, dull, or matte; matte papers have a rougher finish than dull papers, which are very smooth but do not undergo the tremendous pressure under which glossy papers are made.

It's always a good idea to do a test run with the selected design, paper stock, and press. Even if the paper is rated for use in a digital press, it might not present the design well. For example, printing color images on a glossy stock won't necessarily result in glossy images; the toner of a digital press will appear dull against the paper's gloss. Experience tells us that such a paper reproduces images very nicely when used in an offset press, but this could be an expensive assumption to make with a digital print run if the client didn't like the results. This effect can be taken advantage of if the desired result is a dull image area, mimicking the effect of applying a dull spot varnish to an image area on an offset press.

Dull and matte coated papers work well with toner-based printing since their relative dullness is close to that of toner. Additional gloss-enhancing features may be available on some digital presses. Uncoated papers print well in digital presses, but using an uncoated stock will greatly exaggerate the deficiencies of a toner-based system in areas of heavy coverage, which may show uneven areas and may end up with a glossy effect anyway because so much toner is piled on the paper in areas of heavy coverage. Digital presses that use liquid toners will produce images that exhibit the gloss characteristics of the paper better than those which use dry toners.

Large areas of solid black are especially difficult to print smoothly on a digital press. Adding percentages of the three other process colors to black creates what's known as a "rich black." This is a technique long used in conventional printing to create a deeper, more solid black than can be reproduced with just black ink or toner alone. The typical formula for a rich black in offset printing is 100% black, 60% cyan and 40% each of magenta and yellow. Consult the print provider to obtain the suggested formula for rich black that reproduces the best on a particular digital press—they are just a little bit different from one another. Be aware of issues related to heavy toner coverage such as flaking and cracking in fold areas.

Paper and paper grain
Paper grain is an inherent result of the papermaking process. As the paper pulp is conveyed along the wire belt in a Fourdrinier (paper-making) machine, most of the paper fibers naturally align themselves in the direction of the belt, resulting in grain—it's analogous to tossing a box of wooden toothpicks into a fast-moving stream, because the toothpicks will eventually align with the direction of the current.

It's easy to see why paper grain direction is important by taking an ordinary index card and folding it in half one way, then the other. The fold against the grain will be lumpy and ragged; the one with the grain will be smooth. It's always the printer's goal to fold jobs with the grain, but sometimes it's not always possible because cutting a job to fold with the grain would result in excessive waste, especially in sheetfed offset-printed jobs. Folding against the grain can result in cracking of the toner and even the paper if a heavy score is not applied before folding.

The other potential problem with paper grain has to do with paper's amazing affinity for moisture. As ambient humidity increases, paper fibers will swell as much as four to five times in width (against the grain) as in length (with the grain). Books bound against the grain in a dry environment and then subjected to normal levels of humidity will have pages that resist turning, that exhibit waviness on the free edges and buckling or distortion on the bound edge, and the book looks badly bound because it is badly bound.

Lithographic printers prefer to run large sheets of paper with the grain along the axis of the press's cylinders, because the paper will expand slightly from front to back due to the moisture present in the fountain solution used on most lithographic presses, and adjustments can be made on the press to compensate for this growth. There aren't any adjustments that can be made for side to side expansion of the paper.

Dehydrated paper is a significant issue with digital printing because heat from the toner fusing process drives most of the moisture out of the paper, a problem shared with the heatset web offset process. Paper is hydrophilic and will immediately absorb moisture if it has been heated and dried out.

Heatset web presses use chill rollers to reduce the paper temperature and encourage rehydration, and some use rehydration units to replenish the moisture lost in the drying process. It's also possible to rehydrate paper naturally by letting it set awhile in an area of sufficient humidity, but once wavy, dehydrated paper has been dried out for more than 72 hours, the damage becomes permanent.

Digital presses can be operated in office environments, where the air is usually quite dry. If a book is digitally printed, perfect-bound, shrink-wrapped and shipped to a customer in, for example, Miami, the book will swell up like a sponge (and might even fall apart if it has been bound against the grain) within 24 hours of exposure to high humidity.

For these reasons, paper should be properly conditioned before printing, and left in its original wrappings until needed. Printed sheets should be kept at room temperature (20-22°C/68-72°F) and moderate relative humidity, about 50%, for a few hours before it is bound and shipped, if possible. Press-specific issues apply to the Xeikon DCP/32 and its derivatives. The paper web on this press is only 12.6"/320mm in width, so any job that requires a two-up imposition of US Letter (8.5x11-inch) or A4 pages on one sheet will require that the sheet be printed along the grain of the web, and it will be folded against the grain.

The wide-format Xeikon DCP/50 has a web width of 20"/500mm, which can accommodate a transverse two-up imposition that can be folded with the grain. Indigo sheetfed presses can handle a maximum sheet size of 12.6"x18.2"/320mm x 464mm, which means that a similar two-up imposition will usually be printed along the grain and folded against it, unless grain-short paper is used, where the grain direction is along the short dimension of the sheet.

Fit
A job that requires any post-press work must be set up to accommodate the final format and the available cutting and binding equipment. Typically, a prepress department in a print shop is responsible for ensuring that a job is set up correctly for the shop's finishing equipment, but this function may end up in the designer's lap in an in-house press operation. Things that are of concern here are page orientation, trim areas, any bleeds, gutter space consideration for binding, and potentially paper grain direction.

Some layouts may require a "lap" or a longer edge on one side that is used in certain bindery operations such as saddle stitching, and jobs that are to be perfect-bound need to have extra space added to accommodate the grind-off of the book spine prior to adhesive application. Care must be taken that toner is not deposited in areas that will be used for the application of binding adhesives—the binding will eventually fail because the toner will separate from the paper, or the adhesive bond to the toner will separate.

"Stripping" issues
So-named because the processes were performed by the film stripping department of a print shop, and still are to a certain extent for

conventional printing. These issues include trapping, page imposition, overprints, and knockouts.

Trapping is the deliberate introduction of a bit of distortion into areas of abutting colors to accommodate mechanical misregister in a conventional printing press. For example, a green circle can be "spread" slightly over a black background so if there is any misregistration, it will not be apparent. A black circle over a green background will require that the background be "choked" under the black for the same reason. Spreads and chokes are rarely thicker than a quarter of a point except for packaging applications.

Trapping is usually not an issue with digital color presses, so a program's automatic trapping features should be disabled when creating artwork for a digital printers. Symptoms of unwanted trapping usually manifest as "fat" type, especially at smaller point sizes. If trapping is required, the prepress operator should be responsible for performing this step. High-end trapping systems are intended mostly for conventional printing where the press speeds are much higher and there is more mechanical tolerance in the machinery.

Digital presses typically have very tight registration and don't require trapping except in unusual cases, and some RIPs support in-RIP trapping and only apply it where needed.

Knockouts are areas where one color "knocks out" another, such as red type over a yellow background—an opening in the yellow area is made that matches the red type. Overprints are pretty self-explanatory: instead of knocking out the yellow background, overprinted red type is actually printed over the yellow background. This can be a desired effect, but in general only black type should ever be set to overprint and in fact black type should always be set to overprint. This is the default behavior of most publishing applications.

In each case, the digital prepress professional or the digital press operator can determine if any trapping is required, and how much, so trapping decisions are best left to the person with the most experience. Trapping problems can be avoided by designing with restraint and avoiding too many abutting colors. This is especially important with vignettes or blends, as these are extremely difficult to trap correctly.

Imposition is the process of arranging pages into signatures, which consist of pages laid out on a press sheet or a section of press web in the correct order needed for binding. For example, an 8-page 8.5x 11-inch saddle-stitched newsletter needs to have pages 8 and 1 next to each other on a sheet, with pages 2 and 7 printed on the reverse of the sheet. Imposition is normally a function of the print shop and the designer has never really gotten involved with it, but depending on the operation, such as an in-house print shop, there might not be any-one else to do it. Imposition is a requirement for any documents that will be bound.

Imposition for multi-page variable jobs is a special case. Quark-XPress-based imposition software like INposition Lite from DK&A won't work with most variable software that also uses QuarkXPress because it performs imposition at print time, much like most variable applications perform the merge of static and variable information at print time.

Standalone imposition applications like Imation PressWise and ScenicSoft Preps require a PostScript or PDF file as input, and the types of files generated by many of the variable printing applications will not be acceptable to these programs because they use propri-etary instructions, such as Scitex VPS or Xerox VIPP, and because the special instructions in the variable data stream that define the loca-tion of each object will not be able to reference the right positions on the page if the pages are imposed.

The job must be prepared one of three ways: imposed manually, which isn't as hard as it sounds if a folding dummy of the job is made, with the pages numbered correctly; imposed with a special imposition program, which generates a PostScript file for the RIP; or on the RIP where, if available, imposition software can be used to cor-rectly impose the variable job while keeping the variable links intact.

Text reflow
This is the bane of many a prepress operators' existence: a job comes in, is proofed, and then it's discovered that one word failed to wrap properly, throwing off the rest of the document. Jobs that cross plat-forms are especially vulnerable to text reflow, even when using the same application and the same typefaces. This is especially problem-atic with variable data because of imported text.

This can be a very expensive mistake if it is discovered after the job has been printed, and the cost of reprinting the job will be the responsibility of the client if the client has approved a proof containing the error, even if the reflow was introduced at the print shop.

Specific to variable printing is the case of variable text that overflows a text box, causes ugly word breaks, or is missing completely. Designers need to prepare for worst-case eventualities: a surname that's 18 letters long, a field accidentally left blank, a new product that has a much longer description that its predecessor, and so on. Variable layouts should be tested with sample data that contains, within reason, the longest anticipated text string.

Legal issues concerning the transfer of digital typefaces can prevent the use of client-supplied font files. Adobe, for example, allows the customer to transfer typefaces to a printer as long as the printer has also purchased the same typefaces. Situations arise where a client might supply her own copy of, for example, Century Old Style, which may be ever so slightly different than the version of Century Old Style that the printer purchased a year earlier. Whose copy of the font is to be used?

The Adobe typeface license does not address this issue directly, but it's safe to assume that a license for a typeface isn't locked with a ball and chain to one specific version of the otherwise identical typeface.

Adobe does allow users to convert a PostScript Type 1 font into a TrueType font for their own use, and also allows users to embed fonts in EPS files, PostScript print files, and PDF files, as long as the resulting file with the embedded font is not modified further and the font is used only for displaying or printing the document.

All variable jobs should be proofed by printing them, with "live" data if possible, to a PostScript laser printer. Designers working without the database should request sample data records from clients for proofing purposes and should also ask clients what, potentially, the longest possible field might be.

Designers should also anticipate odd word breaks, especially with variable type in large point sizes. Consider these headlines, each with a variable word in them:

> Free Oil Change
> for Your Kia!
>
> Free Oil Change
> for your Mercedes-
> Benz!
>
> Free Oil Change for
> your Mercedes-Benz!

In a narrow column, the second headline breaks awkwardly, but changing the line break avoids that problem. This can be accomplished by determining the length of the variable text and choosing an alternative layout from a set of pages, which is possible with Darwin and Focus Gold. Other applications might require a separate run for long field contents.

From the Adobe Typeface Licensing Frequently-Asked Questions (FAQ): "What is Adobe's position on users and service bureaus sharing typefaces and why? *Adobe's licensing policy on transporting typeface software with print jobs to service bureaus is unchanged. Customers are allowed to give their typeface files to a service bureau along with a print job IF AND ONLY IF the service bureau already owns a valid license for the typeface. This allowance is to ensure that the customer's revision of the typeface software is the one used to image the print job (Adobe does revise its typefaces periodically). Customers are not allowed to give typefaces to service bureaus who do not already own valid licenses for the typefaces. Adobe's position, shared by the partners we license typefaces from, is that our business in typefaces is in part built by receiving compensation for typefaces when they are imaged. Owning licenses for the typefaces is an essential part of the cost of doing business as a service bureau. When you image a font you obtain value from that font, and are required to own a license for that font.*"

8

Production and Workflow Considerations

Preparing for the variable print run
Check the list—The source database should contain only the required information, be exported to a tab-delimited ASCII file, and it should be in the exact state as defined by the project and production managers. Image files specific to each record should be included in a field in each data record if that is the method an application uses for defining variable images; specific text files that might need to be swapped in should be treated the same way.

If possible, proper names, street names, and city names should be verified and corrected. People with uncommon names tend to become annoyed after seeing them spelled incorrectly, or worse, creatively, ten times a week.

CASS-certified software can be used to check all addresses for validity. PostNet barcode generation software can generate numeric PostNet codes from address data and insert this value into a database field, which can be popped into a variable layout and have a PostNet barcode font applied to it.

Check the images—Variable images should be named sensibly to easily identify which image goes with which database record if that is how they are to be assigned.

Scanned images and illustrations should be prepared with the following in mind:

- Images should be saved in uncompressed TIFF or EPS format—most RIPs will choke on PICT, BMP, JPEG, GIF or WMF images. JPEG images can hide in an EPS file unnoticed. Note that the Private-I and PrintShop Mail applications can only work with EPS images.

- Color images should be pre-separated into CMYK TIFF or EPS format unless the RIP supports separation of composite RGB images. This can be a recipe for disaster if not carefully managed, as RGB images will appear on the finished job as black-and-white images if the RIP cannot separate them. It is not necessary to save separated images in the multi-file DCS format; this format is no longer required for separating color images. Check that black-and-white images are saved as "grayscale" mode from Photoshop; sometimes these are represented as RGB, Indexed Color or Lab Color in Photoshop.

- EPS files exported from illustration applications like Adobe Illustrator, MacroMedia FreeHand, and Corel Draw should be checked for the existence of spot or Pantone colors; if found, they must be converted to process colors, unless the job is being run on a digital press that supports spot colors in addition to the standard four process colors. The Indigo E-Print is currently the only digital press that allows up to three spot colors to be printed along with the four process colors, or it can use the high-fidelity six-color IndiChrome process system.

- If EPS files contain imported raster (bitmap) images such as color TIFF files, these must be converted to CMYK color from RGB color if necessary. Linked images placed into illustration files can be included in the exported EPS file by using the application's relevant option for image file handling. This can create large EPS files, but it ensures that the images are contained within the EPS file and don't need to be included separately.

- EPS files should be checked for font requirements. Type in files from Illustrator, FreeHand, and Corel Draw can be converted to outlines to avoid the need to load specific fonts. This is another means of using files from other countries that use non-Roman alphabets; for example, a designer in Japan should convert all Japanese text to paths or outlines before exporting it for use in an English-speaking country where the computers aren't likely to support Japanese text.

Preflighting applications like FlightCheck and Preflight Pro will catch unwanted spot colors and identify missing fonts in documents.

Images and illustrations destined for a common variable-data image container should be saved at the same size as the container for best results. Scaling and rotating images within QuarkXPress causes tremendous processing overhead and can cause the RIP to underdrive the print engine. For example, if a variable picture box is 10cm square, all images should be cropped, rotated, and/or resized in Photoshop to fit within this 10cm square.

Doing this work in Photoshop will also prevent image distortion in the final product, because what is seen in Photoshop is what will be seen on the page. This isn't always the case with images scaled and/or rotated within QuarkXPress.

Images that are enlarged will exhibit pixelization; images that are reduced significantly will soften in appearance. A 4x5-inch 300ppi (pixels or points per inch) image reduced to 20 percent will cause QuarkXPress to send the entire original image at a massively increased resolution, causing a considerable slowdown in processing time. In most cases, digital presses do not require that image resolutions be any higher than 300ppi, and often 200ppi can be used without any noticeable image degradation, although this should be done only if absolutely necessary.

Image resolution is a function of the screen ruling used to print a job and the image's desired magnification or reduction. Typically the image resolution will be twice the screen ruling multiplied by the magnification. A job printed at the common screen ruling of 150 lines per inch at 100 percent magnification will require 300ppi images; a 4x5-inch transparency enlarged 300 percent will require scanning at 900ppi. Most digital presses do not use a fixed line screen due to their relatively low resolution but attempt to emulate the appearance of a fairly fine screen ruling. Because of this, images should not be used for digital printing if their resolution is much below 250ppi.

Sizing images in Photoshop

Assume a variable picture box in the QuarkXPress layout is 3.5 inches square. If the images intended for this box are not already this size along one axis, they must be sized to fit before printing. Here's how to do this in Photoshop:

- Open the original image
- Crop out any unneccesary areas

- Choose Image -> Image Size
- Set the long axis of the image to the size of the picture box, in this case 3.5 inches.

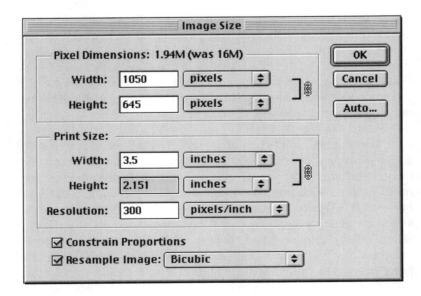

- Maintain proportions and resampling. Digital color presses will not require any image to be more than 300 pixels per inch for best results. If the resolution is too high, resample the image down to 300ppi. If the resolution is much below 250ppi, be prepared for some pixelization (a rough, jagged appearance) in the final printed piece. Resampling an image to a higher resolution will not provide any benefit to the image quality.
- Convert the image to CMYK if necessary, remembering to check Photoshop's CMYK separation setup for the correct amount of black generation and total ink coverage. This can be provided by the press manufacturer, but typically digital presses cannot print halftones lighter than 3% or heavier than 97%, so all images should reflect the halftone screen range of the particular press.

Scanning, color correction, and color conversion
Scanned color images may require some adjustment to achieve a good reproduction, and they may need to be converted from RGB color to CMYK color. Color correction especially is outside the scope of this book, but a few guidelines apply when scanning that usually produce accurate results without a lot of post-scan work. These guidelines apply to both drum scanners and flatbed scanners.

Unless the scanned images are to be repurposed for other uses, such as a Web page or an on-screen presentation, they should be scanned in CMYK, not RGB. Bear in mind that the maximum solid ink density that can be achieved on a digital color press is generally less than 1.2, so color images should be adjusted to accommodate this limitation. Images used for offset printing will need adjustment of the total tonal range for optimum reproduction on a digital press.

Before a digital press is placed into operation, a tone reproduction analysis, a gray balance test, and a dot gain test must be performed to determine the press's color reproduction characteristics. This process is also called "fingerprinting" the press, and is performed on all presses regardless of the printing technology used. Color corrections cannot be accurately performed unless the press's color reproduction characteristics are known. Consult a trained color expert or press consultant for details of these tests.

- Determine the maximum and minimum dot areas that the press is capable of reproducing. SWOP guidelines specify a 5–95% dot size range; a digital press may or may not be able to reproduce higher or lower dot values.These values are determined by a tone reproduction test. SWOP values for total ink coverage (the total amount of ink that can be printed on a sheet with a given printing technology and a given paper type) is 280%. Total ink coverage is usually specified as a smaller amount of the total of the maximum of all four process colors, which is 400%.

> *What is SWOP? It stands for Specifications for Web Offset Publications, a set of specifications designed to produce consistent reproduction of publications printed on #5 coated groundwood paper (that annoyingly slick, crinkly stuff many magazines are printed on) using a heatset web offset press. Similar industry-standard specifications exist for non-heatset web offset (SNAP), sheetfed offset (GRACoL), flexographic (FIRST), and gravure (GAA) printing. There is currently no analogous set of specifications for digital printing.*

- Non-heatset web offset presses (including newspaper presses) are limited to about 240% total ink coverage, while sheetfed lithographic presses can print up to 300% total ink coverage. No process can print a full 100% of each process color—paper would sag, buckle, or just fall apart before this limit was reached. Toner-based digital presses are limited to about 240% total toner coverage for any given area on a sheet, and total toner coverage much above this amount may result in the toner cracking or flaking off the sheet. Check with the printing service for coverage limits.
- These total ink/toner coverage values can be specified in the Photoshop Separation Setup preferences, along with choices for UCR and GCR. Those settings are found in the File –> Color Settings –> CMYK Setup . . . menu in Photoshop 5.0.

```
┌─────────────────────────────────────────────────────────────┐
│                        CMYK Setup                            │
├─────────────────────────────────────────────────────────────┤
│  CMYK Model: ● Built-in ○ ICC ○ Tables          ┌─────────┐  │
│  ┌─ Ink Options ──────────────────────────────┐ │   OK    │  │
│  │                                            │ └─────────┘  │
│  │  Ink Colors: │ SWOP (Coated)        │ ⬍ │  │ ┌─────────┐  │
│  │                                            │ │ Cancel  │  │
│  │  Dot Gain: │ Standard    │ ⬍ │ │ 20 │ %  │ └─────────┘  │
│  └────────────────────────────────────────────┘ ┌─────────┐  │
│  ┌─ Separation Options ───────────────────────┐ │ Load... │  │
│  │                                            │ └─────────┘  │
│  │  Separation Type: ● GCR ○ UCR   Gray Ramp: │ ┌─────────┐  │
│  │                                            │ │ Save... │  │
│  │  Black Generation: │ Medium      │ ⬍ │    │ └─────────┘  │
│  │                                            │  ☑ Preview  │
│  │    Black Ink Limit: │ 95 │ %               │              │
│  │                                            │              │
│  │    Total Ink Limit: │ 300 │ %              │              │
│  │                                            │              │
│  │      UCA Amount: │ 0 │ %                   │              │
│  └────────────────────────────────────────────┘              │
└─────────────────────────────────────────────────────────────┘
```

- The Black Ink Limit value specifies the maximum dot area that the black separation will use. Total ink coverage is determined by the Total ink limit setting. The UCA amount setting defines *under-color addition* as a percentage of the total ink coverage. UCA is used to compensate for the loss of ink density in neutral shadow areas. This additional ink produces rich, dark shadows in areas that might appear flat if printed with only black ink. Along with GCR settings, UCA values are best determined by testing, but values of 20–30% should produce satisfactory results.

- Dot gain is less of an issue on toner-based presses than with conventional presses—the toner is dry, is not partially absorbed into the paper, and the process is directly digital to the paper, so no issues arise of dot spread related to film and plate exposure. However, toner does scatter on paper to a certain degree and does not form crisp, hard-edged dots on the paper like ink-printed dots do. As a result, the dot gain techniques used for other printing technologies can be applied to digital printing.

- A dot-gain test using a "raw" uncompensated image should be performed, measured against the actual image data, and the data used to construct a dot gain curve that can be applied in Photoshop or in image scanning software. Some RIPs for digital presses include a selection of dot gain compensation curves, but these should only be used as the basis for starting a dot gain test.

- UCR and GCR are methods of generating the black separation from an RGB image. UCR (Under Color Removal) is an older technique and only operates in shadow areas, replacing combinations of CMY that form neutral gray areas with black. GCR (Gray Component Replacement) is a newer technique that produces more measurable black generation and can be controlled more carefully than UCR. GCR replaces not only neutral grays, but also the *gray component* of three-color process tones with black. The gray component is the third ink in a three-color tone that produces a graying effect as more of that ink is added. With GCR, the gray component ink is replaced with a calculated amount of black ink and does not result in a color shift unless applied incorrectly.

  For example, a picture of a green apple that is scanned as RGB then converted in Photoshop without GCR is primarily cyan and yellow with a small amount of magenta present to add detail to the image. Without the magenta gray component, the image would appear flat and uninteresting. Replacing most of the magenta with black in this case preserves the detail without altering the image's tone. Photoshop allows the user to specify varying levels of GCR from none at all (which results in an image generated by cyan, magenta, and yellow only) through light, medium, heavy, and maximum. Careful testing and press profiling will determine the optimum level of GCR for a particular set of press, image, and paper characteristics.

  The driving force behind the development of UCR and GCR is the fact that black ink or toner is cheaper than cyan, magenta, and yellow ink or toner. The cost savings realized are hard to quantify without a lot of testing, but there are other benefits to applying UCR and especially GCR to an image when separating it. Detail is enhanced, there is less of a muddy appearance in neutral gray areas, and midtones may appear crisper. Most higher-end scanners can apply UCR or GCR during the scanning and separation process, and if available these can be used instead of Photoshop's separation option.

- Highlight areas should be neutralized to C7M5Y5K0. This combination of the four process colors produces a clean, neutral white highlight. Once the highlight area is neutral, the rest of the image should achieve proper gray balance. On occasion further adjustments may be necessary to remove strong color casts. Many high-end scanners have the ability to neutralize color casts automatically.
- Some images may not contain a definable highlight area, so for these a gray scale should be mounted alongside the image on the scanner and used to determine neutrality and gray balance.
- The highlight-to-midtone density range of a normal-key image should be 0.90 (for transparencies) or 0.80 (for reflective artwork) when scanning. This value is called many different things depending on the scanning software used. A high-key image (one that's mostly highlight areas, such as a photograph of soapsuds) might need a shorter highlight-to-midtone range; a low-key image (one that's mostly shadow areas, a black cat in a coalmine for example) might need a longer highlight-to-midtone range. Highlight-to-midtone range adjustments have a significant effect on the image's contrast.
- When possible, unsharp masking should be applied at the scanning stage rather than in Photoshop. Many low-end scanners cannot perform hardware sharpening, so this step must be done in Photoshop after scanning.

Efficient and correct scanning procedures minimize further color correction and other image repair work in Photoshop. A skilled scanner operator can produce images that can be proofed and printed without any further adjustments except for dust and scratch removal.

When scanned images require color correction, the same method of neutralizing highlight areas and achieving correct gray balance used when scanning can often correct many color problems in Photoshop. Further work may be needed using Photoshop's Curves function to remove strong color casts.

Images that arrive in the RGB color space must usually be converted to the CMYK color space before printing. This is a more complicated process than simply choosing Mode -> CMYK from Photoshop's Image menu. Often these images require further work to correct the dynamic range and highlight neutrality. The most important issue in these conversions is the inability of the CMYK color space to accurately reproduce all of the colors available in the RGB color space. Images with bright, vibrant, saturated color can look dull, flat and washed-out after conversion. The most obvious solution is to re-scan the image in the CMYK color space, but if this is not possible, then some compromise must often be made between the original and the CMYK reproduction.

Careful adjustment of Photoshop's CMYK Setup parameters, including the amount of black generation, the type of black ink replacement method used, the amount of undercolor addition, and total ink coverage, can help to mitigate the effects of color space conversion.

Many RIPs support "in-RIP" separation of RGB images into the CMYK color space with the correct dynamic range and possibly highlight neutrality, but they cannot adjust for out-of-gamut RGB colors and the results may not be as pleasing as a manual color space conversion. Careful testing and colorimetry can be used to determine if a RIP's color separation capabilities result in acceptable color reproduction.

Some of the available variable printing applications support OPI (Open Prepress Interface), a means of substituting high-resolution images for low-resolution proxy images on the RIP. In an OPI workflow, high resolution scanned images are saved to the RIP's disk and low resolution proxy images are delivered to the designer for placement in the job layout. This saves a lot of processing time for the designer because the low-resolution files take up a lot less space and are more quickly manipulated in a page layout.

When the job is sent to the RIP, the high-resolution images are substituted for the low-resolution proxies, and any cropping or other image manipulations applied to the proxies are applied to the high resolution images. In a variable printing system, this can save tremendous time if variable images are to be used in the job. Scitex, Agfa, and many other vendors support an OPI workflow.

Color management

Color management systems (CMS) have been around for awhile in varying levels of effectiveness. Apple's ColorSync is probably the most widely used and Microsoft has added its own CMS to Windows 98 called ICM. The idea behind a CMS is to integrate a given device's color characteristics into a workflow to maintain consistent color reproduction on a number of different devices. To work effectively, a profile must be created for each device in a workflow, from the scanner down to the printing press. These profiles are time-consuming to make and require specialized software and equipment such as a colorimeter to create them accurately. Each profile contains information that tells an application how that device reproduces color.

The profile is embedded in a file when it is scanned, and the profile is used by each succeeding application in a digital workflow. For example, using Apple's ColorSync, an image scanned on a profiled scanner can be opened in Photoshop 5 and a specific scanner profile attached to it. From there, the image can be placed into a ColorSync-aware page layout application, along with other images that may have been scanned on a different scanner, or been copied from a PhotoCD. As long as the device-specific profiles are attached to each image, consistent color reproduction can, in theory, be achieved on a number of different output devices such as a digital proofer, an imagesetter, or a digital press. In practice, however, color output that relies on ColorSync can vary, sometimes spectacularly, if a different application is used to drive the same output device.

Color management systems work well in environments where the production system is very tightly controlled, is closed to the outside world, and is operated by trained professionals who are diligent in creating device profiles and in calibrating those devices on a regular basis. Once a job from the outside comes in with images that do not have attached device profiles, the color management model falls apart. Color management software is no substitute for an experienced color reproduction expert.

Common document problems to watch out for

The following production-stoppers are the most common that appear in jobs sent to press. These could be the subject of an entire book on their own; space constraints prevent a full discussion of these issues.

- *Incorrect page construction*—designers often fail to account for correct page geometry, trims, bleeds, folds, and impositions when building pages, resulting in extra time and expense to correct them. Solution—provide designers with templates that contain all required folds, bleeds, trims, and impositions, set to the correct page geometry; train designers in these techniques. Money spent in training is less costly than reprinting a job because it can't be folded or bound.

- *Problems with placed artwork*—illustrations that contain "nested" EPS files, user-defined screen angles, rulings, and halftone dot shapes, can create unusable output and may even cause the RIP to abort the job. Solution—examine source files carefully for objects that have had custom screening or halftoning applied to them. If nested EPS files are found in illustration files, (for example, if an EPS file is placed, not opened, into a FreeHand document which is later exported as an EPS file, the placed EPS file is said to be nested within the other EPS file), they can often be replaced by opening the nested file in an illustration program rather than placing it, if possible, then copying and pasting the file's contents into the target document which can now be exported as a proper EPS file for placement into a page layout application.

- *Placed artwork causes PostScript errors*—complex illustrations may contain too many curve points, which can result in a PostScript limitcheck error during processing in the RIP. FreeHand and Illustrator offer tools that can simplify an illustration's curves and reduce the number of curve points without affecting reproduction. Clipping paths created in Photoshop have a flatness setting, which can be increased if it is determined that the clipping path is causing the limitcheck error.

- *Color-related errors*—RGB images, duplicated spot colors, and spot colors that need to be converted to process colors will definitely create problems when imaging the job. Solution—convert RGB images to CMYK; use a preflight application to detect duplicate spot colors and/or spot colors that must be converted to process color. Open offending files in the originating application and convert spot colors to process colors. If a job is to be run on a spot color-capable press like the E-Print, verify that the spot color inks chosen are actually available for that press.

- *Artwork exhibits banding*—blends, vignettes, and gradients (all essentially the same thing) are a frequent cause of job rework because designers often fail to account for the limitations in the halftoning process used to produce them. The ease of creating these effects in illustration applications has led to a huge increase in their use, and examples of bad blends can be seen in many publications. Solution—use tint values with a fairly wide range, e.g. from 15% to 85% as narrow tint ranges force the use of larger bands of tint value; make the gradient smaller.

   Train graphic designers to mathematically determine whether a given gradient will reproduce without banding. The number of tints an output device can create (N) can be found by dividing the device's output resolution by the screen ruling, and squaring the result. Use this value to determine the actual number of tints available in a given gradient range (T) by multiplying N by the decimal difference of the tint values at each end of the gradient, e.g. in a gradient from 20% to 75% of a single color, the decimal difference is 0.55. If the size of each band of tint is 0.05″/0.12cm or less, the banding will not be noticeable. To find the tint band size, divide the distance between the start and end points of the gradient by T (gradient range).

- *Font problems*—aside from the obvious error of font files missing completely from a job, spacing problems and text rewrap can result from such subtle differences as using a slightly newer version of the same font from the same foundry. Solution—if text reflow or rewrap is detected and the font specified is being used, the creator of the job may be using a different version of the font files, may have used a TrueType version of a PostScript Type 1 font (common with jobs originating on Windows computers that are processed on a Macintosh), or the font may be damaged. Insist that all jobs include all fonts used throughout the publication, and only load client-supplied font files.

- *Other Possible Problems*—hairlines: these are rules in a page layout that have been given the rather nondescript width of a "hairline." Such a rule will print with the thinnest possible line that can be reproduced on an output device. On an 800dpi digital press, this will be 1/800 of an inch, barely visible. Solution: the FlightCheck application will detect hairlines but only reports the page number that contains them. Once found, change all hairlines to 0.25 points.

• Some designers will cover up page elements with "electronic white-out," or a white box. Even if the elements are hidden from view, they must still be sent to the RIP, where they will be processed, then discarded. Files that seem to take an inordinate amount of time to process given the relative complexity of the document should be checked for hidden elements. Likewise, images that are rotated, distorted, scaled, or heavily cropped in a page layout application waste processing time. Images should already be at the right size, orientation, and cropping when placed in a page layout application. Manipulating images after they are placed just results in a lot of RIP churning.

Check the text

All copy should be relevant to the targeted audience and written in an appropriate tone and voice. All textual material must be proofread —do not rely on a spell-checker. Copy can be imported from nearly any word processing application such as Microsoft Word or Corel WordPerfect. Copy that is imported from another platform, for example, from a Windows system to a Macintosh, must be checked for bad character translations.

Sometimes special characters in a word-processing file such as typographer's quotes and accented foreign letters do not convert to the equivalent on another platform unless the same program is available on both systems, for example, Microsoft Word. Files from Word for Windows, when read with Word on a Macintosh, will automatically have any special characters converted and can be saved for importing into a page layout application.

A general workflow for variable printing

1. A marketing manager creates a database marketing plan that includes variable printing.
2. The manager requests a database extract from the database administrator, specifying exactly which records and

fields are to be extracted. Alternatively, a desktop database system can be used to extract the required data for the print run.

3. The manager selects a graphic designer to create a page layout, and works closely with this person to select any variable images to be used in the layout.
4. A layout is created with visible placeholders for variable data, and tested with sample data from the extracted database information and a selection of the variable images. Proofs are generated on a laser printer for approval.
5. The job is bid out and a printer is selected. At this stage it's critical for the printer to communicate with the client regarding the equipment and software used to produce the variable print run. If necessary, the designer needs to obtain any software or support files required to easily transfer the job to the printing service, especially if the database requires some manipulation. This is the reason the database should be delivered to production as close to the final form as possible.
6. The designer transfers all job files to a removable storage medium, including layout files, the database, all images, all fonts used in the job, a laser proof or folding dummy that clearly indicates the final layout of the job, including any folds, trims, or binding.
7. The printer takes the job in and performs a preflight operation to make sure all of the required elements are included and that the job is correctly laid out for the required press and imposition.
8. The job is assigned to a digital press operator who is experienced with producing variable print jobs. A proof of the job should be pulled immediately and submitted to the client for approval. Once approved, the variable job is set up according to the software used and sent to the RIP, and from there to the press.
9. The job is collected and sent to the finishing department for cutting, folding or binding. Any pieces that are spoiled in the finishing process must be saved and returned to the press operator so they can be reprinted.

Naturally, this is a gross simplification of the process. The current problem with defining one efficient workflow for variable printing is that none of the means of doing so are compatible with or in some cases even similar to each other. Until a standardized means of creating and generating variable jobs is defined, each shop's variable workflow will need to be carefully analyzed by a professional. A reputable consultant can be hired to help with the integration of a variable workflow into an existing one, or with the establishment of an in-house variable printing system. As the price of the equipment begins to fall, expect to see more digital color presses brought into corporations and organizations as the internal demand for color and variable printing increases.

Proofing

Prepress proofs have been a staple of the printing business for decades, but a digital press has the ability to print proofs as if they were any other job. The complete layout should be run once on the digital press to be used for the job. At this stage, live variable data is not necessary and all adjustments for text reflow potential have been made. Proofs can also be created on a variety of digital proofers, but these are typically set up to emulate an offset printing press and will not provide accurate simulation of a digital press. It is always preferable to proof on the actual press.

Once made, proofs must be examined carefully. Images should reproduce clearly, type must be correct, and everything must be checked for accuracy. Look for any elements that accidentally overlap, type that isn't exactly where it should be or isn't in the right typeface, vector artwork that reproduces poorly or contains type that is set in a missing typeface, and incorrect telephone numbers or addresses that might be on the master document. Once the client has signed off on the proof, any further errors in the design and layout are the client's responsibility.

Errors in variable text and images can be traced to the database, the rules used to specify variable data, missing or incomplete data fields in a database, but placing the financial responsibility of reprinting a variable job is fraught with problems. No PIA-style terms of sale exists yet for variable printing, so this is an area in which to tread carefully. Proofing the entire job on a laser printer to check for any errors in the data is a possibility but that is likely to take a very long time and most clients aren't likely to page through reams of laser printouts. Or, print to PDF and soft proof the job.

The variable printing shopping list

Here's a minimal suggestion of equipment and software that should be present in the startup of a new digital printing operation:

- Computer workstations—at least one each dedicated to scanning, page and image assembly, and output. The choice of computer platforms will be dictated by several things, but mostly by the requirements of the customers. If most jobs come in from Macintosh computers, it makes sense to have mostly Macs, with one or two Windows workstations. All of these computers must be connected to a local-area network, and all should be equipped with as much memory (RAM) as possible and with at least 4 GB of hard disk space, preferably more.

- A large-format black-and-white laser printer should be available for proofing and should be able to accept paper that is at least 11x17-inch/A3 size. A digital color proofer such as a dye-diffusion or high-end inkjet system isn't really required but it can save some time over proofing a job on a digital press as long as the proofing system is carefully profiled to match the press's characteristics.

- A high-speed data network, such as 100Base-T Ethernet, and a fast file server. There are many options for file servers but the most efficient to operate are those based upon a Unix or Unix-like operating system like Linux. These types of servers can be difficult to set up and administer, but they will provide the best possible throughput. Other options like Windows NT and MacOS X Server are much easier to set up and administer than a Unix server, but this ease of use may exact a performance penalty. Ultimately, the choice of server will be dictated by the needs of the operation, the skill level of personnel, and the requirements of other equipment that may need to work with the file server.

- An archival system—this can be a simple tape backup device like a DAT or DLT tape drive, or can be as complicated as a robotic "jukebox" used to store optical discs. Whatever system is chosen, it must be able to archive finished work in a timely fashion and users must be able to retrieve old jobs quickly and easily.

- A fairly high-end scanner such as the Scitex EverSmart Pro, the Optronics ColorGetter, or less expensive options like the newer Umax large flatbed scanners. Moving large scans across a network can be be a lengthy process, so some managers like to equip scanning workstations with high-capacity removable hard disks that can be "hot-swapped" in and out of a receptacle without having to shut down the computer. Huge files can easily be moved from one station to another using this technology.

- A digital press and ancillary support equipment. Each vendor's requirements for support equipment will differ. Consult press vendors for required equipment and site preparation specifications for electricity, ventilation, and climate controls.
- Post-press finishing—at the very least, a shop should acquire a guillotine cutter, a folder, and a mechanical binding system such as coil or Wire-O. Further investments might include collators, stitchers, adhesive binding machines such as perfect binders or OtaBind systems, trimmers and other equipment. Finishing equipment must be capable of handling the slippery, often static-charged and curl-prone sheets that are produced from a Xeikon-based print engine. Inline or offline finishing should be based on the ability of the equipment to keep up with press output and the impact that inline finishing (such as automatic collation) will have on production speed. Offline finishing is more flexible and is not tied to one particular piece of equipment—if a press goes down, finishing can still continue.
- Software—specific systems will require software of varying abilities. A scanning station will need scanning software and Photoshop; a page assembly station will require QuarkXPress and PageMaker (and any other applications one chooses to support, such as FrameMaker or Ventura); an output station will require imposition and possibly trapping software and any other software peculiar to a specific type of digital press. Press RIPs may require additional software to perform specific functions. Typefaces must be purchased in order to comply with the licensing requirements of Adobe and other digital type vendors.
- Removable media—due to the annoying variety of removable-media devices, such as Zip, Jaz, SyQuest, and magneto-optical drives, a well-equipped shop should be

prepared to accept any media that might be provided by customers. Consider a station that is equipped with Zip, Jaz (the 2 GB model also reads and writes the older 1 GB disks), possibly an optical drive, which come in multiple 5.25-inch and 3.5-inch formats, and an old-fashioned Syquest 5.25-inch removable media drive. SyQuest Technology, Inc., ceased operations under bankruptcy in 1998, but there are millions of old Syquest 44, 88 and 200 MB cartridges still in widespread use. The 200 MB drive can read and write the even older 44 and 88 MB formats— these drives can be found used and at auction.

- Each workstation should also be equipped with a CD-ROM drive, since many jobs are now "burned" to a CD-ROM with a CD writer, which has become an inexpensive mechanism. CD-ROM drives should be compatible with the new CD-R/W format, which allows a special CD to be written over many times, unlike the older CD-R technology, which is a write-once device. A CD recorder or read/write drive should also be considered as a means of easily gathering a client's jobs on one CD as a means of backup or returning requested client files.
- But wait, there's more! Equipment and software usually requires constant upgrading, updating, and replacement. The life expectancy of a computer workstation might be ten years, but its useful life is at best two years. Choose equipment that can be upgraded to future levels of performance, such as computers with processor slots that can accept newer versions of the processor with minimal cost and downtime. Keep abreast of software upgrades and updates; many companies provide free "updaters" on their Web sites that typically fix bugs or add some feature to the product.
- All of this expensive equipment should be depreciated on an accelerated basis—consult an accountant for feasibility. A Xeikon press might be operable in ten years but it surely won't be cost-effective in 2009. None of these digital presses can be expected to last as long as heavy-iron traditional presses, many of which are decades old and still producing profit for their owners.
- Lastly, personnel must be hired to operate all of this stuff. A digital press operator needs to have more experience

with digital production and processes than with traditional press operation. Database experience will be required for adding value to variable printing jobs. Computer operators and scanning technicians can be brought into a digital printing operation with service-bureau skillsets; there's nothing inherently different about scanning and page assembly for digital printing than for traditional printing. The same holds true for finishing operators. The press operator, however, needs thorough, rigorous training and education to become an expert with the equipment.

Future workflow solutions

While the press is running, there's really not much for the operator to do except monitor the press console for any errors. Realistically, most variable printing systems cannot process jobs while printing. Systems like the Barco PrintStreamer and IBM Collator page buffers help to alleviate this problem by taking rasterized pages from the RIP and storing them on a huge array of high-speed hard disk drives, from which the press is fed the data.

This is a fine solution for short-run variable print jobs, and works perfectly in non-variable print runs of up to a few thousand different pages, but a long-run variable job will deplete the page buffer faster than the RIP can replenish it with new pages. Production must stop in this case to allow the RIP to fill up the page buffer again, and while this is occurring no printing can take place.

This is the problem that Varis and Moore have managed to eliminate for full color variable printing; digital press vendors must continue to "push the envelope" of technology to attain a slack-free workflow. Advances like this are critical to the success and efficiency of variable printing as a viable, timely marketing tool.

A PDF-based workflow

Adobe Systems announced its "Extreme" architecture in 1996 as the Supra system, and the technology is just starting to ship as a part of various suppliers' workflows, like Agfa Apogee. Extreme uses the Adobe PDF file format internally and converts all incoming Post-Script files to individual PDF pages. A feature of the system is the Adobe PJTF (Portable Job Ticket Format) that is created and embedded in each PDF page of a job.

The job ticket contains information about the page and instructions on how to process it, including pre- and post-press operations such as trapping, imposition, and finishing operations. It can contain customer information, billing information along with a record of all billable operations, the number of pages in the complete job, and all printing and finishing instructions.

> *"The promise of this technology [Extreme] is that we will bypass all the anxiety about lost fonts and wrong PPDs and landscape versus portrait. It will make printing from PostScript nearly anxiety-free."*
> *—Paul Beyer*

To achieve its presumably high speed, Extreme requires that a job be split into discrete pages that can be quickly processed, called page independence. The only means of breaking a PostScript job into discrete pages is to convert them to PDF. PDF itself speeds up processing because it has already been preprocessed and is similar to the Display List format used internally in PostScript RIPs for quite some time. PDF is a highly efficient, "slim" file format that can be processed very rapidly by a RIP.

It seems counter-productive that a PDF file must first be converted back to PostScript before it is rasterized, but the Extreme RIP is optimized for this process and the PostScript that is generated from a PDF file is much "cleaner" and smaller than the PostScript that was generated by an application. Once the pages have been rasterized they are sent to the Assembler.

The Extreme architecture has five main components:
- The Normalizer—converts incoming PostScript streams to individual PDF pages.
- The Page Store—PDf files created by the Normalizer are sent to the Page Store for short or long term storage.
- The RIP Bank—this is a system of one or more interconnected RIPs. This is where the Extreme architecture really has a chance to shine for variable printing. RIPs can be added at will to bring the entire system up to a processing level that can drive a digital press at full speed while the job is being processed or while another job is being prepared. Imposition, trapping, separation, and OPI image replacement all occur on the RIP Bank.

- The Assembler—manages the RIP Bank and controls the press engine.
- The Coordinator—manages all aspects of a job; sends PostScript files to the Normalizer for conversion to PDF; stores PDF files in the Page Store, and controls the workflow of the entire system.

Extreme holds a great deal of promise for variable printing. With the PDF workflow, an object-caching mechanism, and multiple RIPs, Extreme has the potential to outperform even high-end systems like VariScript using industry-standard applications and the platform-independent PDF file format. Agfa and Scitex have announced systems based on the Extreme technology, but it remains to be seen whether any of these products will be designed for use with digital presses and variable printing.

IBM is currently shipping the black-and-white InfoPrint 4000 which uses the Extreme technology and includes support for variable printing. This machine is capable of printing 464 impressions per minute. Color digital presses have a long way to go before they reach these speeds, and the hardware that drives them must achieve parity with upcoming press engines. The Extreme architecture seems to be the ideal solution to this problem and is based on a completely open system, unlike VariScript and the Moore XLC systems.

Summary
Workflow is the most important aspect of digital printing and especially of personalized and database printing. No longer can service providers deal with only a job at a time—they must have jobs all the time. And they must be totally automated.

Afterword

The sweepstakes is marked "personal & confidential" and includes details on a $1 million drawing. State regulators say people are being duped by such personal appeals because they make you believe that out of the millions and millions of people who have sent in responses, that you have personally come to their attention. Several states have sued the biggest sweepstakes houses, alleging a variety of deceptive practices. Under federal law, no purchase is necessary to enter or win a sweepstakes, and industry representatives note there are disclaimers with the *You May Already be a Winner* promotions. The industry estimates 70 percent of households toss the mailings without entering a contest or buying any magazine subscriptions or other merchandise. Of those who do return the envelope, about 75 percent decline to buy anything.

Personalized and database printing is much more than *you may be a winner*. It is about relationships between buyers and sellers, and the use of paper-based communication to maintain that relationship.

Direct mail is a cost-effective marketing medium. It costs about nine cents to generate one dollar in revenue. Few other media are as effective. 63 percent of marketers predict that their direct mail expenditures will increase in the next year and most say that it will be by about 29 percent.

We are seeing a shift in marketing. The day of mass marketing may be coming to a close. Instead of marketing to the averages, we will market to the differences—thus needing to mass produce run lengths of one. We market to acquire new customers or to retain existing customers. It costs five times as much to get a single new customer as it does to keep a customer you already have; yet, many marketers allocate six times as much to generate new customers.

Build your own Buick!

Client: Buick Motor Division, General Motors

Provider: Thebault-DI division of L.P. Thebault Cos, Parsippany, NJ.

Best Advice: "Adding value with personalization is the only way to profitably sell digital color printing. . . most people who get into digital printing fail to market it properly."

Source Data: Database of Buick owners generated by EDS delivered ready-to-RIP—minor modifications such as converting all-uppercase words to upper and lower-case performed by LPT-DI.

Workflow: Agfa Personalizer-X application, used with QuarkXPress to generate variable documents.

Marketing Plan: Series of four short newsletters.

Newsletter 1: Minimal levels of personalization. Sent to current Buick owners with cars from two- to four-years old, and to selected non-Buick owners based on demographics of age and income. BRC bound into the newsletter—included questions about the type of car interested in, the color, and desired options.

Newsletter 2: Based upon response, or lack of, from first newsletter. Thebault DI used this opportunity for further newsletter personalization. BRC included for further customer profile refinement.

Newsletter 3: Based on data from returned cards from newsletter 2. Showed the exact model and color specified with a banner headline of customer's surname with the model and the color chosen, e.g. "The Smith's new Jade-Green Regal." Additional information such as options and MSRP also printed on piece.

Newsletter 4: Sent only to those who purchased a new Buick. Two different pieces used: one thanking customer for purchase and offering coupons for use at local retail establishments, another that contained a detailed post-sale questionnaire.

Upshot: The program netted about a 25% response rate overall and was responsible for sales of 7,000 Buicks with a $21 million return on an unspecified investment made in the program. Approximately 2 million total pieces mailed, resulting in one car sale for about every 2800 pieces. $21 million in sales—that's a lotta Buicks!

The window of opportunity for highly profitable variable-data printing is wide open. For now, don't tell anyone.

David and Frank

References

British Printer, June 1998, pp. 6–9

CAP Ventures report of Digital VIP, Oct 25, 1998

CAP Ventures report of the VariScript system, Jan 12, 1998

Seybold Report on Publishing Systems, Vol. 27, N° 17.

Seybold Report on Publishing Systems, Vol. 27, N° 21.

Seybold Report on Publishing Systems, Vol. 28, N° 2.

Seybold Report on Publishing Systems, Vol. 28, N° 8.

Seybold Seminars Online, "Variable Data Printing: Where's the Software?" http://www.seyboldsf.com/Events/sf98/transcripts/ETAPE_44.html 12 Nov 1998

Adobe Systems, Inc., "Adobe Typeface Licensing Frequently-Asked Questions (FAQ)" http://www.adobe.com/supportservice/custsupport/NOTES/21ca.htm 30 December 1998

Some material used by permission of PODi.

Index

A

ASCII, 140, 142, 145, 147, 176-177, 184, 189, 192, 201, 224, 235, 244-245, 249, 255, 262, 275
Acrobat Exchange, 159
Adobe Acrobat, 259
Adobe Illustrator, 265, 276
Agfa, 61, 81, 90, 95-96, 109, 122, 126, 149, 161, 170, 175, 179, 202, 203, 215, 264, 267, 284
    P400, 61, 81
    Chromapress, 70, 95-96, 100, 109, 126, 175, 178, 203
    DigiFoil, 95
    Personalizer-X, 149, 161, 170, 175, 198-200, 202-203, 215, 261, 264-265
Apple, 66, 176, 255, 285
Atlas Software BV Printsop Mail/Xeikon Private-I, 175, 223-227, 229-231, 233, 246, 264

B

Barco Graphics, 89, 92, 95, 126, 161, 170, 176, 223, 251, 252-254, 258, 264, 294
    FastRIP/X, 89, 92
    PageStream, 176, 223, 253, 255, 294
    PrintStreamer RIP, 258
    RIP, 252-253
    VIP, 264
    VIP Designer, 251, 254-255
    VIPline, 255
    VIPScript, 254
Battelle Memorial Institute, 64-65, 75
Beck, David, 107
Beyer, Paul, 295
Bitmap File, 63
Bitstream, 95, 176, 250-251, 259, 264
    PageFlex, 95, 176, 250-251, 259, 264
Bixby, W.E., 64
Bloomberg, 162
Boolean, 143, 147, 213
Breakeven Response Rate, 21
Buick, 161-162
Bull Printing Systems, 114

Komori, 126
Kornei, Otto, 75

L
LZW (Lempel-Ziv and Welch), 254
Landa, Benzion, 96
Lettershops, 39, 49
Lexmark, 66, 72
    Lexmark Optra, 66
Liquid Toner, 78-79
List Brokers, 22-23, 49
Lossless Compression, 254
Loyalty Marketing, 36
Lufthansa Airlines, 163-164
    Quick Response Program (QRP), 163

M
Macintosh, 229, 256, 265, 291
    MacOSX Server, 291
Macromedia FreeHand See FreeHand
Magnetic Brush Development, 78
MAN-Roland, 126, 260
    DICO Press, 126, 260
McGraw-Hill, 113
Meadows' Data Merge, 244, 265
Meadows Information Systems, 222, 264
    DataMerge Pro, 264
Meyer, Herbert, 106
Microsoft Word, 170, 288
Mitsubishi, 126
Mono Component Toner, 78
Moore Corporation, 157-159, 296
    Message Master, 261
Motorola/IBM PowerPC, 251
Mystery Return Address, 29

N
National Change of Address (NCOA), 24
NexPress Solutions LLC, 106-108, 259-260
NeXT, 159
Non-Impact Printing, 60-61

O
ODBC (Open Database Connectivity), 135, 251, 256
OOP (Object Oriented Programming), 133
OPI (Open Prepress Interface), 284, 295
Object Oriented Programming See OOP
Oghton, C.D., 64
Olive Garden, 166
Omni-Adast-DI, 126
On-Demand Printing, 59

S

SGML (Standard Generalized Markup Language), 136
SQL (Structures Query Language), 129, 131-132, 134-135, 251, 256
SWOP (Specifications for Web Offset Publications), 279-280
Schaffert, R.M., 64
Schreier, Bernhard, 106
Scitex, 68, 93-94, 102-105, 108, 126-127, 170, 175-176, 186-188, 198, 223, 259, 264, 272, 284, 291
    Darwin, 149, 170, 175-176, 186, 188-194, 214, 264-265, 274
    Eversmart, 291
    Inkjet Systems, 126
    KBA74 Karat, 126
    SX3000 RIP, 197
    Spontane, 102, 126
    VPS, 272
Screening, 252
Sears, 164
Sequin Digital Screening, 100
Self-mailers, 34
Signal Corps., 65
Splash, 105, 187, 222-223
Standard for Web Offset Publications See SWOP
Standard Generalized Markup Language See SGML
Static Layout, 45
Structured Query Language See SQL
Subaru, 158
Sybase, 129
Syquest, 292-293

T

T/R Systems, 105, 126
    MicroPress Cluster Printing System, 105-106, 126
TIFF, 235, 257, 276
Takacs, Peter, 156
Thebault DI, 161-162
Toets 9220, 157-158
Toner Charge, 79
Toner Concentration, 79-80
TrueType, 235, 287
Truncation, 144, 148

U

UAA (Undeliverable as Addressed), 24
USPS (United States Postal Service), 23-24, 39, 159
Undeliverable as Addressed (UAA), 24
U.S. Army Signal Corps., 75
U.S. Postal Service See USPS

V

Variable Printing, 58, 149-154, 156-157, 164, 171
Varis Corporation, 92-93, 170, 255, 258, 264

VariScript, 92-93, 175, 255-258, 264, 296
Ventura Publisher, 265
VIP Binder, 253
VIP Designer See Barco
VIPP (Xerox), 244
Vision's Edge, 204, 264
    Focus Gold, 170, 175, 204-205, 208-209, 211, 213, 264-265, 274

W
Walk, L.E., 64
Whirlpool Corporation, 160-161
Windows, 171, 291
    Windows NT, 291
Wise, E.N., 64, 75

X
XICS (Xerox Integrated Composition System), 61
XML (Extensible Markup Language), 136, 250-251
XPLOR, 112-113
Xeikon, 68, 81-84, 86-93, 101, 108-109, 122-124, 126, 157, 163, 174-175, 178, 187,
    222-223, 228, 252-253, 255, 258, 267, 270, 293
    DCP-1, 68, 81-82, 87, 124
    DCP/32D, 68, 81-83, 89, 91-93, 109, 126, 158, 255, 270
    DCP/50D, 91-92, 94, 102, 109, 126, 255, 258, 270
    PES, 267
    Private-I, 170
Xerographic toner, 80
Xerox, 61, 65-66, 68, 75, 93-94, 96, 101-105, 108-112, 114, 122, 124, 126-127, 166,
    187, 197, 244-245, 255, 258, 264, 266-267, 272
    9700, 61
    DocuColor, 102-103, 124, 126, 175, 244
    DocuColor 40, 104-105, 123, 126, 187, 197, 267
    DocuColor 40, 109, 126
    DocuColor 70, 93-94, 101, 109, 126, 187, 197, 266-267
    DocuColor 100, 94, 109, 126, 187, 197, 267
    DocuPrint 330, 114
    DocuPrint 900, 114
    DocuPrint 1300, 114
    DocuTech, 61, 66, 96, 110-112, 123, 236
    Majestik, 166
    VIPP, 244-245, 255, 258, 264, 272
    Xerox Integrated Composition System (XICS), 61
XTensions See QuarkXPress Xtensions

Y
Yours Truly See Indigo Yours Truly

Z
Zip Codes, 9, 11, 30, 39, 46, 159, 163, 184, 190
    Zip + 4, 23, 159, 184